P9-DMW-780

# Cognitive Computing and Big Data Analytics

Judith Hurwitz
Marcia Kaufman
Adrian Bowles

WILEY

**Cognitive Computing and Big Data Analytics**

Published by
**John Wiley & Sons, Inc.**
10475 Crosspoint Boulevard
Indianapolis, IN 46256
www.wiley.com

Copyright © 2015 by John Wiley & Sons, Inc., Indianapolis, Indiana

Published simultaneously in Canada

ISBN: 978-1-118-89662-4

ISBN: 978-1-118-89678-5 (ebk)

ISBN: 978-1-118-89663-1 (ebk)

Manufactured in the United States of America

10 9 8 7 6 5 4 3 2 1

No part of this publication may be reproduced, stored in a retrieval system or transmitted in any form or by any means, electronic, mechanical, photocopying, recording, scanning or otherwise, except as permitted under Sections 107 or 108 of the 1976 United States Copyright Act, without either the prior written permission of the Publisher, or authorization through payment of the appropriate per-copy fee to the Copyright Clearance Center, 222 Rosewood Drive, Danvers, MA 01923, (978) 750-8400, fax (978) 646-8600. Requests to the Publisher for permission should be addressed to the Permissions Department, John Wiley & Sons, Inc., 111 River Street, Hoboken, NJ 07030, (201) 748-6011, fax (201) 748-6008, or online at http://www.wiley .com/go/permissions.

**Limit of Liability/Disclaimer of Warranty:** The publisher and the author make no representations or warranties with respect to the accuracy or completeness of the contents of this work and specifically disclaim all warranties, including without limitation warranties of fitness for a particular purpose. No warranty may be created or extended by sales or promotional materials. The advice and strategies contained herein may not be suitable for every situation. This work is sold with the understanding that the publisher is not engaged in rendering legal, accounting, or other professional services. If professional assistance is required, the services of a competent professional person should be sought. Neither the publisher nor the author shall be liable for damages arising herefrom. The fact that an organization or Web site is referred to in this work as a citation and/or a potential source of further information does not mean that the author or the publisher endorses the information the organization or website may provide or recommendations it may make. Further, readers should be aware that Internet websites listed in this work may have changed or disappeared between when this work was written and when it is read.

For general information on our other products and services please contact our Customer Care Department within the United States at (877) 762-2974, outside the United States at (317) 572-3993 or fax (317) 572-4002.

Wiley publishes in a variety of print and electronic formats and by print-on-demand. Some material included with standard print versions of this book may not be included in e-books or in print-on-demand. If this book refers to media such as a CD or DVD that is not included in the version you purchased, you may download this material at http://booksupport.wiley.com. For more information about Wiley products, visit www.wiley.com.

**Library of Congress Control Number:** 2014951020

**Trademarks:** Wiley and the Wiley logo are trademarks or registered trademarks of John Wiley & Sons, Inc. and/or its affiliates, in the United States and other countries, and may not be used without written permission. All other trademarks are the property of their respective owners. John Wiley & Sons, Inc. is not associated with any product or vendor mentioned in this book.

**Executive Editor:** Carol Long
**Project Editor:** Tom Dinse
**Technical Editors:** Mike Kowolensko, James Kobielus, Al Nugent
**Production Manager:** Kathleen Wisor
**Copy Editor:** Apostrophe Editing Services
**Manager of Content Development & Assembly:** Mary Beth Wakefield
**Marketing Director:** David Mayhew
**Marketing Manager:** Carrie Sherrill

**Professional Technology & Strategy Director:** Barry Pruett
**Business Manager:** Amy Knies
**Associate Publisher:** Jim Minatel
**Project Coordinator, Cover:** Patrick Redmond
**Proofreader:** Jen Larsen, Word One
**Indexer:** Johnna VanHoose Dinse
**Cover Designer:** Wiley
**Cover Image:** © iStock.com/Andrey Prokhorov

*We would like to dedicate this book to the power of collaboration. We would like to thank the rest of the team at Hurwitz & Associates for their guidance and support: Dan Kirsch, Vikki Kolbe, and Tricia Gilligan.*

*—The Authors*

*To my husband Warren and my two children, Sara and David. I also dedicate this book to my parents Elaine and David Shapiro.*

*—Judith Hurwitz*

*To my husband Matt and my children, Sara and Emily for their support through this writing process.*

*—Marcia Kaufman*

*To Jeanne, Andrew, Chris, and James, whose unfailing love and support allowed me to disappear long enough to write.*

*—Adrian Bowles*

# About the Technical Editors

**Al Nugent** is a managing partner at Palladian Partners, LLC. He is an experienced technology leader and industry veteran of more than three decades. At Palladian Partners, he leads the organization's technology assessment and strategy practices. Al has served as executive vice president, chief technology officer, senior vice president, and general manager of the Enterprise Systems Management business unit at CA Technologies. Previously, he was senior vice president and CTO at Novell, Inc., and has held CTO positions at BellSouth and Xerox. He is an independent member of the Board of Directors for Telogis and Adaptive Computing, and is an advisor to several early/mid-stage technology and healthcare startups. He is a co-author of *Big Data For Dummies* (John Wiley & Sons, 2013).

**James Kobielus** is a big data evangelist at IBM and a senior program director of product marketing and Big Data analytics solutions. He is an industry veteran, a popular speaker, social media participant, and a thought leader in big data, Hadoop, enterprise data warehousing, advanced analytics, business intelligence, data management, and next best action technologies.

**Dr. Michael D. Kowolenko** is currently an industrial fellow at the Center for Innovation Management Studies (CIMS) based at the N.C. State Poole College of Management. His research is focused on the interface of technology and business decision making. Prior to joining CIMS, he was a senior vice president at Wyeth Biotech Technical Operations and Product Supply (TO&PS), providing strategic and operations leadership perspective to ongoing integrated and cross-functional global business decisions.

# About the Authors

**Judith S. Hurwitz** is president and CEO of Hurwitz & Associates, LLC, a research and consulting firm focused on emerging technology including Big Data, cognitive computing, cloud computing, service management, software development, and security and governance. She is a technology strategist, thought leader, and author. A pioneer in anticipating technology innovation and adoption, she has served as a trusted advisor to many industry leaders over the years. Judith has helped these companies make the transition to a new business model focused on the business value of emerging platforms. She was the founder of CycleBridge, a life science software consulting firm, and Hurwitz Group, a research and consulting firm. She has worked in various corporations including Apollo Computer and John Hancock. Judith has written extensively about all aspects of enterprise and distributed software. In 2011, she authored *Smart or Lucky? How Technology Leaders Turn Chance into Success* (Jossey Bass, 2011).

Judith is a co-author on six *For Dummies* books, including *Big Data For Dummies, Hybrid Cloud For Dummies, Cloud Computing For Dummies, Service Management For Dummies,* and *Service Oriented Architecture For Dummies,* 1st and 2nd Editions (all John Wiley & Sons).

Judith holds B.S. and M.S. degrees from Boston University. She serves on several advisory boards of emerging companies. She is a member of Boston University's Alumni Council. She was named a distinguished alumnus at Boston University's College of Arts & Sciences in 2005. She is also a recipient of the 2005 Massachusetts Technology Leadership Council award.

**Marcia A. Kaufman** is COO and principle analyst at Hurwitz & Associates, LLC, a research and consulting firm focused on emerging technology including Big Data, cognitive computing, cloud computing, service management, software development, and security and governance. She has authored major studies on advanced analytics and has written extensively on cloud infrastructure, Big Data, and security. Marcia has more than 20 years of experience in business strategy, industry research, distributed software, software quality, information management, and analytics. Marcia has worked within the financial services, manufacturing, and services industries. During her tenure at Data Resources Inc. (DRI), she developed econometric industry models and forecasts. She holds an A.B. degree from Connecticut College in mathematics and economics and an M.B.A. degree from Boston University.

Marcia is a co-author on six retail *For Dummies* books including *Big Data For Dummies*, *Hybrid Cloud For Dummies*, *Cloud Computing For Dummies*, *Service Management For Dummies*, and *Service Oriented Architecture For Dummies*, 1st and 2nd Edition (all John Wiley & Sons).

**Dr. Adrian Bowles** is the founder of STORM Insights, Inc., a research and advisory firm providing services for buyers, sellers, and investors in emerging technology markets. Previously, Adrian founded the Governance, Risk Management & Compliance Roundtable for the Object Management Group, the IT Compliance Institute with 101 Communications, and Atelier Research. He has held executive positions at Ovum (Datamonitor), Giga Information Group, New Science Associates, and Yourdon, Inc. Adrian's focus on cognitive computing and analytics naturally follows his graduate studies. (His first natural language simulation application was published in the proceedings of the International Symposium on Cybernetics and Software.) Adrian also held academic appointments in computer science at Drexel University and SUNY-Binghamton, and adjunct faculty positions in the business schools at NYU and Boston College. Adrian earned his B.A. degree in psychology and M.S. degree in computer science from SUNY-Binghamton, and his Ph.D. degree in computer science from Northwestern University.

# Acknowledgments

Writing a book on a topic as complex as cognitive computing required a tremendous amount of research. Our team read hundreds of technical articles and books on various aspects of technology underpinning of the field. In addition, we were fortunate to reach out to many experts who generously spent time with us. We wanted to include a range of perspectives. So, we have many people to thank. We are sure that we have left out individuals who we met at conferences and provided insightful discussions on topics that influenced this book. We would also like to acknowledge the partnership and collaboration among the three of us that allowed this book to be written. We would also like to thank our editors at Wiley, including Carol Long and Tom Dinse. We appreciate the insights and assistance from our three technical editors, Al Nugent, James Kobielus, and Mike Kowolenko.

The following people gave generously of their time and insights: Dr. Manny Aparicio; Avron Barr, Aldo Ventures; Jeff Cohen, Welltok; Dr. Umesh Dayal, Hitachi Data Systems; Stephen DeAngelis, Enterra; Rich Y. Edwards, IBM; Jeff Eisen, IBM; Tim Estes, Digital Reasoning; Sara Gardner, Hitachi Data Systems; Murtaza Ghadyali, Reflexis; Stephen Gold, IBM; Manish Goyal, IBM; John Gunn, Memorial Sloan Kettering Cancer Center; Sue Feldman, Synthexis; Dr. Fern Halper, TDWI; Dr. Kris Hammond, Narrative Science; Ed Harbor, IBM; Marten den Haring, Digital Reasoning; Dr. C. Martin Harris, Cleveland Clinic; Dr. Larry Harris; Dr. Erica Hauver, Hitachi Data Systems; Jeff Hawkins, Numenta and The Redwood Center for Theoretical Neuroscience; Rob High, IBM; Holly T. Hilbrands, IBM; Dr. Paul Hofmann, Space-Time Insight; Amir Husain, Sparkcognition, Inc.; Terry Jones, WayBlazer; Vikki Kolbe, Hurwitz & Associates; Michael Karasick, IBM; Niraj Katwala, Healthline Networks, Inc.; Dr. John Kelly, IBM; Natsuko Kikutake, Hitachi Consulting Co., LTD; Daniel Kirsch, Hurwitz & Associates; Jeff

Margolis, Welltok; D.J. McCloskey, IBM; Alex Niznik, Pfizer; Vincent Padua, IBM; Tapan Patel, SAS Institute; Santiago Quesada, Repsol; Kimberly Reheiser, IBM; Michael Rhoden, IBM; Shay Sabhikhi, Cognitive Scale; Matt Sanchez, Cognitive Scale; Chandran Saravana, SAP; Manoj Saxena, Saxena Foundation; Dr. Candy Sidner, Worchester Polytechnic Institute; Dean Stephens, Healthline Networks, Inc.; Sridhar Sudarsan, IBM; David E. Sweenor, Dell; Wayne Thompson, SAS Institute; Joe Turk, Cleveland Clinic; and Dave Wilson, Hitachi Data Systems.

—Judith Hurwitz

—Marcia Kaufman

—Adrian Bowles

# Contents

# Introduction

With huge advancements in technology in the last 30 years, the ability to gain insights and actions from data hasn't changed much. In general, applications are still designed to perform predetermined functions or automate business processes, so their designers must plan for every usage scenario and code the logic accordingly. They don't adapt to changes in the data or learn from their experiences. Computers are faster and cheaper, but not much smarter. Of course, people are not much smarter than they were 30 years ago either. That is about to change, for humans and machines. A new generation of an information system is emerging that departs from the old model of computing as process automation to provide a collaborative platform for discovery. The first wave of these systems is already augmenting human cognition in a variety of fields. Acting as partners or collaborators for their human users, these systems may derive meaning from volumes of natural language text and generate and evaluate hypotheses in seconds based on analysis of more data than a person could absorb in a lifetime. That is the promise of cognitive computing.

## Human Intelligence + Machine Intelligence

Traditional applications are good at automating well-defined processes. From inventory management to weather forecasting, when speed is the critical factor in success and the processes are known in advance, the traditional approach of defining requirements, coding the logic, and running an application is adequate. That approach fails, however, when we need to dynamically find and leverage obscure relationships between data elements, especially in areas in which the volume or complexity of the data increases rapidly. Change, uncertainty, and complexity are the enemies of traditional systems.

Cognitive computing—based on software and hardware that learns without reprogramming and automates cognitive tasks—presents an appealing new model or paradigm for application development. Instead of automating the way we already conduct business, we begin by thinking about how to augment the best of what the human brain can do with new application capabilities. We start with processes for ingesting data from inside and outside the enterprise, and add functions to identify and evaluate patterns and complex relationships in large and sometimes unstructured data sets, such as natural language text in journals, books, and social media, or images and sounds. The result is a system that can support human reasoning by evaluating data in context and presenting relevant findings along with the evidence that justifies the answers. This approach makes users more efficient—like a traditional application—but it also makes them more effective because parts of the reasoning and learning processes have been automated and assigned to a tireless, fast collaborator.

Like the fundamentals of traditional computing, the concepts behind smart machines are not new. Even before the emergence of digital computers, engineers and scientists speculated about the development of learning machines that could mimic human problem solving and communications skills. Although some of the concepts underlying the foundation technologies—including machine intelligence, computational linguistics, artificial intelligence, neural networks, and expert systems—have been used in conventional solutions for a decade or more, we have seen only the beginning. The new era of intelligent computing is driven by the confluence of a number of factors:

- The growth in the amount of data created by systems, intelligent devices, sensors, videos, and such

- The decrease in the price of computer storage and computing capabilities

- The increasing sophistication of technology that can analyze complex data as fast as it is produced

- The in-depth research from emerging companies across the globe that are investigating and challenging long-held beliefs about what the collaboration of humans and machines can achieve

## Putting the Pieces Together

When you combine Big Data technology and the changing economics of computing with the need for business and industry to be smarter, you have the beginning of fundamental change. There are many names for this paradigm shift: machine learning, cognitive computing, artificial intelligence, knowledge management, and learning machines. But whatever you call it, this change is actually the integration of the best of human knowledge about the world with the awesome power of emerging computational systems to interpret massive amounts of a variety of types of data at an unprecedented rate of speed. But it is not enough to interpret or analyze data. Emerging solutions for cognitive computing must gather huge amounts of data about a specific topic, interact with subject matter experts, and learn the context and language of that subject. This new cognitive era is in its infancy, but we are writing this book because of the significant and immediate market potential for these systems. Cognitive computing is not magic. It is a practical approach to supporting human problem solving with learning machines that will change markets and industries.

## The Book's Focus

This book takes a deep look at the elements of cognitive computing and how it is used to solve problems. It also looks at the human efforts involved in evolving a system that has enough context to interpret complex data and processes in areas such as healthcare, manufacturing, transportation, retail, and financial services. These systems are designed as collaboration between machines and humans. The book examines various projects designed to help make decision making more systematic. How do expertly trained and highly experienced professionals leverage data, prior knowledge, and associations to make informed decisions? Sometimes, these decisions are the right ones because of the depth of knowledge. Other times, however, the decisions are incorrect because the knowledgeable individuals also bring their assumptions and biases into decision making. Many organizations that are implementing their first cognitive systems are looking for techniques that leverage deep experience combined with mechanization of complex Big Data analytics. Although this industry is young, there is much that can be learned from these pioneering cognitive computing engagements.

## Overview of the Book and Technology

The authors of this book, Judith Hurwitz, Marcia Kaufman, and Adrian Bowles are veterans of the computer industry. All of us are opinionated and independent industry analysts and consultants who take an integrated perspective on the relationship between different technologies and how they can transform businesses and industries. We have approached the writing of this book as a true collaboration. Each of us brings different experience from developing software to evaluating emerging technologies, to conducting in-depth research on important technology innovations.

Like many emerging technologies, cognitive computing is not easy. First, cognitive computing represents a new way of creating applications to support business and research goals. Second, it is a combination of many different technologies that have matured enough to become commercially viable. So, you may notice that most of the technologies detailed in the book have their roots in research and products that have been around for years or even decades. Some technologies or methods such as machine learning algorithms and natural language processing (NLP) have been seen in artificial intelligence applications for many decades. Other technologies such as advanced analytics have evolved and grown more sophisticated over time. Dramatic changes in deployment models such as cloud computing and distributed computing technology have provided the power and economies of scale to bring computing power to levels that were impossible only a decade ago.

This book doesn't attempt to replace the many excellent technical books on individual topics such as machine learning, NLP, advanced analytics, neural networks, Internet of Things, distributed computing and cloud computing. Actually, we think it is wise to use this book to give you an understanding of how the pieces fit together to then gain more depth by exploring each topic in detail.

## How This Book Is Organized

This book covers the fundamentals and underlying technologies that are important to creating cognitive system. It also covers the business drivers for cognitive computing and some of the industries that are early adopters of cognitive computing. The final chapter in the book provides a look into the future.

- **Chapter 1: "The Foundation of Cognitive Computing."** This chapter provides perspective on the evolution to cognitive computing from artificial intelligence to machine learning.

- **Chapter 2: "Design Principles for Cognitive Systems**." This chapter provides you with an understanding of what the architecture of cognitive computing is and how the pieces fit together.

- **Chapter 3: "Natural Language Processing in Support of a Cognitive System."** This chapter explains how a cognitive system uses natural language processing techniques and how these techniques create understanding.

- **Chapter 4: "The Relationship Between Big Data and Cognitive Computing."** Big data is one of the pillars of a cognitive system. This chapter demonstrates the Big Data technologies and approaches that are fundamental to a cognitive system.

- **Chapter 5: "Representing Knowledge in Taxonomies and Ontologies."** To create a cognitive system there needs to be organizational structures for the content. This chapter examines how ontologies provide meaning to unstructured content.

- **Chapter 6: "Applying Advanced Analytics to Cognitive Computing."** To assess meaning of both structured and unstructured content requires the use of a wide range of analytical techniques and tools. This chapter provides insights into what is needed.

- **Chapter 7: "The Role of Cloud and Distributed Computing in Cognitive Computing."** Without the ability to distribute computing capability and resources, it would be difficult to scale a cognitive system. This chapter explains the connection between Big Data, cloud services, and distributed analytic services.

- **Chapter 8: "The Business Implications of Cognitive Computing."** Why would a business need to create a cognitive computing environment? This chapter explains the circumstances in which an organization or business would benefit from cognitive computing.

- **Chapter 9: "IBM's Watson as a Cognitive System."** IBM began building a cognitive system by initiating a "grand challenge." The grand challenge was designed to see if it could take on the best Jeopardy! players in the world. The success of this experiment led to IBM creating a cognitive platform called Watson.

- **Chapter 10: "The Process of Building a Cognitive Application."** What does it take for an organization to create its own cognitive system? This chapter provides an overview of what the process looks like and what organizations need to consider.

- **Chapter 11: "Building a Cognitive Healthcare Application."** Each cognitive application will be different depending on the domain. Healthcare is the first area that was selected to create cognitive solutions. This chapter looks at the types of solutions that are being created.

- **Chapter 12: "Smarter Cities: Cognitive Computing in Government."** Using cognitive computing to help streamline support services in large cities has huge potential. This chapter looks at some of the initial efforts and what technologies come into play to support metropolitan areas.

- **Chapter 13: "Emerging Cognitive Computing Areas."** Many different markets and industries can be helped through a cognitive computing approach. This chapter demonstrates which markets can benefit.

- **Chapter 14: "Future Applications for Cognitive Computing."** It is clear that we are early in the evolution of cognitive computing. The coming decade will bring many new software and hardware innovations to stretch the limits of what is possible.

# The Foundation of Cognitive Computing

Cognitive computing is a technology approach that enables humans to collaborate with machines. If you look at cognitive computing as an analog to the human brain, you need to analyze *in context* all types of data, from structured data in databases to unstructured data in text, images, voice, sensors, and video. These are machines that operate at a different level than traditional IT systems because they analyze and learn from this data. A cognitive system has three fundamental principles as described below:

- **Learn**—A cognitive system learns. The system leverages data to make inferences about a domain, a topic, a person, or an issue based on training and observations from all varieties, volumes, and velocity of data.

- **Model**—To learn, the system needs to create a model or representation of a domain (which includes internal and potentially external data) and assumptions that dictate what learning algorithms are used. Understanding the context of how the data fits into the model is key to a cognitive system.

- **Generate hypotheses**—A cognitive system assumes that there is not a single correct answer. The most appropriate answer is based on the data itself. Therefore, a cognitive system is probabilistic. A hypothesis is a candidate explanation for some of the data already understood. A cognitive system uses the data to train, test, or score a hypothesis.

This chapter explores the foundations of what makes a system cognitive and how this approach is beginning to change how you can use data to create systems that learn. You can then use this approach to create solutions that change as more data is added (ingested) and as the system learns. To understand how far we have come, you need to understand the evolution of the foundational technologies. Therefore, this chapter provides background information on how artificial intelligence, cognitive science, and computer science have led to the development of cognitive computing. Finally, an overview is provided of the elements of a cognitive computing system.

## Cognitive Computing as a New Generation

Cognitive computing is an evolution of technology that attempts to make sense of a complex world that is drowning in data in all forms and shapes. You are entering a new era in computing that will transform the way humans collaborate with machines to gain actionable insights. It is clear that technological innovations have transformed industries and the way individuals conduct their daily lives for decades. In the 1950s, transactional and operational processing applications introduced huge efficiencies into business and government operations. Organizations standardized business processes and managed business data more efficiently and accurately than with manual methods. However, as the volume and diversity of data has increased exponentially, many organizations cannot turn that data into actionable knowledge. The amount of new information an individual needs to understand or analyze to make good decisions is overwhelming. The next generation of solutions combines some traditional technology techniques with innovations so that organizations can solve vexing problems. Cognitive computing is in its early stages of maturation. Over time, the techniques that are discussed in this book will be infused into most systems in future years. The focus of this book is this new approach to computing that can create systems that augment problem-solving capabilities.

## The Uses of Cognitive Systems

Cognitive systems are still in the early days of evolution. Over the coming decade you will see cognitive capabilities built into many different applications and systems. There will be new uses that emerge that are either focused on horizontal issues (such as security) or industry-specific problems (such as determining the best way to anticipate retail customer requirements and increase sales, or to diagnose an illness). Today, the initial use cases include some new frontiers and some problems that have confounded industries for decades. For example, systems are being developed that can enable a city manager to anticipate when traffic will be disrupted by weather events and reroute that traffic to avoid problems. In the healthcare industry, cognitive systems are under development that can be used in collaboration with a hospital's electronic medical records to test for omissions and improve accuracy. The cognitive system can help to teach new physicians medical best practices and improve clinical decision making. Cognitive systems can help with the transfer of knowledge and best practices in other industries as well. In these use cases, a cognitive system is designed to build a dialog between human and machine so that best practices are learned by the system as opposed to being programmed as a set of rules.

The list of potential uses of a cognitive computing approach will continue to grow over time. The initial frontier in cognitive computing development has been in the area of healthcare because it is rich in text-based data sources. In addition, successful patient outcomes are often dependent on care providers having a complete, accurate, up-to-date understanding of patient problems. If medical cognitive applications can be developed that enable physicians and caregivers to better understand treatment options through continuous learning, the ability to treat patients could be dramatically improved. Many other industries are testing and developing cognitive applications as well. For example, bringing together unstructured and semi-structured data that can be used within metropolitan areas can greatly increase our understanding of how to improve the delivery of services to citizens. "Smarter city" applications enable managers to plan the next best action to control pollution, improve the traffic flow, and help fight crime. Even traditional customer care and help desk applications can be dramatically improved if systems can learn and help provide fast resolution of customer problems.

## What Makes a System Cognitive?

Three important concepts help make a system cognitive: contextual insight from the model, hypothesis generation (a proposed explanation of a phenomenon), and continuous learning from data across time. In practice, cognitive computing enables the examination of a wide variety of diverse types of data and the interpretation of that data to provide insights and recommend actions. The essence of cognitive computing is the acquisition and analysis of the right amount of information in context with the problem being addressed. A cognitive system must be aware of the context that supports the data to deliver value. When that data is acquired, curated, and analyzed, the cognitive system must identify and remember patterns and associations in the data. This iterative process enables the system to learn and deepen its scope so that understanding of the data improves over time. One of the most important practical characteristics of a cognitive system is the capability to provide the knowledge seeker with a series of alternative answers along with an explanation of the rationale or evidence supporting each answer.

A cognitive computing system consists of tools and techniques, including Big Data and analytics, machine learning, Internet of Things (IoT), Natural Language Processing (NLP), causal induction, probabilistic reasoning, and data visualization. Cognitive systems have the capability to learn, remember, provoke, analyze, and resolve in a manner that is contextually relevant to the organization or to the individual user. The solutions to highly complex problems require the assimilation of all sorts of data and knowledge that is available from a variety of structured, semi-structured, and unstructured sources including, but not limited to, journal articles, industry data, images, sensor data, and structured data from operational and transactional databases. How does a cognitive system leverage this data? As you see later in this chapter, these cognitive systems employ sophisticated continuous learning techniques to understand and organize information.

---

### DISTINGUISHING FEATURES OF A COGNITIVE SYSTEM

Although there are many different approaches to the way cognitive systems will be designed, there are some characteristics that cognitive systems have in common. They include the capability to:

- Learn from experience with data/evidence and improve its own knowledge and performance without reprogramming.

- Generate and/or evaluate conflicting hypotheses based on the current state of its knowledge.

- Report on findings in a way that justifies conclusions based on confidence in the evidence.

- Discover patterns in data, with or without explicit guidance from a user regarding the nature of the pattern.

- Emulate processes or structures found in natural learning systems (that is, memory management, knowledge organization processes, or modeling the neurosynaptic brain structures and processes).

- Use NLP to extract meaning from textual data and use deep learning tools to extract features from images, video, voice, and sensors.

- Use a variety of predictive analytics algorithms and statistical techniques.

---

## Gaining Insights from Data

For a cognitive system to be relevant and useful, it must continuously learn and adapt as new information is ingested and interpreted. To gain insight and understanding of this information requires that a variety of tools understand the data no matter what the form of the data may be. Today, much of the data required is text-based. *Natural Language Processing (NLP)* techniques are needed to capture the meaning of unstructured text from documents or communications from the user. NLP is the primary tool to interpret text. Deep learning tools are required to capture meaning from nontext-based sources such as videos and sensor data. For example, time series analysis analyzes sensor data, whereas a variety of image analysis tools interpret images and videos. All these various types of data have to be transformed so that they can be understood and processed by a machine. In a cognitive system these transformations must be presented in a way that allows the users to understand the relationships between a variety of data sources. Visualization tools and techniques will be critical ways for making this type of complex data accessible and understandable. *Visualization* is one of the most powerful techniques to make it easier to recognize patterns in massive and complex data. As we evolve to cognitive computing we may be required to bring together structured, semi-structured, and unstructured sources to continuously learn and gain insights from data. How these data sources are combined with processes for gaining results is key to cognitive computing. Therefore, the cognitive system offers its users a different experience in the way it interacts with data and processes.

## Domains Where Cognitive Computing Is Well Suited

Cognitive computing systems are often used in domains in which a single query or set of data may result in a hypothesis that yields more than one possible answer. Sometimes, the answers are not mutually exclusive (for example, multiple, related medical diagnoses where the patient may have one or more of the indicated disorders at the same time). This type of system is probabilistic, rather than deterministic. In a *probabilistic system*, there may be a variety of answers, depending on circumstances or context and the confidence level or probability based on the system's current knowledge. A *deterministic system* would have to return a single answer based on the evidence, or no answer if there were a condition of uncertainty.

The cognitive solution is best suited to help when the domain is complex and conclusions depend on who is asking the question and the complexity of the data. Even though human experts might know an answer to a problem, they may not be aware of new data or new circumstances that will change the outcome of an inquiry. More advanced systems can identify missing data that would change the confidence level of an answer and request further information interactively to converge on an answer or set of answers with sufficient confidence to help the user take some action. For example, in the medical diagnostic example, the cognitive system may ask the physician to perform additional tests to rule out or to choose certain diagnoses.

**DEFINING NATURAL LANGUAGE PROCESSING**

Natural Language Processing (NLP) is the capability of computer systems to process text written or recorded in a language used for human communication (such as English or French). Human "natural language" is filled with ambiguities. For example, one word can have multiple meanings depending on how it is used in a sentence. In addition, the meaning of a sentence can change dramatically just by adding or removing a single word. NLP enables computer systems to interpret the meaning of language and to generate natural language responses.

Cognitive systems typically include a knowledge base (corpus) that has been created by ingesting various structured and unstructured data sources. Many of these data sources are text-based documents. NLP is used to identify the semantics of words, phrases, sentences, paragraphs, and other linguistic units in the documents and other unstructured data found in the corpus. One important use of NLP in cognitive systems is to identify the statistical patterns and provide the linkages in data elements so that the meaning of unstructured data can be interpreted in the right context.

For more information on natural language processing, see Chapter 3, "Natural Language Processing in Support of a Cognitive System."

## Artificial Intelligence as the Foundation of Cognitive Computing

Although the seeds of artificial intelligence go back at least 300 years, the evolution over the past 50 years has had the most impact for cognitive computing. Modern *Artificial Intelligence (AI)* encompassed the work of scientists and mathematicians determined to translate the workings of neurons in the brain into a set of logical constructs and models that would mimic the workings of the human mind. As computer science evolved, computer scientists assumed that it would be possible to translate complex thinking into binary coding so that machines could be made to think like humans.

Alan Turing, a British mathematician whose work on cryptography was recognized by Winston Churchill as critical to victory in WWII, was also a pioneer in computer science. Turing turned his attention to machine learning in the 1940s. In his paper called "Computing Machinery and Intelligence" (written in 1950 and published in *Mind,* a United Kingdom peer-reviewed academic journal), he posed the question, "Can machines think?" He dismissed the argument that machines could never think because they possess no human emotion. He postulated that this would imply that "the only way to know that a man thinks is to be that particular man. . . ." Turing argued that with advancement in digital computing, it would be possible to have a learning machine whose internal processes were unknown, or a black box. Thus, "its teacher will often be very largely ignorant of quite what is going on inside, although he will still be able to some extent to predict his pupil's behavior."

In his later writing Turing proposed a test to determine if a machine possessed intelligence, or could mimic the behaviors we associate with intelligence. The test consisted of two humans and a third person that inputted questions for the two people via a typewriter. The goal of the game was to determine if the game players could determine which of the three participants was a human and which was a "typewriter" or a computer. In other words, the game consisted of human/machine interactions. It is clear that Turing was ahead of his time. He was making the distinction between the ability of the human to intuitively operate in a complex world and how well a machine can mimic those attributes.

Another important innovator was Norbert Weiner, whose 1948 book, *Cybernetics or Control and Communication in the Animal and the Machine*, defined the field of cybernetics. While working on a World War II research project at MIT, he studied the continuous feedback that occurred between a guided missile system and its environment. Weiner recognized that this process of continuous feedback occurred in many other complex systems including machines, animals, humans, and organizations. Cybernetics is the study of these feedback mechanisms. The feedback principle describes how complex systems (such as the guided missile system) change their actions in response to their environment. Weiner's theories on the relationship between intelligent behavior and feedback mechanisms led him to determine that machines could simulate human feedback mechanisms. His research and theories had a strong influence on the development of the field of AI.

Games, particularly two-person zero-sum perfect information games (in which both parties can see all moves and can theoretically generate and evaluate all future moves before acting), have been used to test ideas about learning behavior since the dawn of AI. Arthur Lee Samuel, a researcher who later went to work for IBM, developed one of the earliest examples. He is credited with developing the first self-learning program for playing checkers. In his paper published in the *IBM Journal of Research and Development* in 1959, Samuel summarized his research as follows:

> *Two machine-learning procedures have been investigated in some detail using the game of checkers. Enough work has been done to verify the fact that a computer can be programmed so that it will learn to play a better game of checkers than can be played by the person who wrote the program. Furthermore, it can learn to do this in a remarkably short period of time (8 or 10 hours of machine-playing time) when given only the rules of the game, a sense of direction, and a redundant and incomplete list of parameters which are thought to have something to do with the game, but whose correct signs and relative weights are unknown and unspecified. The principles of machine learning verified by these experiments are, of course, applicable to many other situations.*

Samuel's research was an important precursor to the work that followed over the coming decades. His goal was not to find a way to beat an opponent in checkers, but to figure out how humans learned. Initially, in Samuel's checkers experiment, the best he achieved was to have the computer play to a draw with the human opponent.

In 1956, researchers held a conference at Dartmouth College in New Hampshire that helped to define the field of AI. The participants included the most important researchers in what was to become the field of AI. The participants included Allen Newell and Herbert A. Simon of Carnegie Tech (Carnegie Mellon University), Marvin Minsky from MIT, and John McCarthy (who left MIT in 1962 to form a new lab at Stanford). In their proposal for the Dartmouth event, McCarthy et al. outlined a fundamental conjecture that influenced AI research for decades: "every aspect of learning or any other feature of intelligence can in principle be so precisely described that a machine can be made to simulate it." (McCarthy, John; Minsky, Marvin; Rochester, Nathan; Shannon, Claude (1955), "A Proposal for the Dartmouth Summer Research Project on Artificial Intelligence.") Also in 1956, Allen Newell, Herbert Simon, and Cliff Shaw created a program called the "Logic Theorist" that is possibly the first AI computer program. It was created to prove mathematical theorems by simulating certain human problem-solving capabilities.

Herbert Simon, who won the Nobel Prize for Economics in 1978, had an ongoing interest in human cognition and decision making that factored into all his research. He theorized that people are rational agents who can adapt to conditions. He assumed that there could be a simple interface between human knowledge and an artificially intelligent system. Like his predecessors, he assumed that it would be relatively easy to find a way to represent knowledge as an information system. He contended that transition to AI could be accomplished by simply adapting rules based on changing requirements. Simon and his colleagues such as Alan Newell assumed that a simple adaptive mechanism would allow intelligence to be captured to create an intelligent machine.

One of Simon's important contributions to the burgeoning field was an article he wrote about the foundational elements and the future of capturing intelligence. Simon laid out the concept of natural language processing and the capability of computers to mimic vision. He predicted that computers would play chess at the grand master level. (Allen Newell, Cliff Shaw, Herbert Simon. "Chess Playing Programs and the Problem of Complexity." *IBM Journal of Research and Development*, Vol. 4, No. 2, 1958.)

Although many of the early endeavors were wildly optimistic, they did send the field of AI in the right direction. Many of the computer scientists assumed that within 20 years computers would be capable of mimicking cognitive processes fundamental to learning. When many commercial AI start-ups failed to create ongoing businesses in the 1980s, it became clear that new research and more time were needed to fulfill expectations for commercial applications in the field of AI. Scientists and researchers continued to innovate in areas such as symbolic reasoning, expert systems, pattern recognition, and machine learning. In addition, there were extensive developments in related and parallel areas such as robotics and neural networks.

Another significant contributor to AI research was Professor Edward Feigenbaum. In 1965, after joining the computer science faculty at Stanford University, Feigenbaum and Nobel laureate Joshua Lederberg started the DENDRAL project, which was later referred to as the first expert system. The project's importance to the field of AI is based on the framework that was created for other expert systems to follow. Feigenbaum said that the DENDRAL project was important because it showed that "the dream of a really intelligent machine was possible. There was a program that was performing at world class levels of problem-solving competence on problems that only Ph.Ds. solve—these mass spectral analysis problems." Today, expert systems are used in the military and in industries such as manufacturing and healthcare.

## EXPERT SYSTEMS DEFINED

Expert system technology has been around for decades and gained popularity in the 1980s. An *expert system* captures knowledge from domain experts in a knowledge or rules base. The developer of an expert system needs to determine the rules in advance. Occasionally, there are confidence factors applied to the data in the knowledge base. When changes occur, the expert system needs to be updated by a subject matter expert. An expert system is most useful when there is an area of knowledge that will not change dramatically over time. After data is ingested into the system, it can be used to assess different hypotheses and determine the consequences of an assertion. In addition, an expert system can use fuzzy logic as a way to assess the probability of a specific rule included within the system. Often, expert systems are used as a classification technique to help determine how to manage unstructured data.

The U.S. Defense Advanced Research Projects Agency (DARPA) funded much of the underlying research in AI. The agency is responsible for the development of new technologies that can be used by the military. Prior to 1969, millions of dollars were provided for AI research with limited or no direction as to the type of research activities. However, after 1969, DARPA funding was legally restricted to be applied to specific military projects such as autonomous tanks and battle management systems. Expert systems were designed to provide guidance to personnel in the field. Many of these AI systems codified best practices by studying historical events. For example, in the late 1980s DARPA sponsored the FORCES project, which was part of the Air Land Battle Management Program. This was an expert system designed to help field personnel make decisions based on historical best practices. A commander using the system could ask, "What would General Patton do now?" This system was not actually deployed, but provided good experience for knowledge-based defense projects that were built later.

During the 1970s and 1980s there were significant periods of time when it became difficult for scientists to receive funding for AI projects. Although military-based research continued to be funded by DARPA, commercial based funding was almost non-existent. In some cases, computer scientists looking for grants for research would use the term "expert systems" or "knowledge-based systems" rather than AI to help ensure funding. However, subfields of AI including machine learning, ontologies, rules management, pattern matching, and NLP continued to find their way into a myriad of products over the years. Even the Automated Teller Machine (ATM) has evolved to incorporate many of these technologies.

One of the early commercial projects that took AI and machine learning back into prominence was a project initiated by American Express. The project was designed to look for patterns of fraud in credit card transactions. The results of the project were wildly successful. Suddenly, a technology approach that had been maligned was showing business value. The secret ingredient that made the project work was that American Express fed this system a massive amount of data. Typically, companies found it much too expensive to store this much data. American Express gambled that the investment would be worth the price. The results were dramatic. By detecting patterns that would result in fraud, American Express saved an enormous amount of money. The American Express project leveraged machine learning combined with huge volumes of data to determine that fraud was about to take place and stopped those transactions. This was one of the early indications that machine learning and pattern-based algorithms could become an engine for business transformation. It was the beginning of the reinvestment in the emerging field of machine learning—a field that took its foundation from the concepts of AI.

AI is focused on determining how to represent knowledge in a way that the data can be manipulated so that people can make inferences from that knowledge. The field has evolved over the decades. Today, most of the focus is on the area of machine learning algorithms that provide a mechanism to allow computers to process data in a methodical way. But much of the focus of machine learning is dealing with ambiguity because most data is unstructured and open to many different interpretations.

## Understanding Cognition

Understanding how the human brain works and processes information provides a blueprint for the approach to cognitive computing. However, it is not necessary to build a system that replicates all the capabilities of the human brain to serve as a good collaborator for humans. By understanding cognition we can build systems that have many of the characteristics required to continuously learn and adapt to new information. The word *cognition*, from the Latin root gnosis, meaning to know and learn, dates back to the 15th century. Greek philosophers were keenly interested in the field of deductive reasoning.

With cognitive computing, we are bringing together two disciplines:

- **Cognitive science**—The science of the mind.

- **Computer science**—The scientific and practical approach to computation and its applications. It is the systematic technique for translating this theory into practice.

The main branches of cognitive science are psychology (primarily an applied science, in helping diagnose and treat mental/behavioral conditions) and neurology (also primarily applied, in diagnosis/treatment of neurological conditions). Over the years, however, it became clear that there was a critical relationship between the way the human brain works and computer engineering. For example, cognitive scientists, in studying the human mind, have come to understand that human cognition is an interlinking system of systems that allows for information to be received from outside inputs, which is then stored, retrieved, transformed, and transmitted. Likewise, the maturation of the computer field has accelerated the field of cognitive sciences. Increasingly, there is less separation between these two disciplines.

A foundational principle of cognitive science is that an intelligent system consists of a number of specialized processes and services (within the human brain) that interact with each other. For example, a sound transmits a signal to the brain and causes a person to react. If the loud sound results in pain, the brain learns to react by causing the human to place her hands over her ears or by moving away. This isn't an innate reaction; it is learned as a response to a stimulus. There are, of course, different variations in cognition, depending on differences in genetic variations. (A deaf person reacts differently to sound than a person who hears well.) However, these variations are the exception, not the rule.

To make sense of how different processes in the brain relate to each other and impact each other, cognitive scientists model cognitive structures and processes. There isn't a single cognitive architecture; rather, there are many different approaches, depending on the interaction model. For example, there may be an architecture that is related to human senses such as seeing, understanding speech, and reacting to tastes, smells, and touch. A cognitive architecture is also directly tied to how the neurons in the brain carry out specific tasks, absorb new inputs dynamically, and understand context. All this is possible even if there is sparse data because the brain can fill in the implied information. The human brain is architected to deal with the mental processes of perception, memory, judgment, and learning. Humans can think fast and draw conclusions based on their ability to reason or make inferences from the pieces of information they are given.

Humans have the ability to make speculative conjectures, construct imaginative scenarios, use intuition, and other cognitive processes that go beyond mere reasoning, inference, and information processing. The fact that humans have the ability to come up with a supposition based on sparse data points to the brilliance of human cognition. However, there can be negative consequences of this inference. The human may have a bias that leads to conclusions that are erroneous. For example, the human may look at one research study that states that there are some medical benefits to chocolate and conclude that eating a lot of candy will be a good thing. In contrast, a cognitive architecture will not make the mistake of assuming that one study or one conclusion has an overwhelming relevance unless there is actual evidence to draw conclusions. Unlike humans, machines do not have bias unless that bias is programmed into the system.

Traditional architectures rely on humans to interpret processes into code. AI assumes that computers can replace the thinking process of humans. With cognitive computing, the human leverages the unique ability of computers to process, manage, and associate information to expand what is possible.

## Two Systems of Judgment and Choice

It is quite complicated to translate the complexity of human thought and actions into systems. In human systems, we are often influenced by emotion, instinct, habits, and subconscious assumptions about the world. *Cognition* is a foundational approach that leverages not just how we think, but also how we act and how we make decisions. Why does one doctor recommend one treatment whereas another doctor recommends a completely different approach to the same disease? Why do two people raised in the same household with a similar experience grow up to have diametrically opposed views of the world? What explains how we come to conclusions and what does this tell us about cognition and cognitive computing?

One of the most influential thinkers on the topic is Dr. Daniel Kahneman, an Israeli-American psychologist and winner of the 2002 Nobel Memorial Prize in Economic Sciences. He is well known for his research and writing in the field of the psychology of judgment and decision making. One of his greatest contributions to cognitive computing is his research on the cognitive basis for common human errors that arise from heuristic and biases. To understand how to apply cognition to computer science, it is helpful to understand Kahneman's theory about how we think. In 2011, he published a book, *Thinking Fast and Slow*, which provides important insights for cognitive computing. The following section provides some insights into Kahneman's thinking and how it relates to cognitive computing. Kahneman divides his approach to judgment and reasoning into two forms: System 1: Intuitive thinking, and System 2: Controlled and rule-centric thinking.

This next section describes these two systems of thought and how they relate to how cognitive computing works. System 1 thinking is the type of intuitive reasoning that can be analogous to the type of processing that can be easily automated. In contrast, System 2 thinking is the way we process data based on our experiences and input from many data sources. System 2 thinking is related to the complexities of cognitive computing.

## System 1—Automatic Thinking: Intuition and Biases

System 1 thinking is what happens automatically in our brains. It uses our intuition to draw conclusions. Therefore, it is relatively effortless. System 1 thinking begins almost from the moment we are born. We learn to see objects and understand their relationships to ourselves. For example, we associate our mother's voice with safety. We associate a loud noise with danger. These associations form the basis of how we experience the world. The child with a cruel mother will not have the same association with the mother's voice as the child with the kind mother. Of course, there are other issues at play as well. The child with a kind mother may have an underlying mental illness that causes irrational actions. An average child who associates a loud noise with fun may not feel in danger. As people learn over time, they begin to assimilate automatic thinking into their way of operating in the world. The chess protégée who becomes a master automatically learns to make the right moves. The chess master not only knows what his next move should be but also can anticipate what move his opponent will do next. That chess master can play an entire game in his mind without even touching the chessboard. Likewise, emotions and attitudes about the world are automatic, as well. If a person is raised in a dangerous area of a city, he will have automatic attitudes about those people around him. Those attitudes are not something that he even thinks about and cannot easily be controlled. These attitudes are simply part of who he is and how he has assimilated his environment and experiences.

The benefit of System 1 thinking is that we can take in data from the world around us and discover the connections between events. It is easy to see that System 1 is important to cognitive computing because it allows us as humans to use sparse information we collect about events and observations and come to rapid conclusions. System 1 can generate predictions by matching these observations. However, this type of intuitive thinking can also be inaccurate and prone to error if it is not checked and monitored by what Kahneman calls System 2: the ability to analyze massive amounts of information related to the problem being addressed and to reason in a deliberate manner. Combining System 1 intuitive thinking with System 2 deep analysis is critical for cognitive computing. Figure 1-1 shows the interaction between intuitive thinking and deep analysis.

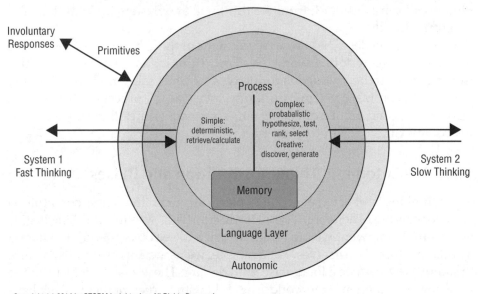

Copyright (c) 2014 by STORM insights, Inc. All Rights Reserved.

**Figure 1-1:** Interaction between intuitive thinking and deep analysis

## System 2—Controlled, Rule-Centric, and Concentrated Effort

Unlike System 1 thinking, System 2 thinking is a reasoning system based on a more deliberate process. System 2 thinking observes and tests assumptions and observations, instead of jumping to a conclusion based on what is assumed. System 2 thinking uses simulation to take an assumption and look at the implications of that assumption. This type of system requires that we collect a lot of data and build models that test System 1 intuition. This is especially important because System 1 thinking is typically based on a narrow view of a situation: a silo. Although an idea may appear to be good and plausible when viewed from a narrow perspective, when viewed in context with other data, conclusions often change. Drug trials are an excellent example of this phenomenon. A potential cancer treatment seems promising. All the preliminary data indicates that the drug will eradicate the cancer cells. However, the treatment is so toxic that it also destroys healthy cells. System 1 thinking would assume that the fact that cancer cells are destroyed is enough to determine that the drug should immediately be put on the market. However, System 1 thinking often includes bias. Although it may appear that an approach makes sense, the definition of the problem may be ill-defined. System 2 thinking slows down the evaluation process and looks at the full context of the problem, collects more data across silos, and comes up with a solution. Because System 2 is anchored in data and models, it takes into account those biases and provides a better outcome. Predicting outcomes is a complex business issue because so many factors can change outcomes. This is why it is important to combine intuitive thinking with computational models.

## Understanding Complex Relationships Between Systems

Because of the advent of cognitive computing, we are beginning to move beyond the era in which a system must be designed as a unified environment intended to solve a specific, well-defined problem. In this new world, complex systems are not necessarily massive programs. Rather, they may be developed as modular services that execute specific functions and are intended to operate based on the actions and the data from specific events. These adaptive systems are designed so that they can be combined with other elements at the right time to determine the answer to a complex problem. What makes this difficult is the requirement to integrate data from a variety of sources. The process begins with the physical ability to ingest data sources. However, the real complexity is both the integration process and the process of discovering relationships between data sources. Unstructured text-based information sources have to be parsed so that it is clear what content is the proper nouns, verbs, and objects. This process of categorization is necessary so that the data can be consistently managed. Data from unstructured sources such as images, video, and voice have to be analyzed through deep analytics of patterns and outliers. For example, recognition of human facial images may be facilitated by analyzing the edge of the image and identifying for patterns that can be interpreted as objects—such as a nose versus an eye. Analysis is done to get a central category based on evaluating all the data in context. The key to success in this complicated process is to ingest enough data in these categories so that it is possible to apply a machine-learning algorithm that can continue to refine the data. The broader the knowledge area is, the more difficult this process will be.

When data is combined from a variety of sources, it must be categorized into some sort of database structure. It is most helpful to have an approach that is highly interdisciplinary and provides a framework to help individuals find answers to some fundamental questions based on continually refining the elements of the information sources that are most relevant. For example, if the system can decipher a proper noun and then find verbs and the object of that verb, it will be easier to determine the context for the data so that the user can make sense of that data and apply it to a problem domain.

---

**ANALYZING IMAGES, VIDEO, AND AUDIO**

The human brain has the ability to automatically translate images into meaning. A doctor who is trained to read an x-ray can interpret differences in results in hundreds of patients in near-real time. The untrained individual can possibly recognize a picture of a person he has only met twice. Being able to extract data from images, videos, and speech is an important issue in gaining understanding of all types of data. This type of analytics has been helped significantly with the advent of cloud-based services. These services make it possible to scale advanced analytics on everything from machine vision, speech recognition, and the ability to gain insights into real-time streaming of images and video. In a cognitive system it is critical to be able to analyze this information to gain insights into information that is not text based. For example, analyzing image data from thousands of faces may identify a criminal or terrorist. Analyzing motion and sound data may provide insights into the severity of an earthquake. Using sophisticated algorithms help determine patterns in this type of unstructured or semi-structured data.

## Types of Adaptive Systems

Cognitive systems are intended to address real-world problems in an adaptive manner. This adaptive systems approach is intended to deliver relevant data-driven insights to decision makers based on advanced analysis of the data. The knowledge base is managed and updated as needed to ensure that the full semantic context of the data is leveraged in the analytic process. For example, the system could be looking at the stock market and the complex set of information about individual companies, statistics about performance of economies, and competitive environments. The goal of the adaptive system would be to bring these elements together so that the consumer of that system gains a holistic view of the relationship between factors. An adaptive system approach can be applied to medicine so that a physician can use a combination of learned knowledge and a corpus of knowledge from clinical trials, research, and journal articles to better understand how to treat a disease.

The combination of computer and human interactions enables cognitive systems to gain a dynamic and holistic view of a specific topic or domain. To be practical, many elements have to come together with the right level of context and right amounts of information from the right sources. These elements have to be coordinated based on the principles of self-organization that mimic the way the human brain assimilates information, draws conclusions, and tests those conclusions. This is not simple to execute. It requires that there is enough information from a variety of sources. The system must therefore discover, digest, and adapt a massive amount of data. The system must look for patterns and relationships that aren't visible to the unassisted human. These types of adaptive systems are an attempt to mimic the way the human brain makes associations—often on sparse data.

## The Elements of a Cognitive System

A cognitive system consists of many different elements, ranging from the hardware and deployment models to machine learning and applications. Although many different approaches exist for creating a cognitive system, there are some common elements that need to be included. Figure 1-2 shows an overview of the architecture for a cognitive system, which is described in the next section. Chapter 2, "Design Principles for Cognitive Systems," goes deeper into a discussion of each of these elements.

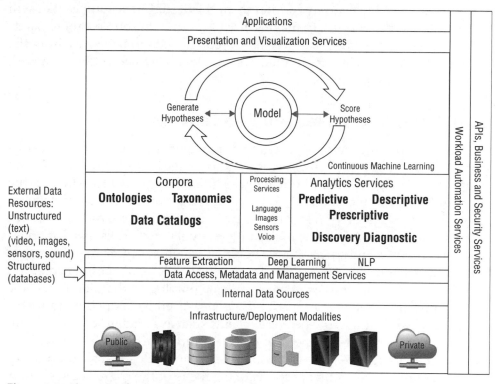

**Figure 1-2:** Elements of a cognitive system

## Infrastructure and Deployment Modalities

In a cognitive system it is critical to have a flexible and agile infrastructure to support applications that continue to grow over time. As the market for cognitive solutions matures, a variety of public and private data need to be managed and processed. In addition, organizations can leverage Software as a Service (SaaS) applications and services to meet industry-specific requirements. A highly parallelized and distributed environment, including compute and storage cloud services, must be supported.

## Data Access, Metadata, and Management Services

Because cognitive computing centers around data, it is not surprising that the sourcing, accessing, and management of data play a central role. Therefore, before adding and using that data, there has to be a range of underlying services. To prepare to use the ingested data requires an understanding of the origins and lineage of that data. Therefore, there needs to be a way to classify the characteristics of that data such as when that text or data source was created and by whom. In a cognitive system these data sources are not static. There will be a variety of internal and external data sources that will be included in the corpus. To make sense of these data sources, there needs to be a set of management services that prepares data to be used within the corpus. Therefore, as in a traditional system, data has to be vetted, cleansed, and monitored for accuracy.

## The Corpus, Taxonomies, and Data Catalogs

Tightly linked with the data access and management layer are the corpus and data analytics services. A *corpus* is the knowledge base of ingested data and is used to manage codified knowledge. The data required to establish the domain for the system is included in the corpus. Various forms of data are ingested into the system (refer to Figure 1-2). In many cognitive systems, this data will primarily be text-based (documents, textbooks, patient notes, customer reports, and such). Other cognitive systems include many forms of unstructured and semi-structured data (such as videos, images, sensors, and sounds). In addition, the corpus may include ontologies that define specific entities and their relationships. *Ontologies* are often developed by industry groups to classify industry-specific elements such as standard chemical compounds, machine parts, or medical diseases and treatments. In a cognitive system, it is often necessary to use a subset of an industry-based ontology to include only the data that pertains to the focus of the cognitive system. A taxonomy works hand in hand with ontologies. A *taxonomy* provides context within the ontology.

## Data Analytics Services

Data analytics services are the techniques used to gain an understanding of the data ingested and managed within the corpus. Typically, users can take advantage of structured, unstructured, and semi-structured data that has been ingested and begin to use sophisticated algorithms to predict outcomes, discover patterns, or determine next best actions. These services do not live in isolation. They continuously access new data from the data access layer and pull data from the corpus. A number of advanced algorithms are applied to develop the model for the cognitive system.

## Continuous Machine Learning

Machine learning is the technique that provides the capability for the data to learn without being explicitly programmed. Cognitive systems are not static. Rather, models are continuously updated based on new data, analysis, and interactions. A machine learning process has two key elements: hypothesis generation and hypothesis evaluation. Machine learning is discussed in detail in Chapter 2.

### Hypothesis Generation and Evaluation

A *hypothesis* is a testable assertion based on evidence that explains some observed phenomenon. In a cognitive computing system, you look for evidence to support or refute hypotheses. You need to acquire data from various sources, create models, and then test how well the models work. This is done through an iterative process of training the data. Training may occur automatically based on the systems analysis of data, or training may incorporate human end users. After training, it begins to become clear if the hypothesis is supported by the data. If the hypothesis is not supported by the data, the user has several options. For example, the user may refine the data by adding to the corpus, or change the hypothesis. To evaluate the hypothesis requires a collaborative process of constituents that use the cognitive system. Just as with the creation of the hypothesis, the evaluation of results refines those results and trains again.

## The Learning Process

To learn from data you need tools to process both structured and unstructured data. For unstructured textual data, NLP services can interpret and detect patterns to support a cognitive system. Unstructured data such as images, videos, and sound requires deep learning tools. Data from sensors are important in emerging cognitive systems. Industries ranging from transportation to healthcare use sensor data to monitor speed, performance, failure rates, and other metrics and then capture and analyze this data in real time to predict behavior and change outcomes. Chapter 2 discusses the tools used to process the varied forms of data analyzed in a cognitive system.

## Presentation and Visualization Services

To interpret complex and often massive amounts of data requires new visualization interfaces. *Data visualization* is the visual representation of data as well as the study of data in a visual way. For example, a bar chart or pie chart is a visual representation of underlying data. Patterns and relationships in data are easier to identify and understand when visualized with structure, color, and such. The two basic types of data visualizations are static and dynamic. In either or both cases, there may also be a requirement for interactivity. Sometimes looking at the visualized representation of the data is not enough. You need to drill down, re-position, expand and contract, and so on. This interactivity enables you to "personalize" the views of the data so that you can pursue non-obvious manifestations of data, relationships, and alternatives. Visualization may depend on color, location, and proximity. Other critical issues that impact visualization include shape, size, and motion. Presentation services prepare results for output. Visualization services help to communicate results by providing a way to demonstrate the relationships between data.

A cognitive system brings text or unstructured data together with visual data to gain insights. In addition, images, motion, and sound are also elements that need to be analyzed and understood. Making this data interactive through a visualization interface can help a cognitive system be more accessible and usable.

## Cognitive Applications

A cognitive system must leverage underlying services to create applications that address problems in a specific domain. These applications that are focused on solving specific problems must engage users so that they gain insights and knowledge from the system. In addition, these applications may need to infuse processes to gain insight about a complex area such as preventive maintenance or treatment for a complex disease. An application may be designed to simulate the smartest customer service agent. The end goal is to turn an average employee into the smartest employee with many years of experience. A well-designed cognitive system provides the user with contextual insights based on role, the process, and the customer issue they are solving. The solution should provide the users insights so they make better decisions based on data that exists but is not easily accessible.

# Summary

A cognitive computing system is intended to provide a platform to solve hypotheses based on learning from data. These systems are best used to solve problems in data-rich domains. A probabilistic approach to systems design is helping to create a new generation of systems that will focus on helping make sense of a complex world.

# Design Principles for Cognitive Systems

In a cognitive computing system, the *model* refers to the corpus and the set of assumptions and algorithms that generate and score hypotheses to answer questions, solve problems, or discover new insights. How you model the world determines what kind of predictions you can make, patterns and anomalies you can detect, and actions you can take. The initial model is developed by the designers of the system, but the cognitive system will update the model and use the model to answer questions or provide insights. The *corpus* is the body of knowledge that machine learning algorithms use to continuously update that model based on its experience, which may include user feedback.

A cognitive system is designed to use a model of a domain to predict potential outcomes. Designing a cognitive system involves multiple steps. It requires an understanding of the available data, the types of questions that need to be asked, and the creation of a corpus comprehensive enough to support the generation of hypotheses about the domain based on observed facts. Therefore, a cognitive system is designed to create hypotheses from data, analyze alternative hypotheses, and determine the availability of supporting evidence to solve problems.

By leveraging machine learning algorithms, question analysis, and advanced analytics on relevant data, which may be structured or unstructured, a cognitive system can provide end users with a powerful approach to learning and decision making. Cognitive systems are designed to learn from their experiences with data. A typical cognitive system uses machine learning algorithms to build models for answering questions or delivering insight. The design of a cognitive system needs to support the following differentiating characteristics:

- Access, manage, and analyze data in context.
- Generate and score multiple hypotheses based on the system's accumulated knowledge. A cognitive system may generate multiple possible solutions to every problem it solves and deliver answers and insights with associated confidence levels.
- The system continuously updates the model based on user interactions and new data. A cognitive system gets smarter over time in an automated way.

This chapter describes the major components that enable cognitive computing systems to learn, note the dependencies between these components, and outline the processes found within each component.

## Components of a Cognitive System

A cognitive computing system has an internal store of knowledge (the corpus) and interacts with the external environment to capture additional data and to potentially update external systems. As discussed in Chapter 1, "The Foundation of Cognitive Computing," cognitive systems represent a new way of gaining insight from a diverse set of data resources. Cognitive systems may use Natural Language Processing to understand text, but also need other processing, deep learning capabilities, and tools to understand images, voice, videos, and location. These processing capabilities provide a way for the cognitive system to understand data in context and make sense of a particular domain area of knowledge. The cognitive system generates hypotheses and provides alternative answers or insights with associated confidence levels. In addition, a cognitive system needs to be capable of deep learning that is specific to subject areas and industries. The life cycle of a cognitive system is an iterative process. This iterative process requires the combination of human best practices and training of the data.

Figure 2-1 shows a representation of the typical elements in a cognitive computing system. This is intended as a general guide to cognitive computing architectures. In practice, cognitive components, APIs, and packaged services will emerge over time. However, even as services become embedded into systems, these elements will remain as the underpinning.

Now start your exploration of the design of a cognitive computing system by analyzing the corpus. Because the corpus is the knowledge base for the cognitive system, you are going to build a model of a specific domain by defining the corpus.

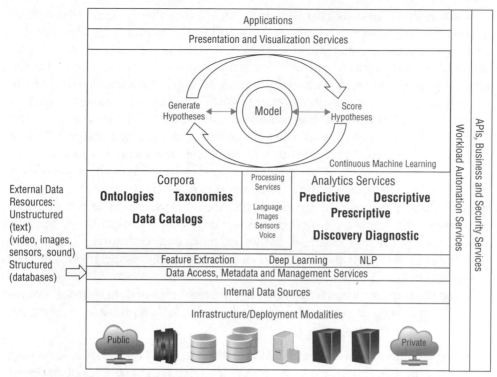

**Figure 2-1:** Architecture of a cognitive system

## Building the Corpus

A *corpus* is a machine-readable representation of the complete record of a particular domain or topic. Experts in a variety of fields use a corpus or corpora for tasks such as linguistic analysis to study writing styles or even to determine authenticity of a particular work. For example, the complete works of William Shakespeare might be a corpus of interest to someone studying literature in the English Renaissance of the 16th and 17th century. For a researcher studying theatrical productions of the same period, it might be necessary to use the Shakespeare corpus plus several others that cover the works of his contemporaries. Such a collection of corpora can quickly become unwieldy if they come from different sources, have different formats, and particularly if they include a large volume of information that is irrelevant to the domain being studied. For example, someone studying theatrical productions might not be interested in the Shakespearean sonnets. Deciding what to leave out is as important as what to include.

In a cognitive computing application, the corpus or corpora represent the body of knowledge the system can use to answer questions, discover new patterns or relationships, and deliver new insights. Before the system is launched, however, a base corpus must be created and the data ingested. The contents of this base corpus constrain the types of problems that can be solved, and the organization of data within the corpus has a significant impact on the efficiency of the system. Therefore, you need a good understanding of the domain area for your cognitive system before determining the required data sources. What types of problems do you want to solve? If the corpus is too narrowly defined, you may miss out on new and unexpected insights. If data is trimmed from the external sources before they are imported into the corpus, they won't be used in the generation or scoring of hypotheses, which is at the heart of machine learning. The corpus needs to include the right mix of relevant data resources that can enable the cognitive system to deliver accurate responses in the expected timeframe. When developing a cognitive system, it's a good idea to err on the side of gathering more data or knowledge because you never know when the discovery of an unexpected association will lead to important new knowledge.

Given the importance placed on having the right mix of data sources, a number of questions have to be addressed early in the design phase for a cognitive computing system:

- Which internal and external data sources are needed for the specific domain areas and problems to be solved? Will external data sources be ingested in whole or in part?

- How can you optimize the organization of data for efficient search and analysis?

- How can you integrate data across multiple corpora?

- How can you ensure that the corpus is expanded to fill in knowledge gaps in your base corpus? How can you determine which data sources need to be updated and at what frequency?

The choice of which sources to include in the initial corpus is critical. Sources ranging from medical journals to Wikipedia may now be efficiently imported in preparation for the launch of a cognitive system. In addition, it may be equally important to ingest information from videos, images, voice, and sensors. These sources are ingested at the data access layer (refer to Figure 2-1). Other data sources may also include subject-specific structured databases, ontologies, taxonomies, and catalogs.

If the cognitive computing application requires access to highly structured data created by or stored in other systems such as public or proprietary databases, another design consideration is how much of that data to import initially. It is also important to determine whether to update or refresh the data periodically, continuously, or in response to a request from the system when it recognizes that more data can help it provide better answers.

In many fields, taxonomies are used to capture hierarchical relationships between elements of interest. For example, a taxonomy for the U.S. Generally Accepted Accounting Principles (GAAP) represents the accounting standards in a hierarchical structure that capture the relationships between them. An *ontology* is similar to a taxonomy, but generally represents more complex relationships, such as the mapping between symptoms and diagnostic criteria in the Diagnostic and Statistical Manual of the American Psychiatric Association. When such a generally accepted taxonomy or ontology exists in a field, it may be useful to import that structure with its data—in whole or in part—rather than creating a novel structure for the same data. Chapter 5, "Representing Knowledge in Taxonomies and Ontologies," discusses the roles of taxonomies and ontologies in more detail.

During the design phase of a cognitive system, a key consideration is whether to construct a taxonomy or ontology if none already exist for the domain. Having such a structure may simplify the operation of the system and make it more efficient. However, if the designers are responsible for ensuring that a taxonomy or ontology is complete and up to date, it may be more effective to have the system continuously evaluate relationships between domain elements rather than have the designers build that into a hard-coded structure.

The choice of data structures can greatly impact the performance of the system on repetitive tasks such as knowledge retrieval for generating and scoring hypotheses. It is therefore advisable to model or simulate typical workloads during the design phase before committing to specific structures. A data catalog, which includes metadata such as semantic information or pointers, may be used to manage the underlying data more efficiently. The catalog is, as an abstraction, more compact and generally faster to manipulate than the much larger database it represents.

In the examples and diagrams, when referring to corpora, it should be noted that these can be integrated into a single corpus when doing so will help simplify the logic of the system or improves performance. Much like a system can be defined as a collection of smaller integrated systems, aggregating data from a collection of corpora results in a single new corpus. Maintaining separate corpora is typically done for performance reasons, much like normalizing tables in a database to facilitate queries, rather than attempting to combine tables into a single, more complex structure.

## Corpus Management Regulatory and Security Considerations

Data sources and the movement of that data are increasingly becoming heavily regulated, particularly for personally identifiable information. Some general issues of data policies for protection, security, and compliance are common to all applications, but cognitive computing applications learn and derive new data or knowledge that may also be subject to a growing body of state, federal, and international legislation.

When the initial corpus is developed, it is likely that a lot of data will be imported using extract-transform-load (ETL) tools. These tools may have risk management, security, and regulatory features to help the user guard against data misuse or provide guidance when sources are known to contain sensitive data. The availability of these tools doesn't absolve the developers from responsibility to ensure that the data and metadata is in compliance with applicable rules and regulations. Protected data may be ingested (for example, personal identifiers) or generated (for example, medical diagnoses) when the corpus is updated by the cognitive computing system. Planning for good corpus management should include a plan to monitor relevant policies that impact data in the corpus. The data access layer tools described in the next section must be accompanied by or embed compliance policies and procedures to ensure that imported and derived data and metadata remain in compliance. That includes consideration of various deployment modalities, such as cloud computing, which may distribute data across geopolitical boundaries.

## Bringing Data into the Cognitive System

Unlike many traditional systems, the data that is ingested into the corpus is not static. You need to build a base of knowledge that adequately defines your domain space. You begin populating this knowledge base with data you expect to be important. As you develop the model in the cognitive system, you refine the corpus. Therefore, you will continuously add to the data sources, transform those data sources, and refine and cleanse those sources based on the model development and continuous learning. This next section discusses how both data sources that are internal to an organization and those that are external to the organization can be used to build a corpus.

### Leveraging Internal and External Data Sources

Most organizations already manage huge volumes of structured data from their transactional systems and business applications, and unstructured data such as text contained in forms or notes and possibly images from documents or corporate video sources. Although some firms are writing applications to monitor external sources such as news and social media feeds, many IT organizations are not yet well equipped to leverage these sources and integrate them with internal data sources. Most cognitive computing systems will be developed for domains that require ongoing access to integrated data from outside the organization.

Just as an individual learns to identify the right external sources to support decision making—from newspapers to network news to social media on the Internet—a cognitive computing system generally needs to access a variety of frequently updated sources to keep current about the domain in which it operates. Also, like professionals who must balance the news or data from these external sources against their own experience, a cognitive system must learn to weigh the external evidence and develop confidence in the source as well as the content over time. For example, a popular magazine with articles on psychology may be a valuable resource, but if it contains data that is in conflict with a refereed journal article on the same topic, the system must know how to weigh the opposing positions. All data sources that may be useful should be considered and potentially ingested. However, this does not mean that all sources will be of equal value.

In healthcare, for example, electronic medical records (EMRs) can provide valuable source information. Although individuals are not always accurate in their own recollections, a database that aggregates findings from a broad spectrum of EMRs and case files may contain information about relationships between combinations of symptoms and disorders or diseases that would be missed if a doctor or researcher had access only to the records from their own practice or institution. In telecommunications, a company might want to use a cognitive system to anticipate machine failures based on internal factors, such as traffic and usage patterns, and on external factors such as severe weather threats that are likely to cause overloads and physical damage. You see more examples of integrating internal and external data sources in Chapter 12, "Smarter Cities: Cognitive Computing in Government." The important thing to remember at the design stage is that with experience, a cognitive computing system should identify and request additional data from external sources when that data will enable it to make better decisions or recommendations. Determining the right data at the right time to make a decision may always be problematic, but with a cognitive computing system, every request for more data will be based on an immediate need.

## Data Access and Feature Extraction Services

The data access level of the diagram shown in Figure 2-1 depicts the main interfaces between the cognitive computing system and the outside world. Any data to be imported from external sources must come through processes within this layer. Cognitive computing applications may leverage external data sources in formats as varied as natural language text, video images, audio files, sensor data, and highly structured data formatted for machine processing. The analogy to human learning is that this level represents the senses. The feature extraction layer has to complete two tasks. First, it has to identify relevant data that needs to be analyzed. The second task is to abstract data as required to support machine learning.

The data access level is shown as separate but closely bound to the feature extraction level to reinforce the idea that some data must be captured and then analyzed or refined before it is ready to be integrated into a corpus suitable for a particular domain. Any data that is considered unstructured—from video and images to natural language text—must be processed in this layer to find the underlying structure. Feature extraction and deep learning refer to a collection of techniques—primarily statistical algorithms—used to transform data into representations that capture the essential properties in a more abstract form that can be processed by a machine learning algorithm. For example, image data generally starts as a sparse binary representation that captures data about individual pixels but doesn't directly represent the underlying objects in the image. A digital image of a cat or a cat scan would be useless to a veterinary or a radiology cognitive computing system until the underlying structure was identified and represented in more meaningful way. Similarly, unstructured text becomes useful input to a cognitive system only when its meaning has been uncovered by a Natural Language Processing System (NLP is covered in detail in Chapter 3, "Natural Language Processing in Support of a Cognitive System").

Although these layers appear as a straightforward process of importing and refining data, it should be noted that external sources may be added or removed based on their value in hypothesis generation and scoring over time. For example, a medical diagnosis system may add a new external source of case files or delete a journal if it is found to provide unreliable evidence. For cognitive systems that provide evidence to support hypotheses in regulated industries, the data access layer processes or the corpora management services should maintain a log or other state data so that an auditor can determine what was "known" at any point in time. This would be important, for example, if a recommendation from the cognitive system was followed by a practitioner and resulted in harm (from a medical misdiagnosis to a poor recommendation by an accountant).

## Analytics Services

Analytics refers to a collection of techniques used to find and report on essential characteristics or relationships within a data set. In general, the use of an analytic technique provides insights about the data to guide some action or decision. A number of packaged algorithms such regression analysis are widely used within solutions. Within a cognitive system, a wide range of standard analytics components are available for descriptive, predictive, and prescriptive tasks within statistical software packages or in commercial component libraries. A variety of tools that support various tasks within cognitive computing systems are available (refer to Figure 2-1). A cognitive computing system generally has additional analytical components embedded in the machine learning cycle algorithms. Chapter 6, "Applying Advanced Analytics to Cognitive Computing," goes into detail about the relevant analytical methods.

# Machine Learning

Continuous learning without reprogramming is at the heart of all cognitive computing solutions. Although the techniques used to acquire, manage, and learn from data vary greatly, at their core most systems apply algorithms developed by researchers in the field of machine learning. Machine learning is a discipline that draws from computer science, statistics, and psychology.

## Finding Patterns in Data

A typical machine-learning algorithm looks for patterns in data and then takes or recommends some action based on what it finds. A pattern may represent a similar structure (for example, elements of a picture that indicate a face), similar values (a cluster of values similar to those found in another data set) or proximity (how "close" the abstract representation of one item is to another). *Proximity* is an important concept in pattern identification or matching. Two data strings representing things or concepts in the real world are "close" when their abstract binary representations have similar characteristics.

Cognitive computing systems use machine-learning algorithms based on inferential statistics to detect or discover patterns that guide their behavior. Choosing the basic learning approach to adopt—detection versus discovery of patterns—should be based on the available data and nature of the problem to be solved. Machine learning typically uses *inferential statistics* (the basis for predictive, rather than descriptive analytics) techniques.

Next, look at two complementary approaches to machine learning that use patterns in different ways: supervised and unsupervised learning. Deciding when to use one or both of these approaches for a specific system depends on the attributes of available data and the goals of the system.

Finding the right machine learning algorithm or algorithms for a cognitive computing application starts with a few questions:

- Is there an existing source of data and associations between data elements to solve my problem?
- Do I know what kind of patterns my data contains?
- Can I give examples of how I would identify and exploit these patterns manually?

When all these questions can be answered in the affirmative, you have a good candidate for a supervised learning system.

## Supervised Learning

*Supervised learning* refers to an approach that teaches the system to detect or match patterns in data based on examples it encounters during training with sample data. The training data should include examples of the types of patterns or question-answer pairs the system will have to process. Learning by example, or *modeling*, is a powerful teaching technique that can be used for training systems to solve complex problems. After the system is operational, a supervised learning system also uses its own experience to improve its performance on pattern matching tasks.

Supervised learning can be used with data that is known to predict outcomes and results. Supervised learning requires an external system—the developer or user—that can evaluate or create a sample data set that represents the domain of data that the system will encounter when it is operational.

In supervised learning, the job of the algorithm is to create a mapping between input and output. The supervised learning model has to process enough data to get to the wanted level of validation, usually expressed as accuracy on the test data set. Both the training data and independent test data should be representative of the type of data that will be encountered when the system is operational. The starting point usually includes noisy data (data that includes a lot of extraneous details that are irrelevant) in the beginning that can be culled as it is trained. There needs to be enough training data so that it is possible to pinpoint the well-conceived hypothesis from the hypothesis class. Achieving this goal with supervised data requires good optimization methods to find that correct hypothesis from the training data. Biases and assumptions are always reflected in a training data set that may affect the performance of the system. It may be necessary to retrain a system when topics or responses drift from the model created by the original assumptions.

The primary applications for supervised learning are in systems that solve classification or regression problems. Solving these problems manually requires a person to recognize patterns based on experience or evidence, and identify one or more answers that satisfy all the constraints of the problem (classification problem) or fill in expected values (regression problem). Experienced people do this well, from a travel agent finding just the right vacation elements for a regular customer to a realtor predicting a selling price on a house. The appeal of supervised learning systems for cognitive computing is that they can operate on much larger data sets than humans can handle, so they are not only more efficient, they also can become more effective than humans with sufficient experience. The learning process begins with an established set of data and an understanding of how that data is organized, including the relationships between attributes of questions and answers. It can then proceed with inductive learning to generalize from the specific examples. Therefore, for supervised learning, the developer needs to begin with a model where the parameters are discoverable from the data set that is used for training.

In a classification system, the goal is to find a match between a set of objectives and a discrete solution. For example, in a cognitive travel application, it is necessary to learn about the desires of travelers and provide suggestions and recommendations for travel. The matching algorithm then compares these features with the data from many other travel requests over time. The algorithm might take into account whether it is a return customer or someone logging on for the first time. Through a question-and-answer process, the system can begin to gain an understanding of who the customer is and what type of offerings would be of interest to the customer. Therefore, the system needs to identify the relevant attributes of that person so that it can begin to narrow down the set of possible responses.

Over time, the system adds more and more data from a large population of users. The learning process begins to see more patterns and builds the connections and context. The algorithms, for example, gain insights into relationships between different categories or clusters of travelers and their preferences. The more data sources that are included in the corpus, the better the learning system can be at suggesting options that will satisfy travelers.

In contrast with classification problems, regression problems require the system to determine the value of a continuous variable, such as price. The system must determine a value based on similar data with known answers. For example, using data about recent automobile sales in a geographic area, including make, model, mileage, and condition, a system can provide an estimate of a specific automobile's selling price by finding a near match with simple regression analysis. This is a typical predictive analytics problem. A supervised learning system can be taught to look for additional attributes that correlate with price and offer more precision as it learns from experience with more data.

## Reinforcement Learning

*Reinforcement learning* is a special case of supervised learning in which the cognitive computing system receives feedback on its performance to guide it to a goal or good outcome. Unlike other supervised learning approaches, however, with reinforcement learning, the system is not explicitly trained with sample data. In reinforcement learning, the system learns to take next actions based on trial and error. Some typical applications of reinforcement learning include robotics and game playing. The machine learning algorithms assess the goodness or effectiveness of policies or actions, and reward the most effective actions. A sequence of successful decisions results in reinforcement, which helps the system generate a policy that best matches the problem being addressed.

Reinforcement learning for cognitive computing is most appropriate where a system must perform a sequence of tasks and the number of variables would make it too difficult to develop a representative training data set. For example, reinforcement would be used in robotics or a self-driving car. The learning algorithm must discover an association between the reward and a sequence of events leading up to the reward. Then the algorithm can try to optimize future actions to remain in a reward state. Although animals can be rewarded with praise, food, or even cash, the reward function in a machine-learning environment is numerical or logical in nature.

## Unsupervised Learning

*Unsupervised learning* refers to a machine learning approach that uses inferential statistical modeling algorithms to *discover* rather than *detect* patterns or similarities in data. An unsupervised learning system can identify new patterns, instead of trying to match a set of patterns it encountered during training. Unlike supervised learning, unsupervised learning is based solely on experience with the data rather than on training with sample data. Unsupervised learning requires the system to discover which relationships among data elements or structures are important by analyzing attributes like frequency of occurrence, context (for example, what has been seen or what has occurred previously), and proximity.

Unsupervised learning is the best approach for a cognitive computing system when an expert or user cannot give examples of typical relationships or question-answer pairs as guides to train the system. This may be due to the complexity of the data, when there are too many variables to consider, or when the structure of the data is unknown (for example, evaluating images from a surveillance camera to detect which person or persons are behaving differently from the crowd). The system first has to identify the actors, then their behaviors, and then find anomalies.

Unsupervised learning is also appropriate when new patterns emerge faster than humans can recognize them so that regular training is impossible. For example, a cognitive computing system to evaluate network threats must recognize anomalies that may indicate an attack or vulnerability that has never been seen before. By comparing the current state of the network with historical data, an unsupervised learning system can look for changes or a state it has never seen before and flag that as suspect activity. If the activity is benign, the system can learn from that experience not to flag that state if it sees it again in the future.

In essence, with unsupervised learning you begin with a massive amount of data, and without preconceived notions about the patterns, relationships, or associations that may be found. In unsupervised learning, you expect that the data will reveal the patterns and anomalies through statistical analysis. Therefore, the goal of unsupervised learning is to discover patterns in the data in the absence of an explicit training model. This type of learning requires sophisticated mathematics and often requires the use of clustering (gathering like data elements) and hidden Markov models (finding patterns that appear over a space of time, such as speech). Unsupervised learning is typically used in areas such as vision analysis, imaging, and bioinformatics for gene or protein sequencing.

Unlike supervised learning, there is no distinction between training and test data, and there is no specific training data that incorporates the patterns being sought in fresh test data.

**USING UNSUPERVISED DISCOVERIES TO DRIVE SUPERVISED LEARNING**

For some domains, a hybrid approach that uses both supervised and unsupervised learning components will be the most effective approach. When an unsupervised learning system detects interesting patterns, knowledge about the associations and relationships within the patterns may be used to construct training data for a supervised learning system. For example, the retail system mentioned that could detect interesting relationships between price and profitability could result in the discovery of a relationship that would be used to train a supervised learning system that recommends items to a customer. For the retailer, combining these two systems could form a virtuous cycle of retail knowledge, each improving the performance of the other over time.

## Hypotheses Generation and Scoring

A *hypothesis* in science is a testable assertion based on evidence that explains some observed phenomenon or relationship between elements within a domain. The key concept here is that a hypothesis has some supporting evidence or knowledge that makes it a plausible explanation for a causal relationship. It isn't a guess. When a scientist formulates a hypothesis as an answer to a question, it is done in a way that allows it to be tested. The hypothesis actually has to predict an experimental outcome. An experiment or series of experiments that supports the hypothesis increases confidence in the ability of the hypothesis to explain the phenomenon. This is conceptually similar to a hypothesis in logic, generally stated as "if P then Q", where "P" is the hypothesis and "Q" is the conclusion.

In the natural sciences we conduct experiments to test hypotheses. Using formal logic we can develop proofs to show that a conclusion follows from a hypothesis (or that it does not follow). In a cognitive computing system we look for evidence—experiences and data or relationships between data elements—to support or refute hypotheses. That is the basis for scoring or assigning a confidence level for a hypothesis. If a cognitive computing hypothesis can be expressed as a logical inference, it may be tested using mechanical theorem proving algorithms. Typically, however, cognitive computing applications solve problems in domains with supporting data that are not so neatly structured. These domains, like medicine and finance, have rich bodies of supporting data that are better suited to statistical methods like those used in scientific experimental design.

Figure 2-2 shows a virtuous cycle of hypotheses generation and scoring. Here the plural "hypotheses" indicates that cognitive systems can generate multiple hypotheses based on the state of data in the corpus at a given time. In general, these can then be evaluated and scored in parallel. In a system such as IBM's Watson, for example, 100 independent hypotheses may be generated in a single cycle. Each may be assigned to a separate thread or core for scoring. That enables the system to leverage parallel hardware architectures and optimize parallel workloads. Of course, conceptually a system could generate and score all hypotheses sequentially. The parallel architecture and workload design of Watson is discussed in detail in Chapter 9, "IBM's Watson as a Cognitive System."

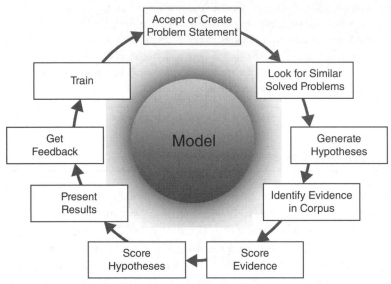

**Figure 2-2:** The continuous machine learning process

## Hypothesis Generation

The discussion about the scientific method said that a hypothesis is formulated to answer a question about a phenomenon based on some evidence that made it plausible. The experimental process is designed to test whether the hypothesis applies in the general case, not just with the evidence that was used to develop the hypothesis. In a typical cognitive computing system, there are two key ways a hypothesis may be generated. The first is in response to an explicit question from the user, such as "What might cause my fever of 102 and sore throat?"

In this scenario, the cognitive computing application must look for plausible explanations. It could, for example, start by presenting all the possible conditions in which you might expect to see these symptoms. (Each condition would be a candidate hypothesis explaining the symptoms.) Alternatively, it may recognize that there are too many answers to be useful and request more information from the user to refine the set of likely causes. This approach to hypothesis generation is frequently used when the goal is to detect a relationship between cause and effect in a domain in which there is a known set of causes and a known set of effects, but there are so many combinations that the mapping of all causes to all effects is an intractable problem for humans to solve. Typically, this type of cognitive computing system will be trained with an extensive set of question/answer pairs. The process of hypothesis generation is one of generating candidate hypotheses that appear to have a similar relationship to the user's question as the relationship between known correct question-answer pairs from the training data set.

The second type of hypothesis generation does not depend on a user asking a specific question. Instead, the system constantly looks for anomalous data patterns that may indicate threats or opportunities. Detecting a new pattern creates a hypothesis based on the nature of the data. For example, if the system is monitoring network sensors to detect threats, a new pattern may create a hypothesis that this pattern is a threat, and the system must either find evidence to support or refute that hypothesis. If the system is monitoring real-time stock transactions, a new pattern of buying behavior may indicate an opportunity. In these systems, the type of hypotheses that will be generated depends on assumptions of the system designers rather than on the actions of the users. Both types of application have the system generate one or more hypotheses based on an event, but in the first case, the event is a user question, and in the second it is driven by a change in the data itself.

## Hypothesis Scoring

At this point, you have seen how cognitive computing systems build a corpus of relevant data for a problem domain. Then, in response to a user question or change in the data, the system generates one or more hypotheses to answer a user's question or explain a new data pattern.

The next step is to evaluate or score these hypotheses based on the evidence in the corpus, and then update the corpus and report the findings to the user or another external system. Hypothesis scoring is a process in which the representation of the hypothesis is compared with data in the corpus to see what evidence exists to support the hypothesis, and what may actually refute it (or rule it out as a valid possible explanation). In fact, scoring or evaluating a hypothesis is a process of applying statistical methods to the hypothesis-evidence pairs to assign a confidence level to the hypothesis. The actual weights that are assigned to each piece of supporting evidence can be adjusted based on experience with the system and feedback during training and during the operational phase. If none of the hypotheses score above a predetermined threshold, the system may ask for more evidence (a new diagnostic blood test, for example) if that information could change the confidence in the hypothesis. Techniques for measuring the proximity of two data elements or structures for pattern matching, such as the fit between two hypothesis-evidence pairs, generally rely on a binary vector representation (such as a sparse distributed representation [SDR]) that can be manipulated using matrix algebra with readily available tools.

The generation/scoring loop may be set to continue until a user is satisfied with the answer or until the system has evaluated all options. The next section shows how machine learning algorithms guide this loop in practice. You need to remember that although the system generates and scores the hypotheses based on the evidence, in most cases the user actually provides feedback on the answer that may be viewed as scoring the process. This ongoing interaction between user and system provides a virtuous cycle of learning for man and machine.

## Presentation and Visualization Services

As a cognitive computing system cycles through the hypothesis generation and scoring cycle, it may produce new answers or candidate answers for a user. In some situations, the user may need to provide additional information. How the system presents these findings or questions will have a big impact on the usability of the system in two ways. First, when presenting data supporting a hypothesis such as a medical diagnosis or recommended vacation plan, the system should present the finding in a way that conveys the most meaning with the least effort on the part of the user and support the finding with relevant evidence. Second, when the system requires additional details to improve its confidence in one or more hypotheses, the user must present that data in a concise and unambiguous way. The general advantage for visualization tools is their capability to graphically depict relationships between data elements in ways that focus attention on trends and abstraction rather than forcing the user to find these patterns in the raw data.

Following are three main types of services available to accomplish these goals.

- Narrative solutions, which use natural language generation techniques to tell a story about the data or summarize findings in natural language. This is appropriate for reporting findings or explanations about the evidence used to arrive at a conclusion or question.

- Visualization services present data in nontext forms, including:
  - Graphics, ranging from simple charts and graphs to multidimensional representations of relationships between data.
  - Images, selected from the data to be presented or generated from an underlying representation. (For example, if feature extraction detects a "face" object, a visualization service could generate a "face" or pictograph from a standard features library.)
  - Gestures or animation of data designed to convey meaning or emotion.

- Reporting services refers to functions that produce structured output, such as database records, that may be suitable for humans or machines.

Some data may naturally lend itself to only one of these options, but often the system may convey the same information in multiple formats. The choice of which tools or formats should ultimately be made by the user, but as a system learns preferences based on user choices in ongoing interactions, it can use the most commonly requested formats as defaults for individual users.

## Infrastructure

The infrastructure/deployment modalities layer referred to in Figure 2-1 represents the hardware, networking, and storage foundation for the cognitive computing application. As noted in the discussion on emerging neuromorphic hardware architectures in Chapter 14, "Future Applications for Cognitive Computing," most cognitive computing systems built in the next decade will primarily use conventional hardware. The two major design considerations for cognitive computing infrastructure decisions are:

- **Distributed Data Management**—For all but the smallest applications, cognitive computing systems can benefit from tools to leverage distributed external data resources and to distribute their operational workloads. Managing the ongoing ingestion of data from a variety of external sources requires a robust infrastructure that can efficiently import large quantities of data. Based on the domain, this may be a combination of structured and unstructured data available for batch or streaming ingestion. Today, a cloud-first approach to data management is recommended to provide maximum flexibility and scalability.

- **Parallelism**—The fundamental cognitive computing cycle of hypothesis generation and scoring can benefit enormously from a software architecture that supports parallel generation/scoring of multiple hypotheses, but performance ultimately depends on the right hardware. Allocating each independent hypothesis to a separate hardware thread or core is a requirement in most cases for acceptable performance as the corpus scales up and the number of hypotheses increases. Although performance improvements should be seen within the system as it learns, the rate of data expansion in the corpus generally outpaces this performance improvement. That argues strongly for the selection of hardware architecture that supports relatively seamless expansion with additional processors.

## Summary

Designing a cognitive system requires bringing together many different elements, beginning with the corpus of data. To create a system that provides an interface between humans and machines means that the system must learn from data and human interaction through an iterative process. The system must be designed so that users can interact with the system both through a language or a visual interface.

# Natural Language Processing in Support of a Cognitive System

One of the aspects that distinguish a cognitive system from other data-driven techniques is the capability to manage, understand, and analyze unstructured data in context with the questions being asked. In many organizations as much as 80 percent of the data that is collected and stored is unstructured. To make good decisions, these documents, reports, e-mail messages, speech recordings or images, and videos must be understood and analyzed to make good decisions. For example, in medical journals there are millions of articles published in a single year that can offer new treatment options. In the retail market, there are billions of social media conversations that are leading indicators of future trends. There is important information that is buried inside voice and video recordings that can have an impact on a variety of fields. Unlike structured database data, which relies on schemas to add context and meaning to data, unstructured information must be parsed and tagged to find the elements of meaning. Tools for this process of identifying the meaning of the individual words include categorization, thesauri, ontologies, tagging, catalogs, dictionaries, and language models.

In a cognitive system, the developer needs to generate and test hypotheses and provide alternative answers or insights with associated confidence levels. Often the body of knowledge used within the cognitive system is text-based. In this situation, Natural Language Processing (NLP) techniques interpret the relationships between massive amounts of natural language elements.

The availability of large amounts of unstructured content is critical to creating a meaningful model of information to support continuous learning. Keep in mind, as discussed in Chapter 2, "Design Principles for Cognitive Systems," not all unstructured data is text. There is a requirement in some cognitive computing systems to support images, video, speech, and sensor data, depending on how the data will be used. Although the focus of this chapter is on the ability to use NLP techniques to support the continuous learning life cycle, other approaches are emerging to manage and process information that is not text-based.

## The Role of NLP in a Cognitive System

NLP is a set of techniques that extract meaning from text. These techniques determine the meaning of a word, phrase, sentence, or document by recognizing the grammatical rules—the predictable patterns within a language. They rely, as people do, on dictionaries, repeated patterns of co-occurring words, and other contextual clues to determine what the meaning might be. NLP applies the same known rules and patterns to make inferences about meaning in a text document. Further, these techniques can identify and extract elements of meaning, such as proper names, locations, actions, or events to find the relationships among them, even across documents. These techniques can also be applied to the text within a database and have been used for more than a decade to find duplicate names and addresses or analyze a comment or reason field, for instance, in large customer databases.

### The Importance of Context

Translating unstructured content from a corpus of information into a meaningful knowledge base is the task of NLP. *Linguistic analysis* breaks down the text to provide meaning. The text has to be transformed so that the user can ask questions and get meaningful answers from the knowledge base. Any system, whether it is a structured database, a query engine, or a knowledge base, requires techniques and tools that enable the user to interpret the data. The key to getting from data to understanding is the quality of the information. With NLP it is possible to interpret data and the relationships between words. It is important to determine what information to keep and how to look for patterns in the structure of that information to distill meaning and context.

NLP enables cognitive systems to extract meaning from text. Phrases, sentences, or complex full documents provide context so that you can understand the meaning of a word or term. This context is critical to assessing the true meaning of text-based data. Patterns and relationships between words and phrases in the text need to be identified to begin to understand the meaning and actual intent of communications. When humans read or listen to natural language text, they automatically find these patterns and make associations between words to determine meaning and understand sentiment. There is a great deal of ambiguity in language, and many words can have multiple meanings depending on the subject matter being discussed or how one word is combined with other words in a phrase, sentence, or paragraph. When humans communicate information there is an assumption of context.

For example, imagine that a truck driver wants to use a cognitive system to plan a trip. He obviously needs to know the best route to travel. However, it would be even better if he could know what weather patterns are anticipated in the week of his trip. He also would like to anticipate any major construction projects that he should avoid. It would also be helpful to understand which routes prohibit trucks that weigh more than 10 tons. The truck driver may collect the answers to these questions. However, it would require him to access multiple systems, search different databases, and ask targeted questions. Even when the truck driver finds all the answers, they are not correlated together to provide the optimal travel route based on his requirements at a specific point in time. The same truck driver will have entirely different questions two weeks later. This time the truck driver may be planning his return after delivering merchandise, and he wants to build a vacation into his plans. The recipient (the truck driver) is required to bring context and understanding to the fragmented information he is gathering.

Now look at the example of a lung cancer specialist who is reviewing an MRI. Although some MRIs provide precise information to diagnose a problem, there are many shades of gray. The specialist may want to compare the MRI results to other patients that appear to have similar conditions. The specialist has treated lung cancer patients for many years and has certain hypotheses about the most appropriate treatments. However, one specialist cannot possibly keep up with all the new research and new treatments that are discussed in technical journals. That specialist needs to ask the cognitive system to look for the anomalies that appear in several MRIs. She may want to ask deeper questions to see what other specialists have experienced in treating the same type of lung cancer. She may want to ask for evidence and conduct a dialog with the cognitive system to understand context and relationships.

Both these examples point out the complexities of gaining insight from text and language. Written text often excludes history, definitions, and other background information that would help the reader understand more of the context for the text. The reader of the text brings his own level of experience to help understand the meaning. Therefore, humans use their understanding of the world to make the connections to fill in the context. Of course, depending on the level of knowledge and the expertise required for the text, some text may not be understood without additional information or training. NLP tools rely on rules of language to determine meaning and extract elements. When combining NLP tools in the context of cognitive systems, these tools have to work with a system where the data is dynamic by definition. This means that the system is designed to learn from examples or patterns; therefore language has to be interpreted based on context.

An NLP system begins with letters, words, and some predefined knowledge store or dictionary that helps to define what words mean. A word by itself lacks context. An NLP builds layers of contextual understanding by first looking to the left and right of that word to identify verb phrases, nouns, and other parts of speech. To build up the layers of understanding, the NLP can extract elements of meaning that can answer questions such as:

- Is there a date? When was the text generated?
- Who is speaking?
- Are there pronouns in the text? To whom or what do they refer?
- Are there references to other documents in the text?
- Is there important information in a previous paragraph?
- Are there references to time and place?
- Who or what is acting, and who/what is being acted upon?

What are the relationships of the entities (people, places, and things) to each other (usually indicated by verbs)? It is important to distinguish the actor and recipient of transitive verbs. (For example, who is doing the hitting and who is getting hit.)

There are many layers to the process of understanding meaning in context. Various techniques are used such as building a feature vector from any information that can be extracted from the document. Statistical tools help with information retrieval and extraction. These tools can help to annotate and label the text with appropriate references (that is, assigning a name to an important person in the text). When you have a sufficient amount of annotated text, machine learning algorithms can ensure that new documents are automatically assigned the right annotations.

## Connecting Words for Meaning

The nature of human communications is complicated. Humans are always transforming the way language is used to convey information. Two individuals can use the same words and even the same sentences and mean different things. We stretch the truth and manipulate words to interpret meaning. Therefore, it is almost impossible to have absolute rules for what words mean on their own and what they mean within sentences. To understand language we have to understand the context of how words are used in individual sentences and what sentences and meanings come before and after those sentences. We are required to parse meaning so that understanding is clear. It is not an easy task to establish context so that those individuals asking questions and looking for answers gain insights that are meaningful.

**THE HISTORY OF NLP**

The desire to achieve techniques for transforming language has been around for decades. In fact, some historians believe that the first attempt to automate the translation from one language to the next occurred as early as the 17th century. From the 1940s to the late 1960s, much of the work in NLP was targeted to machine translation—translating between human languages. However, these efforts discovered a number of complexities that couldn't yet be addressed, including syntactic and semantic processing. The primary technique for translating in those years came through using dictionaries to look up words that would then be translated to another language—a slow and tedious process. This problem led computer scientists to devise new tools and techniques focused on developing grammars and parsers with a focus on syntax. The 1980s saw the evolution of more practical tools such as parsers and grammars to allow systems to better understand not just words but the context and meaning of those words. Some of the most important topics that were developed during the 1980s were the notions of word sense disambiguation, probabilistic networks, and the use of statistical algorithms. In essence, this period saw the beginning of moving from a mechanical approach to natural language into a computational and semantic approach to the topic. The trends in NLP in the past two decades have been in language engineering. This movement has coincided with the growth of the web and the expansion of the amount of automation in text as well as spoken language tools.

## Understanding Linguistics

NLP is an interdisciplinary field that applies statistical and rules-based modeling of natural languages to automate the capability to interpret the meaning of language. Therefore, the focus is on determining the underlying grammatical and semantic patterns that occur within a language or a sublanguage (related to a specific field or market). For instance, different expert domains such as medicine or laws use common words in specialized ways. Therefore, the context of a word is determined by knowing not just its meaning within a sentence, but sometimes by understanding whether it is being used within a particular domain. For example, in the travel industry the word "fall" refers to a season of the year. In a medical context it refers to a patient falling. NLP looks not just at the domain, but also at the levels of meaning that each of the following areas provide to our understanding.

## Language Identification and Tokenization

In any analysis of incoming text, the first process is to identify which language the text is written in and then to separate the string of characters into words (*tokenization*). Many languages do not separate words with spaces, so this initial step is necessary.

## Phonology

*Phonology* is the study of the physical sounds of a language and how those sounds are uttered in a particular language. This area is important for speech recognition and speech synthesis but is not important for interpreting written text. However, to understand, for instance, the soundtrack of a video, or the recording of a call center call, not only is the pronunciation of the words important (regional accents such as British English or Southern United States), but the intonation patterns. A person who is angry may use the same words as a person who is confused; however, differences in intonation will convey differences in emotion. When using speech recognition in a cognitive system, it is important to understand the nuances of how words are said and the meaning that articulation or emphasis conveys.

## Morphology

*Morphology* refers to the structure of a word. Morphology gives us the stem of a word and its additional elements of meaning. Is it singular or plural? Are the verbs first person, future tense, or conditional? This requires that words be partitioned into segments known as *morphemes* that help bring understanding to the meaning of terms. This is especially important in cognitive computing, since human language rather than computing language is the technique for determining answers to questions. Elements in this context are identified and arranged into classes. There are elements including prefixes, suffixes, infixes, and circumfixes. For example, if a word begins with "non-" it has a specific reference to a negative. There is a huge difference in meaning if someone uses the verb "come" versus the verb "came." Combinations of prefixes and suffixes can be combined to form brand new words with very different meanings. Morphology is also used widely in speech and language translation as well as the interpretation of images. Although many dictionaries have been created to provide explanations of different constructions of words in various languages, it is impossible for these explanations to ever be complete (each human language has its own context and nuances that are unique). In languages such as English, rules are often violated. There are new words and expressions created every day.

This process of interpreting meaning is aided by the inclusion of a lexicon or repository of words and rules based on the grammar of a specific language. For example, through a technique called parts of speech tagging or tokenization, it is possible to encapsulate certain words that have definitive meaning. This may be especially important in specific industries or disciplines. For example, in medicine the term "blood pressure" has a specific meaning, However, the words blood and pressure when used independently can have a variety of meanings. Likewise, if you look at the elements of a human face, each component may independently not provide the required information.

## Lexical Analysis

*Lexical analysis* within the context of language processing is a technique that connects each word with its corresponding dictionary meaning. However, this is complicated by the fact that many words have multiple meanings. The process of analyzing a stream of characters from a natural language requires a sequence of *tokens* (a string of text, categorized according to the rules as a symbol such as a number or comma). Specialized *taggers* are important in lexical analysis. For example, an *n-gram tagger* uses a simple statistical algorithm to determine the tag that most frequently occurs in a reference corpus. The analyzer (sometimes called a *lexer*) categorizes the characters according to the type of character string. When this categorization is done, the lexer is combined with a parser that analyzes the syntax of the language so that the overall meaning can be understood.

The lexical syntax is usually a regular language whose alphabet consists of the individual characters of the source code text. The phrase syntax is usually a context-free language whose alphabet consists of the tokens produced by the lexer. Lexical analysis is useful in predicting the function of grammatical words that initially could not be identified. For example, there might be a word like "run" that has multiple meanings and can be a verb or a noun.

## Syntax and Syntactic Analysis

*Syntax* applies to the rules and techniques that govern the sentence structure in languages. The capability to process the syntax and semantics of natural language is critical to a cognitive system because it is important to deduct inferences about what language means based on the topic it is being applied to. Therefore, although words may have a general meaning when used in conversation or written documents, the meaning may be entirely different when used in context of a specific industry. For example, the word "tissue" has different definitions and understanding based on the context of its use. For example, in biology, tissue is a group of biological cells that perform a specific function. However, a tissue can also be used to wrap a present or wipe a runny nose. Even within a domain context, there can still be word-sense ambiguity. In a medical context, "tissue" can be used with skin or a runny nose.

Syntactical analysis helps the system understand the meaning in context with how the term is used in a sentence. This syntactic analysis or parsing is the overall process for analyzing the string of symbols in a natural language based on conforming to a set of grammar rules. Within computational linguistics, *parsing* refers to the technique used by the system to analyze strings of words based on the relationship of those words to each other, in context with their use. Syntactical analysis is important in the question-answering process. For example, suppose you want to ask, "Which books were written by British women authors before the year 1800?" The parsing can make a huge difference in the accuracy of the answer. In this case, the subject of the question is books. Therefore, the answer would be a list of books. If, however, the parser assumed that "British woman authors" was the topic, the answer would instead be a list of authors and not the books they wrote.

## Construction Grammars

Although there are many different approaches to grammar in linguistics, construction grammar has emerged as an important approach for cognitive systems. When approaching syntactical analysis, the results are often represented in a grammar that is often written in text. Therefore, interpretation requires a grammar model that understands text and its semantics. Construction grammar has its roots in cognitive-oriented linguistic analysis. It seeks to find the optimal way to represent relationships between structure and meaning. Therefore, construction grammar assumes that knowledge of a language is based on a collection of "form and function pairings." The "function" side covers what is commonly understood as meaning, content, or intent; it usually extends over both conventional fields of semantics and pragmatics. Construction grammar was one of the first approaches that set out to search for a semantically defined deep structure and how it is manifested in linguistic structures. Therefore, each construction is associated with the principle building blocks of linguistic analysis, including phonology, morphology, syntactic, semantics, pragmatics, discourse, and prosodic characteristics.

## Discourse Analysis

One of the most difficult aspects of NLP is to have a model that brings together individual data in a corpus or other information source so that there is coherency. It is not enough to simply ingest vast amounts of data from important information sources if the meaning, structure, and intention cannot be understood. Certain assertions may be true or false depending on the context. For example, people eat animals, but people are animals, and in general don't eat each other. However, timing is important to understanding context. For example, during the 18th century, cigarette smoking was thought to be beneficial to the lungs. Therefore, if someone were ingesting an information source from that period of time, it would assume that smoking was a good thing. Without context there would be no way to know that premise of that data was incorrect. Discourse is quite important in cognitive computing because it helps deal with complex issues of context. When a verb is used, it is important to understand what that verb is associated with in terms of reference. Within domain-specific sources of data you need to understand the coherence of related information sources. For example, what is the relationship between diabetes and sugar intake? What about the relationship between diabetes and high blood pressure? The system needs to be modeled to look for these types of relationships and context.

Another application for discourse analysis is the capability to understand the "voice of the customer" using sentiment analysis to determine the real feelings and intents being expressed by customers online. The ability to understand the full spectrum of customer issues is well suited for an NLP-focused application. This type of application helps bring together a lot of highly structured and less structured customer information to gain a full understanding of how that customer feels about the company. Is the customer happy? Can this customer get the right level of support? Does the vendor come across as a provider who understands his customer?

## Pragmatics

*Pragmatics* is the aspect of linguistics that tackles one of the fundamental requirements for cognitive computing: the ability to understand the context of how words are used. A document, an article, or a book is written with a bias or point of view. For example, the writer discussing the importance of horses in the 1800s will have a different point of view than the writer talking about the same topic in 2014. In politics, two documents might discuss the same topic and take opposite sides of the argument. Both writers could make compelling cases for their point of view based on a set of facts. Without understanding the background of the writer, it is impossible to gain insight into meaning. The field of pragmatics provides inference to distinguish the context and meaning about what is being said. Within pragmatics, the structure of the conversation within text is analyzed and interpreted.

## Techniques for Resolving Structural Ambiguity

*Disambiguation* is a technique used within NLP for resolving ambiguity in language. Most of these techniques require the use of complex algorithms and machine learning techniques. Even with the use of these advanced techniques, there are no absolutes. Resolution of ambiguity must always deal with uncertainties. We can't have complete accuracy; instead, we rely on the probability of something being most likely to be true. This is true in human language and also in NLP. For example, the phrase, "The train ran late," does not mean that the train could "run"; rather the train was expected to arrive at the station later than it was scheduled. There is little ambiguity in this statement because it is a commonly known phrase. However, others phrases are easily misunderstood. For example, examine the phrase, "The police officer caught the thief with a gun." One might decide that it was the police officer that used a gun to arrest the thief. However, it may well have been the thief was using the gun to commit a crime. Sometimes, the truth of meaning can be hidden inside a complicated sentence.

Because cognitive computing is a probabilistic rather than a deterministic approach to computing, it is not surprising that probabilistic parsing is one way of solving disambiguation. Probabilistic parsing approaches use dynamic programming algorithms to determine the most accurate explanation for a sentence or string of sentences.

## Importance of Hidden Markov Models

One of the most important statistical models for processing both image and speech understanding are *Markov Models*. Increasingly, these models are fundamental to understanding the hidden information inside images, voice, and video. It is now clear that it is complicated to gain a clear understanding of the meaning that is often hidden within language. While the human brain automatically understands how to cope with the fact that the real meaning of a sentence may be indirect, "The cow jumped over the moon" may seem like an impossible task if the sentence were read literally. However, the sentence refers to a song for young children and is intended to be unrealistic and silly. The human mind calculates the probability that this sentence is intended to be a literal action between the cow and the moon. The human understands through the context of their environment, which may dictate a specific interpretation.

The way systems interpret language requires a set of statistical models that are an evolution of a model developed by A.A. Markov in the early 1900s. Markov asserted that it was possible to determine the meaning of a sentence or even a book by looking at the frequency that words would occur in text and the statistical probability that an answer was correct. The most important evolution of Markov's model for NLP and cognitive computing is Hidden Markov Models (HMMs).

The premise behind HMMs is that the most recent data will tell you more about your subject than the distant past because the models are based on the foundations of probability. HMMs therefore help with predictions and filtering as well as smoothing of data. Hidden Markov Models (HMMs) are intended to interpret "noisy" sequences of words or phrases based on probabilistic states. In other words, the model takes a group of sentences or sentence fragments and determines the meaning. Using HMMs requires thinking about the sequence of data. HMMs are used in many different applications including speech recognition, weather patterns, or how to track the position of a robot in relationship to its target. Therefore, Markov models are very important for when you need to determine the exact position of data points when there is a very noisy data environment. Applying HMMs allows the user to model the data sequence supported by a probabilistic model.

Within the model, an algorithm using supervised learning will look for repeating words or phrases that indicate the meaning and how various constructs affect the likelihood that a meaning is true. Markov models assume that the probability of a sequence of words will help us determine the meaning. There are a number of techniques used in HMMs to estimate the probability that a word sequence has a specific meaning. For example, there is a technique called maximum likelihood estimation that is determined by normalizing the content of a corpus.

The value of HMMs is that they do the work of looking for the underlying state of sentences or sentence fragments. Therefore, as the models are trained on more and more data they abstract constructs and meaning. The capability to generate probabilities of meaning and the state transition are the foundation of HMM models and are important in cognitive understanding of unstructured data. The models become more efficient in their ability to learn and to analyze new data sources. Although HMMs are the most prevalent method in understanding the meaning of sentences, another technique called maximum entropy is designed to establish probability through the distribution of words. To create the model, labeled training data is used to constrain the model. This classifies the data.

There are a number of approaches that are important in understanding a corpus in context with its use in a cognitive system. The next section examines some of the most important techniques that are being used.

## Word-Sense Disambiguation (WSD)

Not only do you have to understand a term within an ontology, it is critical to understand the meaning of that word. This is especially complex when a single word may have multiple meanings depending on how it is used. Given this complexity, researchers have been using supervised machine learning techniques. A classifier is a machine learning approach that organizes elements or data items and places them into a particular class. There are different types of classifiers used depending on the purpose. For example, document classification is used to help identify where particular segments of text might belong in your taxonomy.

Often classifiers are used for pattern recognition and therefore are instrumental in cognitive computing. When a set of training data is well understood, supervised learning algorithms are applied. However, in situations in which the data set is vast and it cannot easily be identified, unsupervised learning techniques are often used to determine where clusters are occurring. Scoring of results is important here because patterns have to be correlated with the problem being addressed. Other methods may rely on a variety of dictionaries or lexical knowledge bases. This is especially important when there is a clear body of knowledge—in health sciences, for example. There are many taxonomies and ontologies that define diseases, treatments, and the like. When these elements are predefined, it allows for interpretation of information into knowledge to support decision making. For example, there are well known characteristics of diabetes at the molecular level, the evolution of the disease, and well-tested, successful treatments.

## Semantic Web

NLP by itself provides a sophisticated technique for discovering the meaning of unstructured words in context with their usage. However, to be truly cognitive requires context and semantics. Ontologies and taxonomies are approaches that are expressions of semantics. In fact, the capability to combine natural language processing and the semantic web enables companies to more easily combine structured and unstructured data in ways that are more complicated with traditional data analytic methods. The semantic web provides the Resource Description Framework (RDF), which is the foundational structure used in the World Wide Web for processing metadata (information about the origins, structure, and meaning of data). RDF is used as a way to more accurately find data than would be found in a typical search engine. It provides the ability to rate the available content. RDF also provides a syntax for encoding the particular metadata with standards such as XML (Extensible Markup Language) that supports interoperability between data sources. One of the benefits of schemas that are written in RDF is that it provides one set of properties and classes for describing the RDF generated schemas. The semantic web is instrumental in providing a cognitive approach to gaining insights from a combination of structured and unstructured sources of information in a consistent way.

## Applying Natural Language Technologies to Business Problems

Earlier this chapter mentioned two examples where professionals needed to gain insights from text and other unstructured data. NLP provides an important tool that enables humans to interact with machines. While we are at the early stages of cognitive computing, there are a number of applications that are emerging that take advantage of some of the capabilities of NLP in context with a specific use or market. IBM demonstrated with its Jeopardy! game challenge that it is possible to answer questions as they are being asked. This next section provides some examples of how NLP technologies can transform some industries by understanding language in context.

### Enhancing the Shopping Experience

The most successful web-based shopping sites are those that create a satisfying customer experience. Too often, a customer comes to a site looking for a product based on specific requirements. Typical customers use a search capability to find what they are looking for. Customers may have specific requirements. "I want to purchase a brown and black sweater in size 12 that is not made of wool and is made in a country that does not use child labor. The sweater should be delivered in no more than 5 days, and there should not be a shipping charge." Although it is possible to get an answer to each individual question, it will probably require the user to ask at least six different questions. In addition, some questions, such as if the manufacturer of the sweater has a history of using child labor, may require a series of questions. Users are required to bring all the answers together to complete their transaction. Using NLP text analytics tools within a cognitive context, it is possible to understand what users are asking and create a dialog to provide a positive and interactive experience between humans and machine. By evaluating the use of words and the pattern of use, customers can be satisfied.

## Leveraging the Connected World of Internet of Things

As more and more devices, from cars to highways and traffic lights, are equipped with sensors, there will be the ability to make decisions about what actions to take as conditions change. Traffic management is a complex problem in many large metropolitan areas. If city managers can interact with sensor-based systems combined with unstructured data about events taking place (rallies, concerts, and snow storms), alternative actions can be looked at. A traffic manager may want to ask questions about when to reroute traffic under certain circumstances. If that manager can use an NLP interface to a cognitive system, these questions can be answered in context with everything from weather data to density of traffic to the time when an event will start. Individual domains such as traffic routing and weather predictions will each have their own Hidden Markov Models. In a cognitive system it is possible to correlate this data across domains and models. Matching this data with an NLP engine that interprets textual data can result in significant results. The NLP question and answer interface can help the human interact with this complex data to recommend the next best action or actions.

## Voice of the Customer

The capability for companies to understand not only what their customers are saying but also how it will impact their relationship with that customer is increasingly important. One technique companies use to understand customer attitudes is sentiment analysis. *Sentiment analysis* combines text analytics, NLP, and computational linguistics in order to make sense of text-based comments provided by customers. For example, a company can analyze customer sentiment to predict sales for new product offerings from one of its divisions. However, a customer is not simply a customer for a single business unit. Many customers actually will do business with several different business units within the same company. Creating a corpus of customer data across business units can enable the customer service representative to understand all interactions with customers. Many of these interactions will be stored in notes in customer care systems. These same customers may add comments to social media sites and send e-mail messages directly to the company complaining about problems. There are subtleties in how customers use language that need to be understood to get a clear indication of customer intent.

If the customer is sarcastic or uses the word "not" at the end of a sentence, it is not easily translated. Techniques such as Word Sense Disambiguation are used to decompose the words in a sentence and then provide a sense of the words in context. Word Sense Disambiguation and other fundamental NLP techniques can make the difference between understanding customer satisfaction and missing important signals. To be effective, a business needs to understand the true voice of the customer.

Increasingly, customers are making their preferences understood in new ways. For example, there is a growing requirement to understand the content of data from platforms such as YouTube where individuals provide their personal evaluations of products and services based on their experience. Techniques that understand not just the language but also the intent of those words are a critical part of understanding the voice of the customer. Interpreting not only what words the individual uses but also the order of those words and the intonation of their comments is important.

Although traditional text analytics offerings enable managers to understand words in context, they do not provide the context across lines of business, such as data from manufacturing or delivery systems. A business has to understand customers' attitudes about current problems, future requirements, and what competitors are lurking. To try to get deeper insights, businesses use the net promoter scores to determine how positively or negatively customers are feeling. However, without a true cognitive approach, it is typical that a company will miss some key words and phrases that might include a completely different interpretation of the customers' perceptions of the company. This is why techniques such as Hidden Markov Models may be very important in understanding what a customer is really trying to say about a company or its products and services.

Sentiment Analysis is different across industries. For example, the type of clues that you look for in healthcare will be very different than the types of words that will be meaningful in retail. For example, in healthcare the word "hot" may be an indication of a fever. However, in retail, "hot" may refer to a popular product. Document categorization, ontologies, and taxonomies are important in understanding the difference and making sense of words in context.

In addition to looking for clues in documents, companies rely heavily on information from social media to assess what customers are saying to the company and to other customers. These messages may not always mean what they seem to be saying. For example, a Twitter message that says, "This company sure knows how to treat its customers . . . I wish." is a negative comment. This is why it is important to use NLP tools for text analytics and sentiment analysis to truly understand your customers. These same tools can be used for competitive intelligence. These tools can determine if there is more discussion about an emerging company in your market that should not be ignored. Chapter 6, "Applying Advanced Analytics to Cognitive Computing," discusses advanced analytics in detail.

## Fraud Detection

One of the most important applications for NLP and cognitive computing is the detection of fraud. Traditional fraud detection systems are intended to look for known patterns from internal and external threat databases. Determining risk before it causes major damage is the most important issue for companies dealing with everything from hackers to criminal gangs stealing intellectual property. Although companies leverage firewalls and all sorts of systems that put up a barrier to access, these are not always effective. Smart criminals often find subtle techniques that go under the radar of most fraud detection systems. Having the capability to look for hidden patterns and for anomalies is critical to preventing an event from happening.

In addition, leveraging thousands of fraudulent claims documents, an insurance company can be better prepared to detect subtle indications of fraud. NLP-based cognitive approaches can enable the user to ask questions related to the corpus of data that has been designed based on a model of both acceptable and unacceptable behavior. This corpus can be fed with new information about detected schemes happening somewhere in the world. Understanding not only the words but also their context across many data sources can be applied to fraud prevention. Understanding word sense in complex documents and communications can be significant in preventing fraud.

## Summary

Natural Language Processing is one of the technologies that enables humans to understand the meaning of unstructured data. The ability to not just ask questions but to have an ongoing dialog is key to the value of NLP in context with cognitive computing. As you know, there isn't one single, right answer to just about any question in the world. We make conclusions and judgments based on the information we have available. We also make decisions based on the context of that information. This is not an easy challenge. Not all data is text and words. Increasingly, you access content with data embedded in images, videos, speech, gestures, and sensor data. In this case, deep learning techniques are needed to analyze this type of unstructured data.

We are faced with a world in which there is an unending source of data that only grows by the hour. There are new techniques to analyze that data and there are new methods for putting the pieces together. The human mind has the uncanny ability to make the connections between seemingly unrelated events. But humans are flawed in how much information they can find and then ingest at the same time. NLP, when used in combination with machine learning and advanced analytics, can help humans leverage the depth and breadth of human knowledge in new ways.

# CHAPTER 4

# The Relationship Between Big Data and Cognitive Computing

A cognitive computing environment requires sufficient amount of data to discover patterns or anomalies within that data. In many situations a large data set is required. Within a cognitive system it is important to have enough data that the results of analytics are trustworthy and consistent. A cognitive system requires the ingestion and mapping of data so that the system can begin to discover where there are connections between data sources to begin discovering insights. To accomplish the goal of finding insights in data, a cognitive system includes both structured and unstructured data. Structured data, such as data in a relational database, is created for processing by a computer. In contrast, unstructured data in the form of written material, video, and images, is designed for human consumption and interpretation. This chapter explains the role that big data plays in creating cognitive computing systems.

## Dealing with Human-Generated Data

There is nothing new about dealing with large data sets. In normal form database records, the content and structure are intended to minimize redundancy and to preconfigure the relationships between fields. Therefore, a relational database is optimized for the way *systems* interact and interpret data. Originally, data within a cognitive system was intended for *humans* to process. Such data includes everything from journal articles and other documents to videos, audio, and images, to disparate streams of sensor and machine data. This type of data requires a level of processing beyond the capabilities of relational database systems because the goal is to interpret the meaning and create human readable data.

However, until the last few years, it has been both technically and financially difficult to manage terabytes, let alone petabytes of data. In the past, the best that most organizations could do was to capture samples of data and hope that the right data was sampled. However, there were limitations to how much analysis could be done when major data elements might be missing. In addition, the scope of the data needed to gain a deep understanding of business and technical issues has expanded dramatically. Companies want to look into the future and want to predict what will happen next, and they then want to understand the best actions to take. Without big data techniques, cognitive computing would not be nearly as useful.

## Defining Big Data

Big data requires the capability to manage huge amounts of structured and unstructured data at the appropriate speed and within the right time frame to allow insightful analysis. Big data typically consists of data from a variety of related and unrelated sources that can be quite complex. This can result in huge datasets that may be difficult to manage and analyze. The architectural underpinnings of big data environments have to be designed in a highly distributed manner so that data can be managed and processed quickly and efficiently. This requires highly abstracted and open application programming interfaces (APIs) that provide the capability for a variety of data sources to be ingested, integrated, and evaluated. Big data solutions require a sophisticated infrastructure including security, physical infrastructure, and analytics tools.

### Volume, Variety, Velocity, and Veracity

Before delving into the nuances of big data, you need to understand the four foundational characteristics that define the scope and dimension of the issue:

- *Volume* is the characteristic of big data that gets the most attention. Simply put, volume is the quantity of information that needs to be stored and managed. However, volume can vary significantly. For example, the amount of data generated from a Point of Sale (PoS) system is extremely large. However, the data itself is not complex. In contrast, a single medical image has a huge volume of very complex data. This data is semi-structured since its information consists of images that are well defined but do not have the structure of a database.

- *Variety* of data is instrumental in cognitive computing. As mentioned in the introduction to this chapter, data can be structured (traditional database), unstructured (text), or semi-structured (images and sensor data). The variety of data can range from images to sensor data to text files.

- *Velocity* is the speed of data transmission, processing, and delivery. In some situations, a data source needs to be ingested in periodic batches so that it can be analyzed in context with other data elements. In other situations, data needs to be moved in real time with little or no delay. For example, data from sensors may need to move in real time to react to and repair an anomaly.

- *Veracity* is the requirement that data be accurate. Often if an unstructured source such as social media data is ingested, it will include many inaccuracies and confusing language. However, after an initial data analysis is complete, it will be important to analyze content to make sure that the data that is being used is meaningful.

## The Architectural Foundation for Big Data

Because big data is one of the key foundations of a cognitive system, it is imperative to understand the components of a big data technology stack, as illustrated in Figure 4-1. Without a well-designed set of services, the cognitive environment cannot meet enterprise scaling, security, and compliance requirements. Many of the early cognitive systems designs focus on critical areas such as healthcare that require both scale and security to be viable.

**Figure 4-1:** Big data technology stack

## The Physical Foundation for Big Data

Although most of the discussion in this book focuses on the software enablers for cognitive computing, you need to understand that both big data and cognitive computing require a strong foundation of systems that perform without excessive latency. This physical infrastructure incorporates networks, hardware, and cloud services. Increasingly, to gain the performance required to support big data in the context of cognitive computing, big data infrastructure and hardware needs to be brought together. The underlying physical environment of a big data infrastructure needs to be parallelized and redundant (the system is designed to continue working if one component fails). Networking has to be designed so that it can move data quickly. Likewise, storage has to be implemented and configured so that it can move or connect to information at the right speed. Due to the relatively unlimited scale, capacity, and security of private and public clouds, it is likely that they will become a primary delivery and deployment model for data services.

## Security Infrastructure

Security has to be built in to cognitive applications, but that is not enough given the expansive nature of big data and the speed that data sources have to be deployed in many situations. There are many situations, especially when data comes from real-time devices such as sensors and medical devices, when additional security is required. Therefore, the security infrastructure must ensure security when data is in motion and when data is distributed. Often data is culled from a variety of sources and used for different purposes than originally intended. For example, patient information moved to a big data application might not have the right level of protection for private patient data. Therefore, the security infrastructure needs to include the capability to anonymize data so that data such as Social Security numbers and other personal data are hidden. Techniques such as tokenization can be deployed so that unauthorized users cannot access sensitive data.

## Operational Databases

What makes big data complicated is the requirement to use and integrate many different types of databases and data structures. This is also fundamental to creating a cognitive computing system. Although a lot of the data that will be important to a cognitive system will be unstructured, these data may also need to be stored and managed in structured SQL databases. For example, there might be a travel planning application that requires structured data about hotel room availability hosted in a SQL database; likewise in a healthcare application, there might be the need to gain access to databases of drugs implemented in SQL. Therefore, you need to understand the role of both structured and unstructured data as they come together in big data environments.

### Role of Structured and Unstructured Data

Structured data refers to data that has a defined length and format and whose semantics are explicitly defined in metadata, schemas, and glossaries. Much of structured data is stored in traditional relational databases and data warehouses. In addition, even more structured data is machine-generated from devices such as sensors, smart meters, medical devices, and Global Positioning Systems (GPS). These data sources are instrumental in creating cognitive systems.

Unlike structured data, unstructured or semi-structured data does not follow a specified format, and the semantics of these data types are not explicitly defined. Rather, the semantics must be discovered and extracted through techniques such as natural language processing, text analytics, and machine learning. The need to find ways to collect, store, manage, and analyze unstructured data has become increasingly urgent. As much as 80 percent of all data is unstructured, with the amount of unstructured data growing at a rapid pace. These unstructured data sources include data from documents, journal articles and books, clinical trials, customer support systems, satellite images, scientific data (seismic imagery, atmospheric data, and high-energy physics), radar or sonar data, mobile data, website content, and social media sites. All these types of sources are important elements of a cognitive system because they may provide context for understanding a specific issue.

Unlike most relational databases, unstructured or semi-structured data sources are typically not transactional in nature. Unstructured data follows a variety of structures and may be large. These unstructured data are typically used with nonrelational databases such as NoSQL databases and include the following structures:

- *Key-Value Pair (KVP)* databases rely on an abstraction that provides a combination of an identifier or pointer (Key) and an associated data set (Value). KVP are used in lookup tables, hash tables, and configuration files. It is often used with semi-structured data from XML documents and EDI systems. A commonly used KVP database is an open source database called Riak that is used in high-performance situations such as media-rich data sources and mobile applications.

- *Document databases* provide a technique for managing repositories of unstructured and semi-structured data such as text documents, web pages, complete books, and such. These databases are important in cognitive systems because they effectively manage unstructured data either as static entities or as components that can be dynamically assembled. The JSON data-exchange format supports the ability to manage these types of databases. There are a number of important document databases including MongoDB, CouchDB, Cloudant, Cassandra, and MarkLogic.

■ *Columnar databases* are an efficient database structure that stores data in columns rather than rows. This enables a more efficient technique for writing to and reading data from hard disk storage. The objective is to improve the speed of returning the results of a query. Therefore, it is useful when there is a huge amount of data that needs to be analyzed for query purposes. HBase is one of the most popular columnar databases. Based on Google's BigTable (a scalable storage system that supports sparse data sets), it is particularly useful in cognitive computing use cases because it scales easily and is designed to work with sparse and highly distributed data. This data structure is appropriate for high volumes of data that are updated frequently.

■ *Graph databases* make use of graph structures with nodes and edges to manage and represent data. Unlike a relational database, a graph database does not rely on joins to connect data sources. Rather, graph databases maintain a single structure—the graph. The elements of the graph directly refer to each other so that they track relationships even in sparse data sets. Graph databases are used frequently when dependencies between elements need to be maintained in a dynamic fashion. Common applications include biological model interaction, language relationships, and network connectivity. Therefore, they are well suited for cognitive applications. Neo4J is a commonly used open source graph database.

■ *Spatial databases* are those that are optimized to store and query geometric objects that can include points, lines, and polygons. Spatial data is used in Global Positioning Systems (GPS) to manage, monitor, and track positions and locations. It is useful in cognitive systems that often incorporate GPS data into a solution such as robotics or applications that require an understanding of the impact of weather on a situation. The amount of data required in these types of applications is huge.

■ *PostGIS/OpenGEO* is a relational database that includes a specialized layer to support spatial applications such as 3-D modeling and gathering and analyzing data from sensor networks.

■ *Polyglot Persistence* is a specialized case that brings together different database models for specialized situations. This model is especially important for organizations that need to leverage traditional lines of business applications and databases with text and image data sources.

Table 4-1 provides a comparison of the characteristics of SQL and NoSQL databases.

**Table 4-1:** Important Characteristics of SQL and NoSQL Databases

| ENGINE | QUERY LANGUAGE | MAPREDUCE | DATA TYPES | TRANSACTIONS | EXAMPLES |
|--------|----------------|-----------|------------|--------------|----------|
| Key-value | Lucene, Commands | JavaScript | BLOB, semityped | No | Riak, Redis |
| Document | Commands | JavaScript | Typed | No | MongoDB, CouchDB |
| Columnar | Ruby | Hadoop | Predefined and typed | Yes, if enabled | HBase |
| Graph | Walking, Search, Cypher | No | Untyped | ACID | Neo4J |
| Relational | SQL, Python, C | No | Typed | ACID | PostgreSQL, Oracle, DB2 |

## Data Services and Tools

The underlying data services are critical to operationalizing big data. The supporting tool sets are intended to gather and assemble data so that the data can be processed in the most efficient way. There are a set of services that are needed to support integration, data translation, and normalization as well as scaling. These services include the following:

- A distributed filesystem that is needed to manage the decomposition of structured and unstructured data streams. A distributed filesystem is often a requirement for doing complex data analytics when data comes from a variety of sources.

- Serialized services are required to support persistent data storage as well as supporting remote procedure calls.

- Coordination services are essential for building an application that leverages highly distributed data.

- Extract, transform, and load (ETL) services are required to both load and convert structured and unstructured data to support Hadoop (a key technique for organizing big data).

- Workflow services are the technique for synchronizing processing elements across a big data environment.

## Analytical Data Warehouses

Although a considerable amount of big data begins as unstructured sources, there is also a significant amount of information derived from transactional systems and corporate applications built on relational databases. These structured data sources emanate from systems of record including accounting, customer resource management systems, and other industry-specific applications. The data is usually stored in analytical data warehouses or data marts that are typically a subset of the larger corporate relational database systems. They are useful in creating context when combined with largely unstructured data sources.

## Big Data Analytics

Although business intelligence tools have been around for decades, they typically do not provide the type of sophisticated algorithms needed for big data analytics. Chapter 6, "Applying Advanced Analytics to Cognitive Computing," provides an in-depth perspective on advanced analytics. This chapter provides an overview of how analytics helps businesses to improve business knowledge, anticipate change, and predict outcomes. You see how companies are experiencing a progression in analytics maturity levels ranging from descriptive analytics to predictive analytics to machine learning and cognitive computing. One of the foundational principles of a cognitive computing environment is that there will be a variety of data types that need to be brought together to get a full understanding of the field being analyzed. For example, in medical diagnosis it is helpful to understand the environment of the patient (that is, is he a smoker or overweight?) in addition to analyzing test results. In addition, the diagnostician must compare this one case against new research and outcomes for patients with similar diagnoses and treatment plans. There are additional instances in which there is so much data that it is imperative to use visualization techniques.

In general, advanced analytics in a big data and cognitive computing environment requires the use of sophisticated algorithms because in most cases, there is too much data and too much complex analysis required to use a simple query. As discussed earlier in this chapter, big data typically is too massive to fit into a single machine or into the main memory of a single system. Despite this physical limitation, in order to be effective, the implementation of the algorithm must have the right speed or velocity. Fortunately, there are a number of available and emerging algorithms that support big data analytics including:

- **Sketching and streaming**: These algorithms are used when analyzing streaming data from sensors. Data elements are small but must be moved at a fast speed and require frequent updating.

- **Dimensionality reduction**: These algorithms help to convert data that is highly dimensional into much simpler data. This type of reduction is necessary so it will be easier to solve machine learning problems for classification and regression tasks.

- **Numerical linear algebra**: These algorithms are used when data includes large matrices. For example, retailers use numerical linear algebra to identify customer preferences for a large variety of products and services.

- **Compressed sensing**: These algorithms are useful when the data is sparse or signal data from a streaming sensor are limited to a few linear or time-based measurements. These algorithms enable the system to identify the key elements present in this limited data.

In some situations the large volumes of data included in the analytics process may overwhelm the memory capacity of single machine. Due to the nature of distributed systems it is often necessary to decompose problems and process them in separate physical machines. Techniques like Non-Uniform Memory Access (NUMA) help to overcome these limitations by minimizing thrashing and I/O overhead. NUMA allows for discontinuous pools of memory to be treated as one pool of memory. For example, this technique would allow for an algorithm running on one machine to use memory from another computing device. This additional memory would be treated as an extension of the memory on the first device.

# Hadoop

Hadoop has emerged as one of the most important technologies for managing large amounts of unstructured data in an efficient manner because it uses distributed computing techniques. Hadoop enables you to use parallelization techniques to improve efficiency. It is an open-source community, codebase, and market for a big data environment that is designed, among other things, to parallel-execute code written to MapReduce. Text documents, ontologies, social media data, sensor data, and other forms of nontraditional data types can be efficiently managed in Hadoop. As a result, this technology is critical to the development of corpora for cognitive computing systems. The benefit of using Hadoop is that you can quickly transform massive amounts of nontraditional data from raw data to structured data so that you can search for patterns in that data.

Hadoop is particularly useful for managing big data in cognitive computing because it is easy to dynamically scale and make changes quickly. Hadoop provides a way to efficiently handle the problem of taking highly unstructured data and break it up into component parts to then solve the problem and produce results. Hadoop can be implemented on racks of commodity servers or included in a pre-optimized appliance on vendor-specific hardware. Two key components to Hadoop are described here:

- **Hadoop Distributed File System (HDFS):** A data storage cluster that is both highly reliable and low cost used to make it easy to manage related files across different machines.

- **MapReduce engine:** Provides a way to distribute the processing of the analytics algorithms across a large number of systems. After the distributed computation is complete, all the elements are aggregated back together to provide a result.

Why is HDFS useful in big data and cognitive computing environments? HDFS provides a data service that is particularly well-suited to support large data volumes and high-velocity data. One capability of HDFS that speeds up the processing of large data volumes is based on the data that is written. In HDFS, data is written once and then read many times thereafter, rather than the constant read-writes of other filesystems. HDFS works by breaking large files into smaller pieces called *blocks*. Figure 4-2 illustrates an example of a Hadoop cluster.

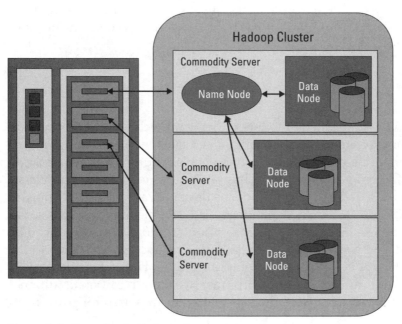

**Figure 4-2:** Example of a Hadoop cluster

These architectural elements are described here:

- **NameNodes:** The role of the NameNode is to keep track of where data is physically stored in the cluster. To maintain this knowledge, the NameNode needs to understand which blocks on which data nodes make up the complete file. The NameNode manages all access to the files, including reads, writes, creates, deletes, and replication of data blocks on the data nodes. In addition, NameNode has the important responsibility of telling the Data Nodes if there is anything for them to do. Because NameNode is critical to keep the HDFS working, it should be replicated to protect against a single point of failure.

■ **Data Nodes:** Data Nodes act as servers that contain the blocks for a set of files. Of the two components, NameNodes have some intelligence, whereas Data Nodes are more simplistic. However, they are also resilient and have multiple roles to play. They store and retrieve the data blocks in the local filesystem of the server. They also store the metadata of a block in the filesystem. In addition, Data Nodes send reports to the NameNode about what blocks are available for file operations. Blocks are stored on Data Nodes.

Hadoop MapReduce is the heart of the Hadoop system. It provides all the capabilities you need to break big data into manageable chunks, process the data in parallel on your distributed cluster, and then make the data available for user consumption or additional processing. And it does all this work in a highly resilient, fault-tolerant manner. You provide input and the MapReduce Engine converts the input into output quickly and efficiently, providing you with the answers you need. Hadoop MapReduce includes several stages or functions that you can implement to help reach your goal of getting the answers you need from big data. The stages include getting data ready, mapping the data, and reducing and combining the data. Figure 4-3 illustrates how Hadoop MapReduce performs its tasks.

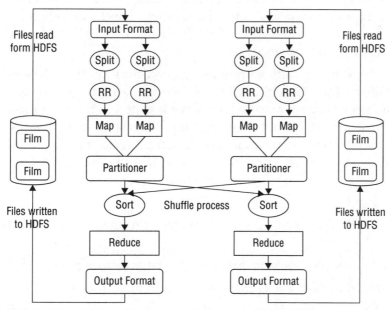

**Figure 4-3:** Workflow and data movement in a small Hadoop cluster

A large and growing ecosystem has developed around Hadoop. This has been extremely advantageous to companies wanting to implement big data initiatives because the technologies in the ecosystem make Hadoop much easier to use. The key tools in the Hadoop ecosystem are described here:

- **Hadoop Yet Another Resource Negotiator (YARN):** Acts as a distributed operating system for big data applications. YARN manages the resources and helps to provide efficient job scheduling and tracking for Hadoop using two services: The ResourceManager (RM) and the Application Master (AM). The RM acts as the arbitrator responsible for distributing resources among all the applications in the system. Each node in the system has a NodeManager that monitors the application's usage of CPU, disk, network, and memory and reports back to the RM. The AM negotiates with the RM regarding resource allocation and works with NodeManagers to execute and monitor tasks.

- **HBase:** A distributed, nonrelational (columnar) database (discussed earlier in this chapter). This means that all data is stored in tables with rows and columns similar to relational database management systems (RDBMSs). It is modeled after Google BigTable and can host large tables (billions of columns/rows) because it is layered on Hadoop clusters of commodity hardware. HBase provides random, real-time read/write access to big data. HBase is highly configurable, providing a great deal of flexibility to address huge amounts of data efficiently. Although the schema must be defined and created before any data can be stored, tables can be altered after the database is up and running. This factor is helpful in big data environments because you don't always know all the details of your data streams in advance.

- **Hive:** A batch-oriented, data-warehousing layer built on the core elements of Hadoop. Hive provides both SQL-like access to structured data and big data analysis with MapReduce. Hive is different from a typical data warehouse in that it is not designed for quick responses to queries. Therefore, it is not appropriate for real-time analytics as complex queries can take hours to complete. Hive is useful for data mining and deeper analytics that do not demand a rapid response.

- **Avro:** A data serialization system.

- **Cassandra**: A scalable multi-master database with no single points of failure.

- **Chukwa:** A data collection system for managing large distributed systems.

- **Mahout:** A scalable machine learning and data mining library.

- **Pig:** A high-level data-flow language and execution framework for parallel computation.

- **Spark:** A fast and general compute engine for Hadoop data. Spark provides a simple and expressive programming model that supports a wide range of applications, including ETL, machine learning, stream processing, and graph computation.

- **Tez:** A generalized data-flow programming framework, built on Hadoop YARN, which provides a powerful and flexible engine to execute an arbitrary DAG of tasks to process data for both batch and interactive use-cases. Tez is being adopted by Hive, Pig and other frameworks in the Hadoop ecosystem, and also by other commercial software (e.g. ETL tools), to replace Hadoop MapReduce as the underlying execution engine.

- **ZooKeeper:** A high-performance coordination service for distributed applications.

## Data in Motion and Streaming Data

Cognitive computing can help businesses to gain value from many types of data that have been hard to interpret and analyze. One of the most important types of data that companies are beginning to work with is data in motion or streaming data. *Streaming data* is a continuous sequence of data that is moving at fast speeds. There are many examples of streaming data ranging from data coming from equipment sensors to medical devices to temperature sensors to stock market financial data and video streams. Streaming data platforms are designed to process this data at high speeds. Speed is of the highest priority when processing streaming data, and it can't be compromised or the results will not be useful. Streaming data is useful when analytics need to be done in real time while the data is in motion. In fact, the value of the analysis (and often the data) decreases with time. For example, if you can't analyze and act immediately, a sales opportunity might be lost or a threat might go undetected.

Many industries are finding ways to gain value from data in motion. In some situations, these companies can take data they already have and begin to use it more effectively. In other situations, they are collecting data that they could not collect before. Sometimes organizations can collect much more of the data that they had been only collecting snapshots of in the past. These organizations use streaming data to improve outcomes for customers, patients, city residents, or perhaps for mankind. Businesses use streaming data to influence customer decision making at the point of sale.

There are some important uses of data streaming today. There will be many more uses as organizations begin to understand the value of leveraging the data created by sensors and actuators. The uses for streaming data include the following:

- In power plant management, there is the need for a highly secure environment so that unauthorized individuals do not interfere with the delivery of power to customers. Companies often place sensors around the perimeter of a site to detect movement. But not all forms of movement represent a threat. For example, the system needs to be able to detect if an unauthorized person is accessing a secure area versus an animal walking around. Clearly, the innocent rabbit does not pose a security risk. Therefore, the vast amount of data coming from these sensors needs to be analyzed in real time so that an alarm is sounded only when an actual threat exists.

- In manufacturing, it will be important to use the data coming from sensors to monitor the purity of chemicals being mixed in the production process. This is a concrete reason to leverage the streaming data. However, in other situations, it may be possible to capture a lot of data, but no overriding business requirement exists. In other words, just because you can stream data doesn't mean that you always should.

- In medical applications, sensors are connected to highly sensitive medical equipment to monitor performance and alert technicians of any deviations from expected performance. The recorded data is continuously in motion to ensure that technicians receive information about potential faults with enough lead time to make a correction to the equipment and avoid potential harm to patients.

- In the telecommunications industry it is critical to monitor large volumes of communications data to ensure that service levels meet customer expectations.

- In the retail industry, point-of-sale data is analyzed as it is created to try to influence customer decision making. Data is processed and analyzed at the point of engagement and maybe used in combination with location data or social media data.

- Understanding the context of data collected is critical in at-risk physical locations. The system has to be able to detect the context of the incident and determine if there is a problem.

- Medical organizations can analyze complex data from medical devices. The resulting analysis of this streaming data can determine different aspects of a patient's condition and then match results against known conditions or other abnormal indicators.

## Analyzing Dark Data

Although the focus has been on the data that is well known and often used by organizations, there is a considerable amount of it that is stored but has never been analyzed or viewed. Called *dark data*, this information is often log data from equipment or security systems. There are often mandates for organizations to store this data. Before the advent of big data approaches such as Hadoop and MapReduce, it was prohibitively expensive to even attempt to analyze the data.

However, there are enormous amounts of valuable data that can help organizations begin to understand patterns that were unknown. For example, machine data stored in these logs may predict when a typical machine will fail based on patterns of temperature, moisture, or other repeated conditions. Having this data available for predictive analysis can help companies know the precise conditions when a machine will fail or when to change a traffic pattern.

## Integration of Big Data with Traditional Data

Although much of the attention in big data has been focused on accessing and analyzing complex unstructured data, it is important to understand that the results of analysis of this data has to be integrated with traditional relational databases, data warehouses, and line of business applications. To create a cognitive system requires that an organization have a holistic view of the required data so that the context is correct.

Therefore, building a cognitive system requires that the massive amounts of data be managed and analyzed. It also requires that there are the right data integration tools and techniques in place to effectively create the corpus. This is not a static process. To be effective, all types of big data must be moved, integrated, and managed based on the problem being addressed.

## Summary

Big data is at the heart of creating an effective cognitive system. There are a variety of different types of big data including structured and unstructured sources. The data is not all the same. There will be important differences in the volume of information, the types of information, and whether it needs to be moved quickly from one place to another. Organizations will have to ensure that when planning to use big data to create the corpus for a cognitive system that the underlying data is accurate and in the right context.

# Representing Knowledge in Taxonomies and Ontologies

Learning from data is at the heart of cognitive computing. If a system cannot use data to improve its own performance without reprogramming, it isn't considered to be a cognitive system. But to do that, there must be a wealth of data available at the heart of the environment, formats for representing the knowledge contained within that data, and a process for assimilating new knowledge. This is analogous to the way a child learns about the world through observation, experience, and perhaps instruction. This chapter looks at some simple knowledge representations before exploring more sophisticated and comprehensive approaches to knowledge representation: taxonomies and ontologies.

## Representing Knowledge

In computer systems as in humans, knowledge may include facts or beliefs and general information. It should also include standard knowledge organizational structures such as ontologies and taxonomies—as well as relationships, rules, or properties that describe objects (nouns) and help to categorize them. For example, we may know that people are animals and Bob is a person, so Bob should have all the properties that we associate with animals. In people, we sometimes equate knowledge with understanding, but that's not the case with computers. Of course, in a computer, it is possible to "know" a lot without "understanding" anything. In fact, that's the basic definition of a *database*: a collection of associated data organized within a computer environment so that it can be easily accessed.

Think for a minute about the smartest people you know. What makes someone smart or intelligent? It's much more than having an encyclopedic memory. Intelligence is the ability to acquire, retain, analyze, develop, communicate, and apply knowledge. One can be intelligent without knowing much—think of a precocious child, who may display signs of intelligence before acquiring much knowledge. Conversely, a person can know plenty of facts but not know how to use those facts to accomplish a goal.

## Developing a Cognitive System

There are many different techniques that are useful in creating a cognitive system. One important technique is to leverage massive amounts of data and analyze the patterns that emerge from that data without providing an explicit query. This issue is covered in Chapter 6, "Applying Advanced Analytics to Cognitive Computing." In essence, you are not telling the system what answer you are looking for. In a 2012 experiment, Google researchers selected at random 10 million images from YouTube videos and used a network of 16,000 processors to look for patterns. Perhaps not surprisingly, this system found a distinct pattern (shading in various points of the image in the same proportion and relationship to other repeated subimages) from among more than 20,000 distinct items in the images. By analyzing these images in detail, looking for such a pattern that was repeated more often than random arrangements of pixels—regardless of color, background, image quality, and so on—it found one promising combination of shadings that appeared frequently enough to be flagged as unique. It "discovered" a generic pattern for images of cats.

Although this experiment verified that it was possible to detect patterns systematically in a big data sample, it was only a beginning. Most cognitive computing systems take a more focused approach. They are designed to learn and provide value to users in a specific field or domain, such as medical diagnosis or customer service. A challenge for these cognitive systems builders is to capture enough relevant knowledge to be useful and to represent it in a way that allows the system to add to the knowledge or refine it with experience.

Each industry and each domain within that industry has its own vocabulary and historical knowledge. These domains include a lot of different types of objects, from systems and parts of the body in medical systems to engine parts in a predictive aircraft maintenance system. Each of the object types may have specific rules that guide their interaction and behavior. For example, an X-ray may be a specific object type that has certain physical properties.

Likewise, a wing nut in an airplane part will be associated with specific rules governing how it may be installed and serviced with other physical components. The process of capturing and representing this knowledge requires experts who understand the vocabulary and rules of their industry well enough to explain them so that they can be codified for machine processing.

However, even with the support of industry experts, it is not possible to capture enough knowledge and nuance to design a system that replicates a complete understanding of an industry or market. Therefore, most cognitive systems start with a meaningful subset of domain knowledge and then dynamically—with experience or training—enhance and refine that basic model. The foundation of this approach is to define taxonomies and ontologies focused on a specific area of knowledge.

Another interesting aspect of creating cognitive systems is "cross-context" understanding. In order to achieve higher levels of cognition, people or systems must be able to correlate data from multiple corpora at the same time. Humans do this type of correlation early on in life with almost no effort. We learn how to ride a bicycle and then we process information about weather, traffic, road conditions, etc. so that we can ride safely and get where we plan to go. In our earlier example about aircraft parts, wouldn't it be appropriate for the cognitive system to connect the parts assembly with safety and historical weather data to better recommend materials or processes?

## Defining Taxonomies and Ontologies

Before getting into the details of how knowledge is managed, it is important to define taxonomies and ontologies. This is covered in more detail later in this chapter ("Explaining How to Represent Knowledge"), but definitions now will provide context. Taxonomies are a hierarchical way of capturing or codifying information within a particular field of study.

You can think of the categories of data within a taxonomy as a set of classification frameworks with common properties. *Hierarchical* refers to a structure or structures where a subcategory, like a subset, inherits all the properties defined in the superset or "top" of the category. A taxonomy typically has a formal way to specify the properties that apply to all elements within each category.

If you were interested in capturing everything that is known about motor vehicles, you could start with a set of motor vehicles, as shown in Figure 5-1, and perhaps divide that into subsets of passenger cars, motorcycles, commercial vehicles, and so on. You could create further categories or subsets for buses, taxis, and so on. This can become quite cumbersome, and the decision of which sets are at the highest levels should reflect the intended use. For example, is it more important to the user that an electric bus carries a lot of people, or that it is powered by electricity? Fortunately, you can factor the data according to usage to simplify development.

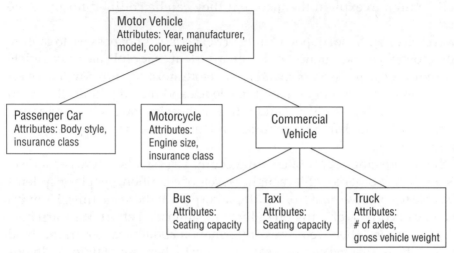

**Figure 5-1:** Motor vehicle types

For example, in a vehicle tracking system, there could be definitions for cars, boats, motorcycles, buses, and trucks. If you are a motor vehicle department and you are tracking registrations to determine ownership and assign fees, there is little information you need about each category. A car may be defined as a vehicle with two axles, and each "instance" of car—representing one actual car in the physical world—would have a weight assigned that could compute registration fees. If your state decides to tax based on other attributes, such as fuel type or EPA fuel ratings, the taxonomy might include those details in each specific car record, or create classes for "fuel efficient" and "gas guzzler" vehicles.

For other applications, the same vehicles may be categorized differently in a taxonomy. For example, an insurance company must calculate a liability class based on properties like horsepower versus weight and body type (convertible versus sedan). The taxonomy for an insurance company could organize the classes differently and have new subclasses tailored to their processing requirements. Certain industries have well-defined, mature taxonomies. The pharmaceutical industry, for example, has detailed taxonomies of compounds used to create a variety of drugs.

In contrast, an *ontology* generally includes all the information you would capture in a taxonomy, but also includes details about rules and relationships between the categories and about criteria for inclusion. An ontology is more likely to include semantic information that can be used to guide decision making. A richer, more fully specified ontology enables more ways that it can be applied to solving problems and decision making.

**THE ROLE OF STATE IN A COGNITIVE SYSTEM**

Before getting into a discussion about how to represent knowledge and how to build a model that can make the connections between elements, you need to understand the concept of state. *State* is the condition of a system at a particular point in time or in a specific situation. As a simple example, a body of water could be in one of three states: solid, liquid, or gas. The state variable is the temperature. To determine what state it was in last month, knowing the temperature at the time (and for a period leading up to that time) would be sufficient. For a cognitive computing system, the state may include many variables, from values for stored knowledge to user logs to configuration data (which modules were actually in place at a particular time). The ability to determine state information or restore a system to a particular state may be an auditing requirement (for example, in a financial services or medical diagnostic system). If the system is used as a cognitive platform for applications, the platform may not need to track state information at all if that is left to the applications themselves.

## Explaining How to Represent Knowledge

Deciding on a knowledge representation scheme—such as taxonomies and ontologies—is a critical step in planning a cognitive computing solution. Simplicity is always a good design goal, but some problem domains are inherently complex, with relationships that are imprecise or that cannot be specified completely. As a general rule, we want to at least capture all the known object types or classes. A *class* defines the properties of a set of elements or instances. The class definition accomplishes the goal of providing information about relationships or behaviors as the system learns. A more robust representation requires more work in the beginning, but it is more flexible when the system is operational.

Domain knowledge within a cognitive computing application may be captured and stored in a variety of data structures, from simple lists, to conventional databases, to documents, to multidimensional purpose-built structures. Cognitive computing system designers can use procedural, list-processing, functional, or object-oriented programming languages to specify and implement these structures. They may use data modeling tools or even specify the knowledge model in a language created just for this purpose. The choice of tools and representations should reflect the types of operations the system will have to perform on the data. As is the case in any application, there may be trade-offs that dictate one approach over another. Optimizing a medical system for fast diagnosis of toxins (poison control, for example) may make it suboptimal for recommending appropriate lifestyle changes based on similar input. It is important to consider typical scenarios and rare but conceivable test cases when defining the knowledge model and the structure you will use to implement it in software.

A single system may actually contain several knowledge repositories, partitioned by the task or by some attribute of a particular class of objects. For example, a predictive maintenance system for a large manufacturing firm may have separate instances for problems with toasters and MRI machines. Knowledge for each machine type could be organized by attributes of the machine, or perhaps by types of fault and their frequency of occurrence.

The logical design for the collection of data structures used to represent knowledge acts as a model for the domain. Some domains are straightforward to model. For example, the game of chess is centuries old and easy to explain and represent but difficult to master. Chess is a two-person, perfect-information, zero-sum game. Players see the same board and can be expected to know the rules and therefore mentally compute possible next moves, limited by their ability to store all the alternatives in their brain's memory.

A system that plays chess has to model the following elements: an 8x8 chessboard and 32 chess pieces, grouped into 6 categories or object types (pawn, rook, knight, bishop, queen, and king). Each category has its own point value and set of permissible behaviors. The system must know the starting location and color of each piece. (Actually, if it "knows" the starting location, it "knows" the color, too.) As the game progresses, the system must ensure or enforce that only legal moves are made and calculate its own best move based on the state of the game. Figure 5-2 shows a variety of representations that could capture the state of a chess game.

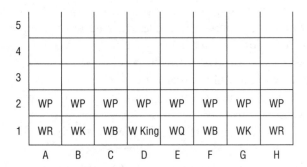

|   | A | B | C | D | E | F | G | H |
|---|---|---|---|---|---|---|---|---|
| 5 | | | | | | | | |
| 4 | | | | | | | | |
| 3 | | | | | | | | |
| 2 | WP | WP | WP | WP | WP | WP | WP | WP |
| 1 | WR | WK | WB | W King | WQ | WB | WK | WR |

Possible first moves

A2 A3, A2 A4, B2 B3, B2 B4, C2 C3, C2 C4, D2 D3, D2 D4
B1 A3, B1 C3

|   | Piece | Place |
|---|-------|-------|
| 1 | WR | A 1 |
| 2 | WK | B 1 |
| 3 | WB | C 1 |
| 4 | W King | D 1 |
|   | ⋮ | ⋮ |
| 30 | BK | F 8 |
| 31 | BB | G 8 |
| 32 | BR | H 8 |

Rules

| Piece | Moves |
|-------|-------|
| Rook | Vertical, horizontal, 1-n |
| Knight | Row +/−2, col +/−1<br>Row +/−1, col +/−2 |
| Bishop | Diagonal 1-n |
|  | ⋮ |

**Figure 5-2:** Representing a chess game

Chess notation has evolved over the years. Today, a Standard Algebraic Notation is commonly used to record physical games by the World Chess Federation. The notation may be used internally in a chess program to capture knowledge about the "state" of the game. This means that the knowledge of the parts and permissible behavior is straightforward. In fact, a program that considers only the current state of the board and evaluates several or even every possible future state before making its next move could beat human champions (who have a limited ability to evaluate future states) without being cognitive—all the rules could be instantiated in code before the first move is made. The brute force approach is possible because the domain is completely specified. At any point in the game, both sides have perfect information and can—in theory—calculate and evaluate every possible subsequent move given sufficient time and memory.

A more sophisticated approach might be adapted to an individual opponent by reviewing every move she played in past games to predict her next move based on how she moved in similar game states (configurations of pieces). Using historical behavior to defend against unconventional strategies would require much more of this historical knowledge. The pieces, behaviors, and game state would be the same with or without considering historical behavior of a particular opponent. All could be represented with simple data structures—a reasonable assignment for a college freshman studying computer science. The difference is in the complexity of knowledge required to select a move based on context. Although the possible moves are always the same for a given state, the choice of moves might differ based on context.

Writing a chess program that can adapt to an individual opponent by evaluating the context of a particular move by comparing it to historical behavior to defend against unconventional strategies would be more complex, but the underlying principles are the same.

Now look at a more difficult domain to represent: automotive diagnostics and repair (Figure 5-3). Every automobile powered by an internal combustion engine (ICE) shares certain properties, components, and major subsystems. Electrical, fuel, ignition, cooling, and exhaust are but a few of the dozen or so commonly recognized subsystems. A cognitive solution for automotive diagnostics would have to represent each component of each system, and possible interactions between them.

Here, classification begins to blur the lines; for example, is an electric fuel pump part of the electrical system or part of the fuel system? Is a coil part of the electrical system or ignition system? For diagnostics, common symptoms must be codified before the system can suggest a cause. Is black smoke coming from the exhaust pipe an indication of an exhaust system failure or a fuel failure? (It is typically fuel.) Is white smoke an exhaust or fuel problem? (Usually neither—it's an indication of a bad gasket allowing water in the combustion chamber.)

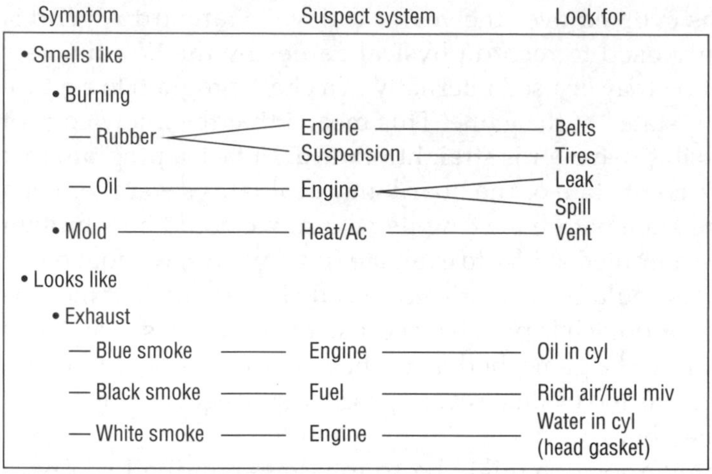

```
       Symptom                Suspect system            Look for

  • Smells like

      • Burning

         — Rubber  ————————  Engine    ————————  Belts
                                Suspension ————————  Tires

         — Oil  ———————————  Engine    ————————  Leak
                                                      Spill

      • Mold  —————————————  Heat/Ac  ————————  Vent

  • Looks like

      • Exhaust

         — Blue smoke  ———— Engine  ———————— Oil in cyl

         — Black smoke ———— Fuel    ———————— Rich air/fuel miv

         — White smoke ———— Engine  ———————— Water in cyl
                                                      (head gasket)
```

**Figure 5-3:** Automotive diagnostics and repair

When it is impractical to capture all the relationships between components, and between component condition and symptoms of failure in advance, a cognitive system can accept feedback and improve its performance. However, this is only practical if the knowledge representation is robust enough to cover all conditions. Decisions made about classification impact how knowledge is stored, which may dictate what types of problems can be easily solved.

So far we have been dealing with relatively simple domains. It is much more difficult to navigate when a domain's experts do not agree on knowledge and rules. For example, in drug discovery there are too many factors and complications to create a straightforward knowledge base. Therefore, it is not surprising that there are practical limits as to what we can process effectively today.

Although some domains are straightforward, others are broad and complicated. For example, though we think of "medicine" as a single domain, it actually consists of a huge number of disciplines. Therefore, you would not expect that there could be a single representation of the knowledge in that domain. You can't represent everything relevant to medicine in one system—that would be like having a 1:1 scale map of the world with views for political boundaries, roads, topography, and weather. In medicine, there are well-defined subsystems (such as circulatory, respiratory, nervous, and digestive), and well-defined diseases, medical conditions, and pathologies that cross these systemic boundaries.

For representing and codifying knowledge, one-half the battle is deciding what to ignore in a specific model. As Marvin Minsky, a pioneer in artificial intelligence and knowledge management, noted in *Artificial Intelligence at MIT: Expanding Frontiers* (Patrick H. Winston, Ed., vol. 1, MIT Press, 1990. Reprinted in *AI Magazine,* Summer 1991):

*To solve really hard problems, we'll have to use several different representations. This is because each particular kind of data structure has its own virtues and deficiencies, and none by itself would seem adequate for all the different functions involved with what we call common sense.*

Therefore, some of the earliest cognitive systems are focused on a single branch of medicine, such as oncology. By focusing on an area of medicine, you can start to partition the domain into manageable and meaningful segments.

As with all branches of medicine, the comprehensive study of oncology requires an understanding of diagnosis, care or treatments, and prevention. Each of these subcategories may be further decomposed and studied in isolation. In practice, that is what leads to professional specialization (knowing more and more about a smaller subset of the field), but to "understand" oncology you must understand the interrelationships between these subcategories. Table 5-1 lists common types of cancers. Each subcategory or cancer type would be associated with disease-specific paradigms for diagnosis and treatment.

**Table 5-1:** Common Types of Cancers

| Common Solid Tumors | Lung, colon, breast, reproductive, stomach, brain |
| --- | --- |
| Hematologic Tumors | Leukemia, lymphoma |
| Connective Tissue Tumors | Sarcoma |

## Managing Multiple Views of Knowledge

In the automobile diagnostic example, you could factor the available knowledge into separate models for each subsystem. Many expert mechanics and maintenance manuals organize their knowledge by subsystems. Asking qualifying questions to rule out one system or another before going deeper into diagnosing a problem within a single system works well and may appear to be an obvious approach. However, there is a danger in partitioning knowledge into subsystems. Partitioning may make it difficult to correctly identify problems when they span multiple subsystems. For example, for healthcare, there might be a subsystem about diagnosing high blood pressure and a second subsystem focused on diabetes. In fact, there is often a correlation between these two subsystems that needs to be taken into account.

In a complex domain like oncology, in which it is more common to have complications involving several subsystems, you may need more than one view or representation to capture all the relevant knowledge. A professional may use books, journals, case notes, and communications with peers to fully understand a new case. Of course, the stored knowledge in the doctor's brain is an amalgam of historical references to these same types of resources.

In a cognitive computing system, you can also capture this type of knowledge and segment it into views that can be linked together to present a more complete view. New discoveries may change the way professionals think about problems, and that in turn may change the way you choose to segment knowledge in your cognitive systems. For example, cancer types and treatments were historically described by parts of the body where they were found. Someone studying a case of liver cancer might not immediately think to try a treatment previously tested and approved for use on another organ. Recently, however, it has become possible to analyze vast quantities of data across organ boundaries and compare cases based on attributes of the patient's genome. Similarity analysis for healthcare diagnostics is an important application of machine-learning algorithms. This has led to the discovery of promising patterns between patients, genomes, cancers, treatments, and outcomes. As a result, new relationships have been found and new treatments have been applied. This type of discovery points out the value in deferring partitioning as long as possible to prevent missing relationships.

## Models for Knowledge Representation

There are many different ways of representing knowledge. It could be as simple as a chart on the wall or as complicated as a full lexicon of terms used in a field along with their representations and definitions. This section provides an overview of taxonomies and ontologies. In addition, it provides some insights into additional knowledge representations that are important in a cognitive system. Within cognitive systems, knowledge representations range from simple trees to ontologies, taxonomies, and semantic webs.

### Taxonomies

A *taxonomy* is a representation of the formal structure of classes or types of objects within a domain. Taxonomies are generally hierarchical and provide names for each class in the domain. They may also capture the membership properties of each object in relation to the other objects. The rules of a specific taxonomy are used to classify or categorize any object in the domain, so they must be complete, consistent, and unambiguous. This rigor in specification should ensure that any newly discovered object must fit into one, and only one, category or object class.

The concept of using a taxonomy to organize knowledge in science is well established. In fact, if you've ever started a guessing game by asking "is it animal, mineral, or vegetable?" you were using Linnaeus' 1737 taxonomy of nature. Linnaeus called those three categories the "kingdoms" in his taxonomy (Figure 5-4). Everything in nature had to fall into one of those categories, which he further divided into class, order, genus, species, and variety. At any level in a taxonomy, there can be no common elements between classes. If there are, a new, common higher-level category is required.

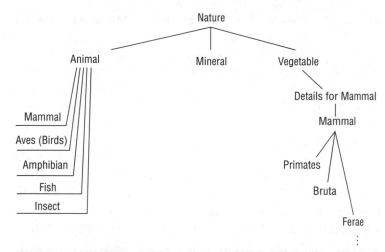

**Figure 5-4:** Taxonomy of nature

Members of any class in the taxonomy inherit all the properties of their ancestor classes. For example, if you know that humans are mammals, you know that they are endothermic (warm-blooded) vertebrates with body hair and produce milk to feed their offspring. Of course, you also know that humans breathe, but you know that because everything in the class mammals belong to the phylum chordata, which are all animals, and animals respire. Inheritance simplifies representation in a taxonomy because common properties need be specified only at the highest level of commonality.

In a cognitive computing system, the reference taxonomy may be represented as objects in an object-oriented programming language or in common data structures such as tables and trees. These taxonomies consist of rules and constructs that will not likely change over time.

## Ontologies

An *ontology* provides more detail than a taxonomy, although the boundary between them in practice is somewhat fuzzy. An ontology should comprehensively capture the common understanding—vocabulary, definitions, and rules—of a community as it applies to a specific domain. The process of developing an ontology often reveals inconsistent assumptions, beliefs, and practices within the community. It is important in general that consensus is reached, or at least that areas of disagreement in emerging fields be surfaced for discussion. In many fields, professional associations codify their knowledge to facilitate communications and common understanding. These documents may be used as the basis of an ontology for a cognitive computing system.

For example, the codes in the Diagnostic and Statistical Manual of Mental Disorders (DSM) of the American Psychiatric Association classify all disorders recognized by the APA. These definitions may change over time. For example, in DSM-5 the diagnosis of attention-deficit/hyperactivity disorder (ADHD) was updated to state that symptoms can occur by age 12 instead of the older view that they had to occur by age 6. That would be a small change in an ontology based on the DSM. A bigger change, as shown in Figure 5-5, was the replacement of four specific disorders (autism, Asperger's, childhood disintegrative disorder, and pervasive developmental disorder not otherwise specified) with a single condition called autism spectrum disorder (ASD). Another major change was the elimination of a "multi-axial" reference system that distinguished between medical and mental disorders. Structural changes like that reflect a change in thinking, which needs to be reflected in any system based on this classification scheme.

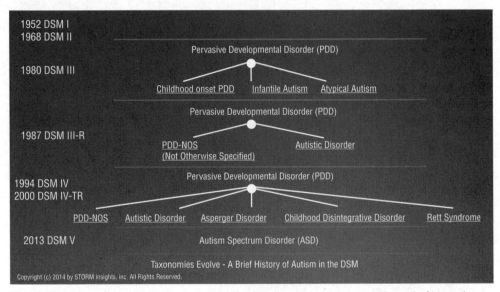

**Figure 5-5:** Taxonomies Evolve—Autism in the Diagnostic and Statistical Manual of Mental Disorders

A practitioner needs to keep up with changing definitions and standards of care, and a cognitive computing system designed to aid a practitioner must update its knowledge base accordingly. For example, a system tracking patient care must account for the fact that a specific disorder no longer exists but has been superseded by another.

As mentioned, sometimes multiple views are necessary, and they must be compatible. In healthcare, we think of three major constituencies: providers, payers, and patients. Their ability to communicate is critical. Continuing with the mental health example, provider/payer communication is accomplished by the DSM mapping to the ICD-9-CM codification used by insurance companies. It also uses codes from the U.S. Clinical Modifications of the World

Health Organization's International Classification of Diseases (ICD) to provide global compatibility.

The process of updating from DSM IV to DSM V required three drafts and generated more than 13,000 comments from the community. That is an extreme case, but virtually all established professions and disciplines have some common codification that can be used as the basis for a cognitive computing ontology.

For a cognitive computing solution, it is critical that industry experts agree on the underlying ontology. If there are disagreements with the structure or content of an ontology, the output of the system is suspect. Practitioners need to determine what information means in context with their requirements; otherwise, the system will not be meaningful. Early ontologies for learning systems were often specified in programming notation, predominantly LISP (LISt Processing, the original lingua franca of artificial intelligence). LISP is still in use, but as larger domains are being specified in greater detail, developers are increasingly turning to a special purpose language. Web Ontology Language (OWL) is a formal ontology specification language supported by open source tools. As with any knowledge representation, the chosen structure imposes limits on what is captured, and what is captured imposes limits on what can be answered.

## Other Methods of Knowledge Representation

In addition to ontologies, there are other approaches to knowledge representation. Two examples are described in the following sections.

### Simple Trees

A *simple tree* is a logical data structure that captures parent-child relationships. In a model where the relationships are rigid and formalized, a simple tree, implemented as a table with (element, parent) fields in every row, is an efficient way to represent knowledge. Simple trees are used frequently in data analytic tools and in catalogs. For example, a retailer's catalog may have 30 or 40 categories of products that it offers. Each category would have a series of elements that are members of that category.

### The Semantic Web

Some members of the World Wide Web Consortium (W3C) are attempting to evolve the current web into a "semantic web" as described by Tim Berners-Lee, et al in *Scientific American* in 2001. In a *semantic web*, everything would be machine usable because all data would have semantic attributes, as described in the W3C's Resource Description Framework (RDF). The current web is basically a collection of structures or documents addressed by uniform resource locators (URLs). When you find something at an address, there is no required uniformity about how it is represented. By adding semantics, you would force structure into everything on the web. If we did have a semantic web, we could use more of what is on the web for a cognitive system without extensive preprocessing to uncover structural information.

It is important to differentiate between semantics and syntax. *Syntax* describes the legal structural relationships between elements. For example, one legal form of a sentence is <subject><predicate>, where <subject> may be a noun phrase and <predicate> may be a verb phrase. According to that rule, "Bob runs quickly" is a valid sentence. ("Bob" is the noun phrase, "runs quickly" is the verb phrase.) However, because syntax is structural, we can substitute any noun for another and still be syntactically valid. "Nose runs quickly" or "The blue glass runs quickly" are similarly valid. That's where semantics—the rules for interpreting or attributing meaning to language—come into play.

When processing natural language or even programming languages, you look at syntax first and then semantics. Does the concept follow logically, and then what is the meaning of those terms as they apply to a specific topic? Syntactically, you are looking for the right word type, but semantically you need to look for meaningful words in context. To identify meaning within data requires that there is a hierarchy that takes enough data so that hidden meanings begin to emerge from the usage and context within the corpus of data. The end result has to be the meaning and intent of the data.

## The Importance of Persistence and State

The concept of state was discussed in terms of modeling and remembering the placement of pieces on a chessboard after a particular move. Without capturing and recording the state of a game, it would be impossible to stop the application and resume it later. Cognitive computing applications—and platforms—may also be "stateful" and remember details about their last interaction with a user, or a cumulative history, or they may be "stateless" and start each session without preconceptions. At a higher level, they may also capture new knowledge each time and preserve it for future sessions with the same or different users. Alternatively, some knowledge may be preserved, whereas some that is related to a specific user may not be retained.

In many situations, knowledge—or beliefs that we treat as facts—changes as we learn more about a field. For example, what we assumed a decade ago about treatments for lung cancer is radically different from what we know today. Therefore, as a field of study matures, early assumptions about relationships may ultimately be proved false, or confidence levels may change. That is an argument for preserving some state attributes or auditing data to reconstruct the state of the system when something was captured as a "fact." For example, a nutrition system giving advice in 2010 would likely have reported that butter was dangerous, but in 2014 new evidence emerged and we "knew" that was false—based on the best available data at the time. In 2020, the state of the practice may swing back to an antifat stance based on new evidence, so it is critical that we capture time information with knowledge.

This concept of statefulness is especially important in a cognitive system in which asking a single question will not resolve an issue. In medical diagnosis of a type of cancer, the practitioner may need to ask a series of related questions. Each question will lead to a follow up question. The system needs to not only know the current question but the context of the previous question. A simple example is instructive. When you use a voice recognition system such as Apple's Siri, you might ask, "Is there a restaurant near where I am walking?" Siri will tell you, "Yes, there is a restaurant within the next block." If you now ask, "Does it serve pizza?" Siri will not know the context and will not provide you with a correct answer.

## Implementation Considerations

The primary consideration in choosing which representations to use requires that you understand what you need to capture for the types of queries you want answers to. For example, if you want to search quickly for part numbers while performing aircraft maintenance, a tree structure might be sufficient. You may not need to know the history of the origins of all the parts that are used. If you need to trace back the manufacturing history of specific parts to identify likely failures based on other issues with parts made in the same batch, you would need a more detailed representation. And if you are looking for possible relationships between diabetes and a specific skin condition—crossing typical knowledge boundaries—you may need to use a sophisticated and more comprehensive ontology.

## Summary

When an organization creates and captures its representation of relevant domain knowledge, that knowledge has to be stored and managed on an ongoing basis. There is no method that works best in every situation. The method used depends on the type of structure within the knowledge, the industry, and many other factors. One certainty is that the size of the data sources will continue to expand and explode over time. Therefore, scalability is a foundational requirement to create cognitive systems that are both trusted and reliable.

As soldiers quickly learn in basic training, when the map and the terrain don't agree, they must believe the terrain. In a cognitive system, when the system's knowledge doesn't reflect reality, the system must be changed. The time to plan for operational changes is in the design phase where knowledge representation decisions are made.

# 6

# Applying Advanced Analytics to Cognitive Computing

Advanced analytics refers to a collection of techniques and algorithms for identifying patterns in large, complex, or high-velocity data sets with varying degrees of structure. It includes sophisticated statistical models, predictive analytics, machine learning, neural networks, text analytics, and other advanced data mining techniques. Some of the specific statistical techniques used in advanced analytics include decision tree analysis, linear and logistic regression analysis, social network analysis, and time series analysis. These analytical processes help discover patterns and anomalies in large volumes of data that can anticipate and predict business outcomes. Accordingly, advanced analytics is a critical element in creating long-term success with a cognitive system that can ask for the right answers to complex questions and predict outcomes. This chapter explores the technologies behind advanced analytics and how they can be leveraged in a knowledge-driven cognitive environment. With the right level of advanced analytics, you can gain deeper insights and predict outcomes in a more accurate and insightful manner.

## Advanced Analytics Is on a Path to Cognitive Computing

The role of analytics in an organization's operational processes has changed significantly over the past 30 years. As illustrated in Table 6-1, companies are experiencing a progression in analytics maturity levels, ranging from descriptive analytics to predictive analytics to machine learning and cognitive computing. Companies have been successful at using analytics to understand both where they have been and how they can learn from the past to anticipate the future. They can describe how various actions and events will impact outcomes. Although the knowledge from this analysis can be used to make predictions, typically these predictions are made through a lens of preconceived expectations. Data scientists and business analysts have been constrained to make predictions based on analytical models that are based on historical data. However, there are always unknown factors that can have a significant impact on future outcomes. Companies need a way to build predictive models that can react and change when there are changes to the business environment.

**Table 6-1:** Analytics Maturity Levels

| ANALYTICS TYPE | DESCRIPTION | EXAMPLES OF QUESTIONS ANSWERED |
|---|---|---|
| Descriptive Analytics | Understand what happens when using analytic techniques on historical and current data. | Which product styles are selling better this quarter as compared to last quarter? Which regions are exhibiting the highest/lowest growth? What factors are impacting growth in different regions? |
| Predictive Analytics | Understand what might happen when using statistical predictive modeling capabilities, including data mining and machine learning. Predictive models use historical and current/real-time data to predict future outcomes. Models look for trends, clusters of behavior, and events. Models identify outliers. | What are the predictions for next quarter's sales by product and region? How does this impact raw material purchases, inventory management, and human resource management? |
| Prescriptive Analytics | Use to create a framework for making a decision about what to do or not do in the future. The "predictive" element should be addressed in prescriptive analytics to help identify the relative consequences of your actions. Use an iterative process so that your model can learn from the relationship between actions and outcomes. | What is the best mix of products for each region? How will customers in each region react to advertising promotions and offers? What type of offer should be made to each customer to build loyalty and increase sales? |
| Machine Learning and Cognitive Computing | Collaboration between humans and machines to solve complex problems. Assimilate and analyze multiple sources of information to predict outcomes. Need depends on the problems you are trying to solve. Improve effectiveness of problem solving and reduce errors in predicting outcomes. | How secure is the city environment? Are there any alerts from the vast amount of information streaming from monitoring devices (video, audio, and sensing devices for smoke or poisonous gases)? Which combination of drugs will provide the best outcome for this cancer patient based on the specific characteristics of the tumor and genetic sequencing? |

The next frontier, which comes with opportunities for enormous change, includes big data analytics and incorporates the technologies of machine learning and cognitive computing. As shown in Figure 6-1, there is a convergence of technologies cutting across analytics and artificial intelligence. One major push for this convergence is the change in the timing and immediacy of data. Today's applications often require planning and operational changes at a fast rate for businesses to remain competitive. Waiting 24 hours or longer for results of a predictive model is no longer acceptable. For example, a customer relationship management application may require an iterative analytics process that incorporates current information from customer interactions and provides outcomes to support split-second decision making, ensuring that customers are satisfied. In addition, data sources are more complex and diverse. Therefore, analytic models need to incorporate large data sets including structured, unstructured, and streaming data to improve predictive capabilities. The multitude of data sources that companies need to evaluate to improve model accuracy includes operational databases, social media, customer relationship systems, web logs, sensors, and videos.

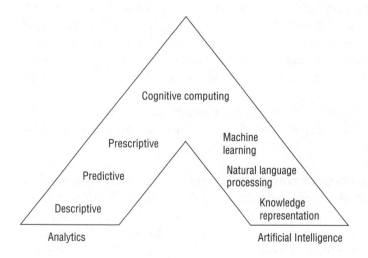

**Figure 6-1:** Converging technologies: analytics and artificial intelligence

Increasingly, advanced analytics is deployed in high-risk situations such as patient health management, machine performance, and threat and theft management. In these use cases the ability to predict outcomes with a high degree of accuracy can mean lives are saved and major crises are averted. In addition, advanced analytics and machine learning are used in situations in which the large volume and fast speed of data that must be processed demands automation to provide a competitive advantage. Typically, human decision makers use the results of predictive models to support their decision-making capabilities and help them to take the right action.

There are situations, however, in which pattern recognition and analytic processes lead to action without any human intervention. For example, investment banks and institutional traders use electronic platforms for automated or algorithmic trading of stocks. Statistical algorithms are created to execute orders for trades based on pre-established policies without humans stepping in to approve or manage the trades. Automated trading platforms use machine learning algorithms that combine historical data and current data that may have an impact on the price of the stock. For example, a trading algorithm may be designed to automatically adjust based on social media news feeds. This approach can provide rapid insight as large volumes of current data are processed at incredibly fast speeds. Although taking action based on this early (and unverified) information may improve trading performance, the lack of human interaction can also lead to erroneous actions. For example, automated trading algorithms have responded to fake or misleading social media news feeds leading to a rapid fall in the stock market. A human would have hopefully taken the time to check the facts.

Meeting business requirements for speed and accuracy of predictions with traditional approaches to analytics has become challenging. With the use of machine learning and cognitive computing, you can develop predictive models that account for relationships, patterns, and expectations that you may have never thought of before. You can move from describing what you see to impacting what you will see.

The following two examples illustrate how companies are using machine learning and analytics to improve predictive capabilities and optimize business results.

- **Analytics and machine learning predict trending customer issues.** The speed of social media can accelerate a small customer issue and grow it into a major complication before a company has time to react. Some companies decrease the time it takes to react to customer concerns by leveraging SaaS offerings that use machine learning to look for trends in social media conversations. The software compares the social media data to historical patterns and then continuously updates the results based on how the predicted pattern compares to actual results. This form of machine learning provides at least 72 hours of advanced warning on trending issues before they are picked up by mainstream media. As a result, marketing and public relations teams can take early action to protect the company's brand and mitigate customer concerns. Media buyers use the service to quickly identify changing customer purchasing trends, so they can determine where they should place their ads in mobile applications and web environments.

- **Analytics and machine learning speed the analysis of performance to improve service level agreements (SLA).** Many companies find it hard to monitor IT performance at fast enough intervals to identify and fix small problems before they escalate and negatively impact SLAs. Using machine learning algorithms, companies can identify patterns of IT behavior and orchestrate its systems and operational processes to become more prescriptive. These systems can learn to adapt to changing customer expectations and requirements. For example, telecommunications companies need to anticipate and prevent network slowdowns or outages so that they can keep the network operating at the speeds required by their customers. However, it can be nearly impossible to identify and correct for interruptions in bandwidth if network monitoring is not done at a sufficiently granular level. For example, with a new machine learning solution offered by Hitachi, telecoms can analyze large streams of data in real time. Hitachi's customers can combine analysis of historical data and real-time analysis of social media data to identify patterns in the data and make corrections in the performance of the network. There are many situations in which this would be helpful to customers. For example, if a streaming video application shows a popular sporting event and the game goes into overtime, an adaptive system could automatically add an additional 15 minutes of bandwidth support, so end users are provided with consistent high-quality service. Machine learning can help the system adapt to a variety of changes and unusual occurrences to maintain quality of performance.

## Key Capabilities in Advanced Analytics

You can't develop a cognitive system without using some combination of predictive analytics, text analytics, or machine learning. It is through the application of components of advanced analytics that data scientists can identify and understand the meaning of patterns and anomalies in massive amounts of structured and unstructured data. These patterns are used to develop the models and algorithms that help determine the right course of action for decision makers. The analytics process helps you understand the relationships that exist among data elements and the context of the data. Machine learning is applied to improve the accuracy of the models and make better predictions. It is an essential technology for advanced analytics, particularly because of the need to analyze big data sources that are primarily unstructured in nature. In addition to machine learning, advanced analytics capabilities including predictive analytics, text analytics, image analytics, and speech analytics are described later in the chapter.

## The Relationship Between Statistics, Data Mining, and Machine Learning

Statistics, data mining, and machine learning are all included in advanced analytics. Each of these disciplines has a role in understanding data, describing the characteristics of a data set, finding relationships and patterns in that data, building a model, and making predictions. There is a great deal of overlap in how the various techniques and tools are applied to solving business problems. Many of the widely used data mining and machine learning algorithms are rooted in classical statistical analysis. The following highlights how these capabilities relate to each other. Machine learning algorithms are covered in the next section in greater detail due to the importance of this discipline to advanced analytics and cognitive computing.

- **Statistics** is the science of learning from data. Classical or conventional statistics is inferential in nature, meaning it is used to reach conclusions about the data (various parameters). Although statistical modeling can be used for making predictions, the focus is primarily on making inferences and understanding the characteristics of the variables. The practice of statistics requires that you test your theory or hypothesis by looking at the errors around the data structure. You test the model assumptions to understand what may have led to the errors with techniques such as normality, independence, and constant variances. The goal is to have constant variances around your model. In addition, statistics requires you to do estimation using confidence values and significance testing—test a null hypothesis and determine the significance of the results, called p–values.

- **Data mining**, which is based on the principles of statistics, is the process of exploring and analyzing large amounts of data to discover patterns in that data. Algorithms are used to find relationships and patterns in the data and then this information about the patterns is used to make forecasts and predictions. Data mining is used to solve a range of business problems such as fraud detection, market basket analysis, and customer churn analysis. Traditionally, organizations have used data mining tools on large volumes of structured data such as customer relationship management databases or aircraft parts inventories. Some analytics vendors provide software solutions that enable data mining of a combination of structured and unstructured data. Generally, the goal of data mining is to extract data from a larger data set for the purposes of classification or prediction. In classification, the idea is to sort data into groups. For example, a marketer might be interested in the characteristics of people who responded to a promotional offer versus those who didn't respond to the promotion. In this example, data mining would be used to extract the data according to the two different classes and analyze the characteristics of each class. A marketer might be interested in predicting those who will respond to a promotion. Data mining tools are intended to support the human decision-making process.

- **Machine learning** uses some of the same algorithms that are used in data mining. One of the key differences in machine learning as compared to other mathematical approaches is the focus on using iterative methods to reduce the errors. Machine learning provides a way for systems to learn and thereby improve both the models and the results of those models. It is an automated approach that provides new ways of searching for data and enables many iterations of a model to occur, quickly improving accuracy. Machine learning algorithms have been used as "black box" algorithms that make predictions for large data sets without requiring a causal interpretation of the fitted model.

## Using Machine Learning in the Analytics Process

Machine learning is essential to improving the accuracy of predictive models in a cognitive environment. These predictive models have a large number of attributes across many observations. The data sets are likely to be unstructured, massive in size, and subject to frequent change. Machine learning enables the models to learn from the data and enhance the knowledge base for a cognitive system. Hundreds or thousands of iterations of a model take place very quickly, leading to an improvement in the types of associations that are made between data elements. Due to their complexity and size, these patterns and associations could have easily been overlooked by human observation. In addition, complex algorithms can be automatically adjusted based on rapid changes in variables such as sensor data, time, weather data, and customer sentiment metrics. The improvements in accuracy are a result of the training process and automation. Machine learning refines the models and algorithms by continuously process-ing new data in real time and training the system to adapt to changing patterns and associations in the data.

Increasingly companies are incorporating machine learning to understand the context of various predictive attributes and how these variables relate to each other. This improved understanding of context leads to greater accuracy in the predictions. Companies are applying machine-learning technology to improve predictive analytics processes that have been in place for many years. For example, the telecommunications industry has used analytics to analyze historical customer information such as demographics, usage, trouble tickets, and products purchased to help predict and reduce churn. Over time the industry progressed from a focus on data mining of structured customer information to include text analytics of historical unstructured information such as comments on customer surveys and notes from call center interactions. Currently, an advanced analytic approach followed by some telecoms brings the unstructured and structured information together to develop a more complete profile of an individual customer. In addition, historical information can be combined with the most current information sourced through social media applications. Machine learning technology is used to train systems to quickly identify those customers that the company is most at risk of losing and develop a strategy to improve retention. Machine learning is applied in many industries including healthcare, robotics, telecommunications, retail, and manufacturing.

Supervised and unsupervised machine learning algorithms are used in a variety of analytics applications. The machine learning algorithm chosen depends on the type of problem being solved and the type and volume of the data required to solve the problem. Typically, supervised learning techniques use labeled data to train a model, whereas unsupervised learning uses unlabeled data in the training process. Machine learning models that are trained on labeled data can then use this training to predict an accurate label for unlabeled data. *Labeled data* refers to the identification or tag that provides some information about the data. For example, unstructured data such as voice recordings could be "labeled" or "tagged" with a name of the speaker or some information about the topic on the recording. Humans often provide the labels to the data as part of the training. Unlabeled data does not include tags, other identifiers, or metadata. For example, unstructured data such as videos, social media data, voice recordings, or digital images would be considered unlabeled if it exists in its raw form without any preconceived human judgments about the data.

### Supervised Learning

Supervised learning typically begins with an established set of data and a certain understanding of how that data is classified. Humans are involved to provide the training, and the analytical model is fit with data that is tagged or labeled. The algorithms are trained using preprocessed examples and then the performance of the algorithms is evaluated with test data. Occasionally, patterns that are identified in a subset of the data can't be detected in the larger population of data. If you fit the model to patterns that exist only in the training subset, then you create a problem called *overfitting*. To protect against overfitting, testing needs to be done against both labeled data and unlabeled data. Using unlabeled data for the test set can help to evaluate the accuracy of the model in predicting outcomes and results. Some applications of supervised learning include speech recognition, risk analysis, fraud detection, and recommendation systems.

The following tools and techniques are often used to implement supervised learning algorithms.

■ **Regression**—Regression models were developed in the statistical community. LASSO regression, Logistic regression, and Ridge regression can be used in machine learning. LASSO is a type of linear regression that minimizes the sum of squared errors. Logistic regression is a variant of standard regression but extends the concept to deal with classification. It measures the relationship between a categorical-dependent variable and one or many independent variables. Ridge regression is a technique used to analyze data with highly correlated independent variables (collinearity). Ridge regression introduces some bias to the estimates in order to reduce the standard errors or misleading variances that result from collinearity with least squares estimates.

■ **Decision tree**—A decision tree is a representation or data structure that captures the relationships among a set of categories. Leaf or end nodes represent the categories, while all other nodes represent "decisions" or questions that refine the search through the tree. A variety of machine learning algorithms are based on traversing decision trees. For example, gradient boosting and random forest algorithms assume that the underlying data is stored as a decision tree. Gradient boosting is a technique for regression problems, which produces a prediction model in the form of an ensemble. Random forest is an algorithm that organizes data using classification and regression trees to look for outliers, anomalies, and patterns in the data. The algorithm builds a model by initially selecting predictors at random and then continuously repeats the process to build hundreds of trees. Random forest is a bagging tool (ensembles of regression trees fit to bootstrap samples) that leads to more accurate models by relying on an iterative approach to many alternative analyses. After the trees are grown, it is possible to identify clusters or segments in data and rank the importance of variables used in the model. Leo Breiman, Statistics Department at the University of California, Berkeley, created this algorithm and described it in a paper published in 2001. Random forest algorithms are used extensively in risk analytics.

■ **Neural networks**—Neural network algorithms are designed to emulate human/animal brains. The network consists of input nodes, hidden layers, and output nodes. Each of the units is assigned a weight. Using an iterative approach, the algorithm continuously adjusts the weights until it reaches a specific stopping point. Errors identified in training data output are used to make adjustments to the algorithm and improve the accuracy of the analytic model. Neural networks are used in speech recognition, object recognition, image retrieval, and fraud detection. Neural networks can be used in recommendation systems like the Amazon.com system that makes selections for the buyer based on previous purchases and searches. Deep neural networks can be used to build models on unlabeled data.

As noted in Chapter 5, "Representing Knowledge in Taxonomies and Ontologies," two recent projects highlight the power of neural networks as discovery and classification engines. The Google Brain project used 16,000 processors in a neural network to discover patterns in images that converged as it learned to recognize cats, without a predefined template for cat images. Microsoft's Project Adam can identify dog breeds from photographs, using asynchronous neural networks.

Neural networks can be challenging to use in environments that require an audit trail or traceability, such as financial services trading systems. Because these systems are designed to learn autonomously, it could be cost-prohibitive to track changes made in a way that would satisfy the requirements of an outside examiner.

- **Support Vector Machine (SVM)**—SVM is a machine learning algorithm that works with labeled training data and output results to an optimal hyperplane. A *hyperplane* is a subspace of the dimension minus one (that is, a line in a plane). SVM is usually used when there are a small number of input features. The features are expanded into higher dimension space. SVM is not scalable to billions of elements of training data. An alternative algorithm for situations with extremely large volumes of training data would be logistic regression.

- **k-Nearest Neighbor (k-NN)**—k-NN is a supervised classification technique that identifies groups of similar records. The k-Nearest Neighbor technique calculates the distances between the record and points in the historical (training) data. It then assigns this record to the class of its nearest neighbor in a data set. k-NN is often selected when there is limited knowledge about the distribution of the data.

### Unsupervised Learning

Unsupervised learning algorithms can solve problems that require large volumes of unlabeled data. As in supervised learning, these algorithms look for patterns in the data that enable an analytics process. For example, in social analytics, you may need to look at large volumes of Twitter messages (tweets), Instagram photos, and Facebook messages to collect adequate information and develop insight into the problem you want to solve. This data is not tagged; and given the large volume, it would take too much time and other resources to attempt to tag all this unstructured data. As a result, unsupervised learning algorithms would be the most likely choice for social media analytics.

Unsupervised learning means that the computer learns based on an iterative process of analyzing data without human intervention. Unsupervised learning algorithms segment data into groups of examples (clusters) or groups of features. The unlabeled data creates the parameter values and classification of the data. Unsupervised learning can determine the outcome or solution to a problem, or it can be used as the first step that is then passed on to a supervised learning process.

The following tools and techniques are typically used in unsupervised learning.

- **Clustering techniques** are used to find clusters that exist in the data sample. Clustering categorizes the variables into groups based on certain criteria (all the variables with X or all the variables without X).

  - The **K-means algorithm** can estimate the unknown means based on the data. This is probably the most widely used unsupervised learning algorithm. It is a simple local optimization algorithm.

  - The **EM-Algorithm for clustering** can maximize the mixture density given the data.

- **Kernel density estimation (KDE)** estimates the probability distribution or the density of a data set. It measures the relationship between random variables. KDE can smooth the data when inferences are made from a finite data sample. KDE is used in analytics for risk management and financial modeling.

- **Nonnegative matrix factorization (NMF)** is useful in pattern recognition and to solve challenging machine learning problems in fields such as gene expression analysis and social network analysis. NMF factorizes a non-negative matrix into two non-negative matrixes of lower rank, and can be used as a clustering or classification tool. Used in one way, it is similar to K-means clustering. With another variation, NMF is similar to probabilistic latent semantic indexing—an unsupervised machine-learning approach for text analytics.

- **Principal Components Analysis (PCA)** is used for visualization and feature selection. PCA defines a linear projection where each of the projected dimensions is a linear combination of the original.

- **Singular Value Decomposition (SVD)** can help to eliminate redundant data to improve the speed and overall performance of the algorithm. SVD can help decide which variables are most important and which ones can be eliminated. For example, assume you have two variables that are highly correlated, such as "humidity index and probability of rain" and, therefore, do not add value to the model when used together. SVD can be used to determine which variable should be kept in the model. SVD is often used in recommendation engines.

- **Self Organizing Map (SOM)** is an unsupervised neural network model that was developed in 1982 by Tuevo Kohonen. SOM is a pattern recognition process. The patterns are learned without any external influences. It is an abstract mathematical model of topographic mapping from the (visual) sensors to the cerebral cortex. It is used to understand how the brain recognizes and processes patterns. This understanding of how the brain works has been applied to machine learning pattern recognition. These techniques have been applied to manufacturing processes.

## Predictive Analytics

Predictive analytics is a statistical or data mining solution consisting of algorithms and techniques that can predict future outcomes. Data mining, text mining, and machine learning can find hidden patterns, clusters, and outliers in both structured and unstructured data. These patterns form the basis of the answers and predictions made with a cognitive system. Predictive modeling uses the independent variables that were identified through data mining and other techniques to determine what is likely to occur under various future circumstances. Organizations use predictive analytics in many ways, including prediction, optimization, forecasting, and simulation. Predictive analytics can be applied to structured, unstructured, and semi-structured data. In predictive analytics, the algorithm you use applies some sort of objective function. For example, Amazon.com uses an algorithm that learns about your buying behavior and makes predictions regarding your interest in making additional purchases.

The focus on analyzing unstructured data represents a change for the use of predictive analytics. Traditionally, statistics and data mining technology have been applied to large databases of structured data. The internal operational systems of record at an organization are typically stored as structured data. However, it is the wide range of data types in unstructured data that represents the majority of data required to form a knowledge base for a cognitive system. These unstructured data sources include e-mails, log files, customer call center notes, social media, web content, video, and literature. Until recently, it has been more difficult for companies to extract, explore, and leverage unstructured data for decision making. Technology advancements such as Hadoop have improved the speed and performance of statistical analysis of unstructured data. The ability to analyze these unstructured data sources is key to the development of cognitive systems.

### Business Value of Predictive Analytics

Companies use predictive analytics to solve many business challenges, including reducing customer churn, improving the overall understanding of customer priorities, and reducing fraud. Businesses can use predictive analytics to target customers that fit a certain profile, and segment customers according to prior purchases and current sentiment. By fine-tuning the models with iterative analytics and machine learning, predictive analytics can improve outcomes for businesses. Table 6-2 illustrates several examples of predictive analytics customer use cases.

**Table 6-2:** Predictive Analytics Use Cases

| USE CASE | EXAMPLE | HOW PREDICTIVE ANALYTICS CHANGES OUTCOMES |
|---|---|---|
| Predicting consumer behavior | A manufacturer can identify patterns in consumer preferences that it could not recognize using traditional analysis of the data. Use of predictive analytics has improved supply chain management and the ability to react to consumer demand. This manufacturer can now predict customer orders 4 months in advance with an accuracy rate of approximately 98 percent. | The company deployed a real-time data warehouse to ensure that multiple sources of data could be well integrated and available at the right time for analytics. The company is building more accurate models using timely data and diverse data types. The models are designed to identify hidden patterns and create accurate forecasts. |
| Sales and inventory forecasting | A large multistore retailer uses advanced analytics to develop models at a faster pace than in the past using larger volumes of data. This company benefited by improving the accuracy of its sales forecasting models and reducing inventories. The company achieved 82 percent accuracy in its forecasting, a major improvement compared to traditional approaches. | This retailer implemented an analytics platform that standardizes and automates a portion of the predictive analytics process. Using this platform, the company can build 500 predictive models per month as compared to 1 model using traditional methods. The increased granularity in its models is yielding greater accuracy. |
| Predicting failures in machinery | A medical equipment manufacturer embeds sensors in its equipment to monitor performance. The recorded data is constantly streamed and analyzed to predict potential failures with enough lead time to make adjustments and avoid harm to patients. | Advanced analytics is used to build sophisticated algorithms that can uncover hidden patterns of failure and monitor sensitive equipment more accurately than traditional methods. The volume of data that needs to be analyzed is large and streaming. |
| Predicting and reducing fraud | An insurance company used advanced analytics to transform its approach to claims processing and improve fraud detection. The company improved its success rate in pursuing fraudulent claims from 50 percent to 90 percent and saved millions of dollars. | Predictive analytics is used to look at the whole claims process differently. Patterns of fraud are analyzed and used to rate the likelihood that each new claim may be fraudulent. Text mining is incorporated into the system to gain insight from analyzing the content of police reports and medical records. |

## Text Analytics

Given the business value of text-based unstructured sources, text analytics is a critical element of cognitive systems. Text analytics is the process of categorizing unstructured text, extracting relevant information, transforming it into structured information, and analyzing it in various ways. The analysis and extraction processes used in text analytics leverage techniques that originate in computational linguistics, natural language processing, statistics, and other computer science disciplines. The text can be extracted and transformed, and then analyzed iteratively to identify patterns or clusters and determine relationships and trends. In addition, the transformed information from text analytics can be combined with structured data and analyzed using various business intelligence or predictive and automated discovery techniques.

The need for businesses to make decisions based on real-time information makes text analytics an increasingly important capability. For example, a telecom provider wanting to understand which customers might be most likely to switch to the competition unless they receive the right incentive needs real-time data on customer sentiment. The accuracy of predictive models that rely on customer sentiment data requires rapid analysis of large volumes of unstructured data. Sentiment scoring and natural language processing engines can build more accurate models and improve the speed of analysis. Machine learning can improve the models' capability to react to sentiment data from social media as it is fed back into the model. Text analytics is widely used to help organizations increase customer satisfaction, build customer loyalty, and predict changes in customer behavior. Text analytics can also improve search capabilities in areas such as faceted navigation.

### Business Value of Text Analytics

The business value of text analytics increases with an organization's capability to understand how to act or make decisions based on the content. Text analytics is used in areas such as marketing analysis, social media analytics, sentiment analysis, market basket analysis, sales forecasting, product selection, and inventory management (see Table 6-3). To take the right action, companies need to understand not only what a customer is saying, but also what the customer's intent might be. Text analytics can help companies listen to what its customers are saying both individually and as a group. Understanding what the customer intends to do next requires deep insight into sentiment at a granular level. This deep listening to a customer is often part of a voice of the customer (VOC) program. For example, by combining knowledge of prior purchases with an analysis of one customer's relationship with others, his buying behavior and high-priority issues, a company is in a better position to take the next best action in any customer interaction.

The goal of a VOC program is to understand customer pain and identify where you may have the greatest challenges with your customers. For example, do you have a new product introduction that is not meeting expectations, or are you having problems with defects? By incorporating text analytics into your VOC program, you can identify changes in customer sentiment quicker. These sentiments may be found in e-mails, customer surveys, and social media. There is often a lot of noise in big data that may contain valuable information on consumer sentiment. Text analytics can reduce the noise by identifying patterns in large volumes of unstructured information, providing an early indicator of changes in customer behavior. In sentiment analytics, the input is text and the output is a sentiment score (scale ranging from positive to negative). The model computes the score with an algorithm. You can look at how sentiment changes over time or how customers view your products compared to competitors.

**Table 6-3:** Text Analytics Use Cases

| Marketing | Churn analysis, voice of the customer, sentiment analysis, customer survey analysis, social media analysis, market research |
| --- | --- |
| Operations | Voice of the employee, document categorization, competitive intelligence |
| Legal/Risk and Compliance | Document categorization, risk analysis, fraud detection, warranty analysis, e-discovery |

## Image Analytics

The sources used to develop knowledge corpora for a cognitive system are likely to include videos, photos, or medical images. There has been an enormous increase in the volume of images created and managed by governments, organizations, and individuals. As a result, image analytics capabilities are important in cognitive computing. The ability to quickly identify clusters and patterns in these images can have a major impact on IT and physical security, healthcare, transportation logistics, and many other areas. For example, facial recognition technology is used to both verify and identify individuals as a means to help prevent fraud and solve crimes. Governments use facial and image analytics to anticipate and prevent terrorist activities. Facial recognition can be used in video indexing to label faces in the video and identify the speakers in the video. Although facial recognition is a significant part of image analytics, cognitive systems will demand the capability to identify content in many different types of images. Image analytics can index and search video events by classifying objects into different categories such as people, animals, and cars, or to look for anomalies in a medical digital image such as an X-ray or CT scan.

Facial recognition was one of the earliest research areas in the field of image analytics. The first system for face recognition was developed in the 1960s. It was only partially automated, however, and there were a lot of manual steps involved. In the late 1980s, Kirby and Sirvich developed a system called Principal Components Analysis (PCA), which compares digitized sections of photos (eigenfaces). Compression techniques eliminate data that is not going to help with the comparison. This research represented a significant advancement, enabling greater automation and improvements in speed and accuracy. There is great deal of ongoing research focusing on this area of technology, and it continues to improve. For example, there are algorithms that focus on the unique skeletal and musculature features in a face. These features have an impact on facial expressions that are consistent over time even as person ages.

Facial recognition is currently a big research area for many technology companies. For example, Facebook's research into facial recognition has resulted in software called DeepFace that is based on an advanced machine learning neural network. The machine learning algorithm analyzes a large number of human faces looking for recurring patterns in facial features such as eyebrows and lips. The learning process for DeepFace is based on a corpus of 4 million photos of faces. Facebook and other companies such as Google and Apple use facial recognition technology to enable users to identify and tag friends in photographs. Facebook's DeepFace project will be used to improve facial recognition capabilities on Facebook. Current test metrics show that DeepFace is almost as accurate as the human brain when comparing two photos to see if the face is the same. With this high level of accuracy there could be many other applications for DeepFace for marketing, sales, and security.

One key aspect of image analytics technology is the capability to detect the edge or the boundaries of objects in images. Edge detection algorithms look for discontinuities in brightness and can be used to segment the images. Some of the most common edge detection algorithms include Sobel, Canny, Prewitt, Roberts, and fuzzy logic. These algorithms are applied to all objects, not just faces. The process of facial recognition begins with finding the face in the image and identifying the facial features. Another aspect is based on determining color segmentation by looking at ratios of skin tone pixels. A face recognition algorithm using Eigenface-Fisher Linear Discriminant (EFLD) and Dynamic Fuzzy Neural Network (DFNN) helps with the dimension of features and classification. It reduces errors compared to previous algorithms. It works well on a face database with different expressions, poses, and illuminations. Machine learning frameworks can improve modeling and classification capabilities of large volumes of images.

Zintera, an emerging company based in San Diego, California, has developed a technology platform to enable image and video processing based on a biophysical neural network model. Zintera's technology requires very sparse training sets so that the neural network models can process images and videos quickly.

There are many potential applications for image analytics in healthcare. For example, IBM has a long-term, grand challenge project called Medical Sieve that incorporates image analytics. The goal of this project is to build a next-generation cognitive assistant with advanced multimodal analytics, clinical knowledge, and reasoning capabilities. Medical Sieve, an image-guided informatics system, will be tuned to assist in clinical decision making in radiology and cardiology. Radiologists typically need to view thousands of images per day, leading to eyestrain and the possibility of a misdiagnosis. Medical Sieve uses sophisticated medical text and image processing, pattern recognition, and machine learning techniques guided by advanced clinical knowledge to process clinical data about the patient and identify anomalies in the images. Finally, it creates advanced summaries of imaging studies, capturing the most critical anomalies that are detected in various views of the images.

## Speech Analytics

Text, image, and speech analytics can be used in a cognitive system to provide the right context to answer a question correctly or make an accurate prediction. Although text analytics is used to gain insight into sentiment, many emotions and attitudes can be easily masked in text. Images and speech can provide many more clues to a person's emotions and anticipated actions. *Speech analytics* is the process of analyzing recorded speech to extract information about the person speaking or the content of his words. Identifying the patterns of words and phrases that are good indicators of emotion and intent to act in a certain way can lead to improved accuracy of predictive models.

Speech analytics has been applied to call center processes for many years. There was significant research in the field of automatic speech recognition (ASR) as early as the 1950s. ASR systems needed to provide accurate information for people with vastly different speech patterns and regional accents without the need for training. Statistical models can create speech-clustering algorithms for different word and sound reference patterns. Although various statistical modeling techniques were applied to solving the problem of ASR, the hidden Markov model (HMM) and the stochastic language model became the most widely used techniques in the 1980s. As call centers developed in the 1990s as an important way to create a more efficient and cost-effective way to properly route calls, companies such as AT&T began using automatic speech recognition technology as part of the call center process.

Automated speech recognition (ASR) is one component of speech analytics. ASR can determine the words and phrases used in an individual's spoken language. This basic analysis can prioritize calls or get an initial understanding of the reason for the call. However, speech analytics is intended to go much deeper to gain more insight into context. Calls are categorized to identify patterns and anomalies. In the call center environment, speech analytics can answer many different types of questions. What is the subject matter discussed? What is the emotional tone of the speech? Is the speaker angry, impatient, or dissatisfied with a product? Are expectations for customer service agent performance met?

## Using Advanced Analytics to Create Value

Ultimately, the goal of deploying advanced analytics processes and cognitive computing is to improve decision making. Companies are using analytics to differentiate from the competition by doing a better job of listening to customers, anticipating their needs, and making highly targeted offers. Government agencies use analytics to differentiate their cities by making them safer, more responsive to citizens' needs, and more ecologically sound. Healthcare organizations use analytics to improve physician training, eliminate unnecessary hospitalizations, and improve overall quality of care. Building the analytics models and cognitive computing environments that support these improvements in decision making requires more data, more accurate data, more refined data, and the ability to manage and interpret data from all input streams at fast speeds.

Figure 6-2 illustrates the trade-offs that companies often need to make to create business value from data. The ability to make faster and more execution-oriented decisions depends on reducing the "degree of difficulty" of interpreting the right data from all input streams. You need to manage the volume and complexity of the data. At the same time, you need to sample high-velocity data in a meaningful way. Raw data as captured by systems and sensors has potential value, but needs to be processed and analyzed to build business value. Referring to Figure 6-2, business value increases as volume, complexity, and speed are managed during the analytics process. The value to an organization comes from acting on the analysis of the data.

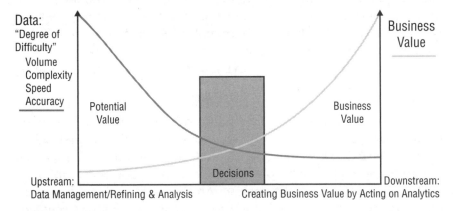

**Figure 6-2:** Refining raw data to create business value

Source: "An Executive Guide to Analytics Infrastructure," January 2014 by STORM Insights, Inc.

## Building Value with In-memory Capabilities

Managing the dimensions of speed, complexity, and volume can be best addressed by an optimization strategy that includes both software and hardware. To scale appropriately to support big data analysis, many companies opt for hardware that is pre-integrated and optimized to run advanced analytics workloads. To achieve business value, the analytical models and predictions need to be fully integrated into operational business processes. All applications need access to the necessary data at the right time. Capabilities such as columnar alignments, graph databases, and in-memory computing can help support advanced analytics. To enhance the speed, shared memory, shared disk, high-speed networks, and optimized storage are valuable techniques.

Platforms that are designed for high-speed and volume analytics may rely on in-memory capabilities. Transaction processing, operational processing, analytics, and reporting and visualization can be integrated within one in-memory platform. It eliminates the time-consuming effort of data extraction and transformation. In-memory analytics provides a way to process large and complex analytic workloads quickly. It can improve application performance. These workloads can be chunked into smaller units and distributed across a parallel system. This approach is used primarily with structured data. In-memory analytics can help to overcome the challenges of trying to visualize and analyze big data at fast enough speeds. For example, with real-time streaming data, in-memory capabilities can ensure that computations are performed in RAM to increase processing times much faster than data access from disk.

Current approaches to model development, advanced analytics, and cognitive computing demand highly scalable architectures. The iterative processes used in machine learning yield more precise results, but at the same time require extreme speeds that can be provided by in-memory computing. With data viewed as the most important asset in advanced analytics, one benefit of using in-memory capabilities is that you eliminate the need to push the data to where the computations are taking place. Managing data sets in-memory means that the data can be used for transaction processing and analytics simultaneously. Organizing the documents for machine learning can be processing-intensive, so executing tasks such as creating tags or labels for documents can process faster in memory. Many companies find that they are building hundreds of models to develop more accurate and customized predictions. In addition, machine learning algorithms typically require complex technical computations on large volumes of data. Leveraging infrastructure with the right power and speed is critical to the success of these predictive models and cognitive systems.

## Impact of Open Source Tools on Advanced Analytics

Open source analytics tools are having a major impact on the growth of predictive analytics at many organizations. The open source software environment and programming language, R, is fast becoming one of the primary tools for data scientists, statisticians, and other enterprise users. R, which is designed for computational statistics and data visualization, is the language of choice for graduate students doing research in advanced analytics and cognitive computing. Strong interest in R has led to a very active open source community. Members of the community share information on models, algorithms, and coding best practices. Users like the flexibility that a special-purpose programming language and environment offers for building custom applications. Some of the benefits of R include its flexibility and adaptability. R is actually an implementation of the statistical programming language S, developed at Bell Laboratories, as a higher-level alternative to using FORTRAN statistical subroutines.

Although R can be complicated to use unless you are an experienced data scientist or statistician, many vendors offer some sort of connection to R that makes it easier to use. Vendors are providing algorithms that are preset and ready to use in model development. The open source community has spawned and supports many projects that form the foundation for advanced analytics applications. For example, two important projects within the Apache Foundation are projects like Cassandra (distributed DBMS) and Spark (an analytics framework for cluster computing in the Hadoop space).

## Summary

Advanced analytics helps the cognitive system gain insight from the corpora and ontologies. For example, machine learning algorithms and predictive modeling are applied to ensure that the cognitive system is constantly learning. The system needs to understand context, provide the right answers to questions, make accurate predictions, and apply the right information at the right time. The actual machine learning algorithms selected will depend on the goals of the analysis. For example, is the cognitive system applied to some aspect of healthcare? Are the goals related to improving medical diagnosis accuracy, reducing costs, reducing re-admission rates after patients are discharged from the hospital, or improving overall health for individuals and communities?

Machine learning algorithms will be applied to help discover the patterns that are important to building a cognitive system that is both accurate and fast. Algorithms for prediction, classification, segmentation, forecasting, sequence pattern discovery, association pattern discovery, geo-spatial and temporal discovery, or pattern detection may all be applied as needed to improve results of the system.

# The Role of Cloud and Distributed Computing in Cognitive Computing

The ability to leverage highly distributed and cost-effective computing services has not only transformed the way software is managed and delivered but also has become the linchpin for commercializing cognitive computing. Large cognitive computing systems require a converged computing environment that supports a variety of types of hardware, software services, and networking elements that have to be workload balanced. Therefore, cloud computing and a distributed architecture are the foundational models required to make large-scale cognitive computing operational. This chapter provides an overview of distributed computing architectures and cloud computing models.

## Leveraging Distributed Computing for Shared Resources

The cognitive computing environment must provide a platform that consolidates a massive amount of information from disparate sources and process that information in a sophisticated manner. The system must also implement advanced analytics to gain insights into complex data. Clearly, a single integrated system would be impractical because of the need to bring so many different elements together. This is where highly distributed environments supporting cloud computing become the delivery platform of choice. The *cloud* is a method of providing a set of shared computing resources including applications, compute services, storage capabilities, networking, software development, variable deployment modalities, and business processes. Cloud computing allows developers to combine distributed computing systems into a set of shared resources that can be used to support large cognitive workloads. To achieve this goal, it is important to base cloud services on standards and standardized interfaces. These interfaces are defined by standards organizations providing a consistent specification that can be widely adopted by cloud providers. This chapter provides insights into the role of distributed cloud services in making cognitive computing a reality.

Consumers of cloud services, including firms building cognitive computing applications, benefit from the shared resource model, which enables them to pay by usage on systems that operate close to peak efficiency. Owning these resources requires an ongoing fixed cost for carrying excess capacity for anticipated peak loads. Having the ability to use these services on demand makes them affordable to a wide range and size of organizations.

## Why Cloud Services Are Fundamental to Cognitive Computing Systems

A cognitive system requires the capability to leverage data sources and complex algorithms. The most efficient and effective means to operationalize cognitive systems is cloud computing because by design, they are built on distributed computing models. Without distributing computing capabilities via the Internet, the World Wide Web (or just "web") would never have existed. In fact, the web was designed to enable researchers to share documents, images, videos, or audio files by simply assigning addresses without regard to the meaning of the content. With cognitive computing the environment is optimized to support a massive amount of data that must be analyzed and organized based on patterns. For example, the source data may be distributed across hundreds of different structured and unstructured information sources. In order to orchestrate the access to these sources, the cloud environment may have a catalog, index, or registry of pointers to the data as well as metadata associated with key resources. There may also be a requirement for analytics that leverage high-powered computing capabilities. An additional benefit of using cloud computing and its underlying distributed model is the ability to access high-powered computing engines to solve complex science, engineering, and business problems on demand. Again, the organization would not have to purchase this high-end system, but rather can consume the computational services only when needed.

# Characteristics of Cloud Computing

Although this chapter covers a number of models of cloud computing, some characteristics are common to all models. These include elasticity and self-service provisioning, metering of service usage and performance, and workload management. In addition, supporting distributed compute capabilities is instrumental to the cloud. All these services are required because of the dynamic nature of the cloud. The cloud is purpose-built so that it can support a number of different workloads and characteristics of those workloads. This section includes a discussion of these capabilities and characteristics.

## Elasticity and Self-service Provisioning

*Elasticity* of a cloud service offers the ability for consumers to increase or decrease the amount of compute, storage, or networking they need to complete a task. Although the notion of adding services is available in other modes of computing, within a cloud environment, elasticity is intended to be an automated service that is controlled by a self-service function. This is especially important when the consumer of a cloud service needs to increase the amount of compute services, for example, when applying an algorithm to a complex set of data. When that calculation is complete, the amount of compute resources can be automatically decreased. Within elasticity are the areas of scaling and distributed processing.

### Scaling

With cloud elasticity you can scale the service to process shifting workloads. The two primary models of scaling are horizontal and vertical. *Horizontal scaling* (often called scaling out or scaling in) means that the same type of service is expanded based on the need of the workload. As more of the same capability is needed, the system allocates more resources. As the need diminishes, those resources are released to the pool. With horizontal scaling, additional servers or blades can be added to support expanding requirements. In contrast, *vertical scaling* (often called scaling up) occurs when one computing resource is expanded, creating a better match between the workload and the computing environment. Rather than adding more servers, a scale-up environment enables you to add additional memory or storage to the existing system environment. Vertical scaling is useful for solving problems with applications requiring highly distributed computing environments. As an example, Hadoop is designed to distribute computation across nodes, so it benefits from scaling up.

### Distributed Processing

With the growth in big data, the ability to distribute processing across compute nodes to gain better performance is increasingly important. Although the idea of a distributed filesystem is not new, new data technologies like NoSQL, HBase, and Hadoop are driving the importance of this capability. Using clusters of machines within a cloud to process complex algorithms is critical. Cognitive computing requires not only ingesting data but also the ability to analyze complex data to provide potential answers to complex problems.

## Cloud Computing Models

Although there is sophisticated technology within cloud computing, you need to understand that cloud computing is a service-provisioning model that is transforming the degree to which companies can access and manage complex technology. The economic benefits of the cloud model are obvious. By providing a shared services model, each user pays only for services used. Within cloud computing models, there are a number of different approaches that are optimized for executing specific tasks for specific workloads. This is analogous to how power grids operate. A large metropolitan area does not have a single power plant to support all customers. Rather there is a system or grid that coordinates a highly decentralized set of power distribution stations supporting different neighborhoods. A well-designed power grid would model the distribution of power based on environmental conditions, consumption patterns, or catastrophic events. Having a shared services model makes a power grid affordable. If you take this analogy a step further, companies and individuals that invest in solar panels connected to a grid may get paid commensurate with the amount of electricity they contribute back to the public power grid. Likewise, in systems such as the World Community Grid, individuals contribute computing resources to help solve major computational problems. In the future, there may be cognitive computing grids where resources are shared across companies, industries, regions, and nations.

There isn't a single model of cloud computing. Rather there are a number of deployment models, including public, private, managed services, and hybrid clouds. Each of these deployment models features such service models as Software as a Service (SaaS), Platform as a Service (PaaS), and Infrastructure as a Service (IaaS). Following is a description of each of these deployment models. The next section provides an overview of the technical underpinnings of each of these models (see Figure 7-1).

### The Public Cloud

The *public cloud* is a utility model of computing typically offered as a shared multitenant environment, in which multiple users physically share a container within a single server. A *multitenant cloud* is a publicly accessible service that is owned and operated by a third-party service provider and is accessed through an Internet connection. The customer pays based on usage or per unit of computing or storage. Therefore, a public cloud is often thought of as a commodity service. Typically, a user gains access to a service through a virtualized image—a combination of computing resources that can run independently from the physical hardware. Public clouds are most efficient when they support common workloads so that the system is automated and optimized for that workload. This is different than a data center where there may be multiple operating systems, and multiple types of applications and workloads. As such, it is difficult to optimize the environment for small numbers of simple workloads. The public cloud can be an effective economic model because it is built on a shared services model. The more customers that public cloud vendors such as Amazon.com, Microsoft Azure, and Google cloud services support, the less they charge per unit of usage. The typical payment model is based on a few cents per megabyte of storage or a unit of compute.

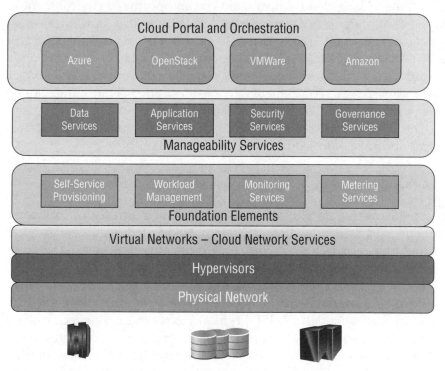

**Figure 7-1:** Foundations of a cloud architecture

One of the key characteristics of a public cloud is that it provides the same level of service and security to all its customers, represented by generalized service level agreements (SLAs). The service provider, therefore, manages its servers, automation, and security as an integrated environment. The customer leveraging these public services has little or no visibility into the resources within the operation of the system.

Well-designed commercial public cloud services tend to offer a reasonable level of service and security. Companies that need to have compliance and governance guarantees because of government regulations may be unable to use a public cloud service. In those cases, private cloud services may be a more viable option for critical customer and financial data. However, other commodity services such as e-mail are often implemented using public cloud services because they are not strategic assets for organizations. Some public cloud service providers offer additional specialized services such as virtual private networks or specialized governance services.

## The Private Cloud

As the name implies, a *private cloud* is managed within a company's data center, and those resources are typically not shared with other companies. Like a public cloud, the private cloud is intended to be an optimized environment so that it supports a single underlying operating system with an optimized set of management and automation services. Like public clouds, the private cloud also provides optimization of workloads to improve manageability and performance. Because a private cloud is controlled internally, it can optimize security based on industry governance requirements. In addition, the private cloud can be established with a specific level of service required to support customers and partners. The company has the capability to implement tools and services to monitor and optimize both security and service levels.

## Managed Service Providers

In addition to private clouds that are owned and operated directly by a company, there are managed service providers (MSPs) that provide dedicated cloud services designed and managed by a third party for the benefit of a specific customer.

Companies that are uncomfortable with public cloud services may not want to operate their own private clouds. In addition, some companies want to leverage a sophisticated set of services that are not resident within their own environment. *Managed Service Providers* (*MSPs*) typically offer industry-specific cloud services available as an ongoing supported service or as an on demand service. These cloud services have characteristics of either a public or a well-architected private cloud in that they offer management, security, and automation. They may offer some services as a multitenant environment but also provide the option of providing customers with their own private hardware environment that is secured just for their use. A managed service provider may provide a cognitive computing service that is specific to one industry such as a technique for analyzing customer churn in a retail environment through the use of a machine-learning algorithm. Therefore, the MSP is a form of private cloud because a single customer can use it on a dedicated, physically partitioned basis.

However, like a public cloud, it can serve multiple customers from a common, albeit physically partitioned, infrastructure.

## The Hybrid Cloud Model

A *hybrid cloud* offers the ability to either integrate or connect to services across public, private, and managed services. In essence, a hybrid cloud becomes a virtual computing environment that may combine virtualized services in a public cloud with services from a private cloud, a managed service vendor, and a data center. For example, a single company may use its data center to manage customer transactions. Those transactions are then connected with a public cloud where the company has created a web-based front end and a mobile interface to allow customers to buy products online. The same company uses a third-party managed service that checks credit for anyone trying to use a credit card to pay for a service. There may also be a series of public cloud-based applications that control customer service details. In addition, the company uses extra compute capabilities from a public cloud provider during peak holiday periods to make sure that the website does not crash when the system becomes overloaded.

Although each of these elements are all designed and operated by individual vendors, they can be managed as a single system. A hybrid cloud can be highly effective because as a distributed system, it can enable companies to leverage a series of services that are the best fit for the task at hand, as shown in Figure 7-2.

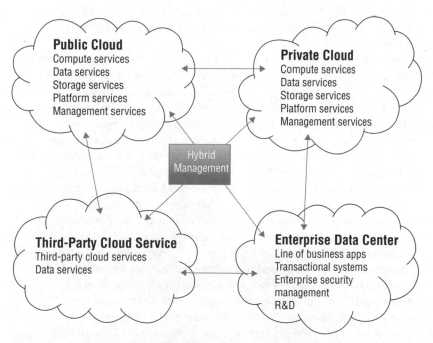

**Figure 7-2:** Hybrid cloud architecture

Whether the cloud model is public or private, they can allocate different cognitive-computing workloads to the optimal service components. Because the performance of a cognitive system can benefit from deployment on a variety of workload-optimized services rather than one unified system, a hybrid cloud model is the most logical and practical approach as these systems grow in production. Cognitive computing can be architected as a series of services that interact and call different services via Application Programming Interfaces (APIs) to execute a process or compute an algorithm in an efficient and cost-effective manner. When companies use big data sets to calculate complex algorithms on an occasional basis, it is often difficult to gain access to enough compute resources at a reasonable cost. For example, in the pharmaceutical industry, drug discovery requires the analysis of massive amounts of data that needs to be both stored and processed. Before cloud computing, these companies had to compromise and select only subsets of data to analyze. They had to be confident that the data they were selecting was the right subset. It was quite possible, however, that the patterns or anomalies might not have appeared in the subset or snapshot of data that they could afford to collect.

## APPLYING CLOUD COMPUTING TO CLINICAL RESEARCH

One of the best ways to understand the benefits of cloud computing for sophisticated research is to look at a clinical research example, such as epilepsy analysis. In the December 10, 2013 issue of the *Journal of the American Medical Informatics Association*, the researchers discuss how they conducted epilepsy research by leveraging cloud-based big data analytics.

Researchers have been conducting research to attempt to discover new treatments for epilepsy (one of the most common neurological disorders). The typical source of data has come from recordings from electroencephalograms (EEG). This data is used to diagnose and evaluate epilepsy patients. If the signals from this data can be analyzed and visualized in real time, researchers can better determine what is happening with a patient before, during, and after an episode. In addition, this data can be correlated with ontologies designed to support conclusions between events and diagnosis.

Researchers working on this project found that if they could move from an integrated application that resided on a desktop to a cloud-based data management system, they could collect more data and analyze that data in real time. The researchers developed the Prevention and Risk Identification of SUDEP Mortality (PRISM) project. This web-based electrophysiology data visualization and analysis platform was called Cloudwave. This public cloud infrastructure integrated a patient information identification system and added a query system. The foundation of the system included the use of parallelized algorithms for computing using the MapReduce framework to interpret the huge volume of data. Data visualization correlates the results with the ontologies and other research such as databases of other risk factors. A query function can make the results accessible to researchers.

Without the support of cloud services and advanced analytics, the researchers would not have analyzed this amount of data in a reasonable timeframe. It would have taken too long and required the purchase of expensive hardware that was not in the budget of the organization. Even more important was that the real-time services were needed only intermittently and therefore a cloud service that could be used on an occasional basis was optimal for the requirements of the project. The organization also found a web service vendor that would support the Health Insurance Portability and Accountability Act (HIPAA) standards.

## Delivery Models of the Cloud

Whether discussing public or private cloud deployment models, a number of important service delivery models define the way consumers and suppliers take advantage of these approaches to computing (refer to Figure 7-2). These models are divided into four different areas because they each provide a different capability that is important to implementing sophisticated services.

### Infrastructure as a Service

As its name implies, *Infrastructure as a Service* (*IaaS*) is the foundational cloud service. IaaS provisions compute, storage, and networking services through either a virtualized image or directly on the computer systems. This is called native (or bare metal) implementation. Although bare metal implementations are frequently used when speed is the most important factor, the typical IaaS model relies on virtualization. A public IaaS service is designed as a self-service environment so that a customer can purchase a service such as compute or storage based on the instance of computing that is needed. Consumers can purchase an instance based on the amount of resources consumed over a specified period of time. When a consumer stops paying for the service, the resource disappears. In a private IaaS environment controlled directly by a company, those provisioned resources would remain in place and will be controlled by the information technology organization.

#### Virtualization

*Virtualization* is the technique that separates resources and services from the underlying physical delivery environment. In a traditional model, the hardware is partitioned through the use of a hypervisor. The *hypervisor* is software that provides a thin layer of code on top of the server that enables system resources to be shared. This means that a single system can support multiple operating systems, infrastructure software, storage, networks, and applications. In addition, the hypervisor enables more services to be supported on the same physical infrastructure. IaaS relies on images that encapsulate the key capabilities required by a consumer to operate a cloud service such as an amount of computing capability or a set amount of storage. The image will include the capability to manage these resources such as add new code or balance the set of resources.

### Software-defined Environment

The goal of IaaS is to optimize the use of system resources so that they can support workloads and applications with the maximum efficiency. A *Software Defined Environment* (*SDE*) is an abstraction layer that unifies the components of virtualization in IaaS so that the components can be managed in a unified fashion. In effect, the SDE is intended to provide an overall orchestration and management environment for the variety of resources used within an IaaS environment. Therefore, an SDE brings together compute, storage, and networking to create a more efficient hybrid cloud environment. It also enables developers to use a variety of types of virtualization within the same environment without the burden of hand-coding the linkages between these services.

### Containers

A *container* consists of an application that is designed to run within IaaS, encapsulated together with its dependencies as a lightweight package ready for deployment. It includes well-defined and standardized Application Programming Interfaces (APIs) to make integration easier. A container is often used within the context of a Software Defined Environment. The use of containers creates an alternative to relying on virtualized images. Unlike virtualization, a container does not require a hypervisor. Several open source projects (e.g., Docker) have emerged in the past few years to facilitate this style of computing.

## Software as a Service

*Software as a Service* (*SaaS*) is a defined application that is operated on a public cloud service. Today, virtually every enterprise software offering is available as SaaS, and it is becoming the de facto approach to desktop applications and personal software, as well. In fact, it is becoming difficult to buy or license some types of software because the SaaS model provides a more predictable revenue stream for the vendors.

SaaS applications are built to take advantage of IaaS. Therefore, like IaaS, SaaS is typically delivered in a multitenancy environment offering load balancing and self-service provisioning. This means that multiple users share a physical computing environment with other users and companies. Their own implementation is partitioned from other users. One of the benefits of SaaS is that the consumer is not responsible for software updates and maintenance of the application. However, unlike a traditional on-premises application, the user does not have a perpetual license for the application. Rather the user pays on a per-user, per month, or per year basis. Many SaaS applications are designed as packaged applications based on a business process such as customer relationship management or accounting. These applications are designed in a modular fashion so that customers can select only what they require. For example, some accounting SaaS applications may have a foundation of a bookkeeping process and can expand into a complex online accounting system. Over the years, more and more areas of software are available as a service, including collaboration, project management, marketing, social media services, risk management, and commerce solutions.

SaaS implementations are expanding beyond the traditional packaged software. Increasingly, most emerging software platforms are implemented as cloud services as the preferred deployment model. One of the most important examples of the power of the cloud for cognitive computing is the advent of big data environments Hadoop and MapReduce that depend on a highly distributed cloud platform to process massive amounts of data. The distributed nature of the cloud enables complex computation to be completed quickly.

Business intelligence (BI) services have been available as cloud services for a number of years. However, the objective of these systems is to provide management with reports that capture historical performance of the business. Advanced analytics offerings are increasingly offered as cloud services. The complexity and amount of data analyzed demands the type of scalable and distributed properties of the cloud. The complex cognitive algorithms used in machine learning and predictive analytics are better served by a cloud infrastructure. One of the benefits of using the cloud for advanced analytics as a service is that it is more affordable for solving complex problems. For example, an analyst might need to build a predictive model to solve a specific problem in a quick timeframe. Rather than purchasing all the hardware and software, the analyst can leverage a sophisticated analytics application in the cloud. The analyst pays only for the capability used for that project. After the project is complete, there is no further financial obligation. The cloud offers the ability to solve a problem that leverages huge amounts of computing capability. There may also be the need to store the data and results from this analysis.

Analytics as a service in the cloud enables business managers or business analysts to leverage an analytics portal that documents best practices. Increasingly, there are offerings on the market that provide the knowledge of the data scientist without the expense of hiring those expensive resources. Many of these offerings enable a data scientist to optimize an algorithm based on the problem being solved. Some of the emerging use cases for analytics in the cloud come from industries such as retail, where managers want to understand what is driving profits in various business units. While it may be a simple question to ask, the answer is extremely complicated. The analysis requires the ingestion of considerable information from a number of internal and external sources, followed by the computation to determine patterns, followed by recommendations for next best actions for issue resolution. A cloud analytic service can codify the best algorithm to apply to a specific analytical goal and the cloud service can access a specific capability on demand. In the future, analytics as a service will generate new models where the analytics service provider will provide services to help analyze a customer's data. In the long run, analytics as a service will enable data providers to provide new cognitive computing offerings. By the end of this decade, the major cognitive computing technologies such as Natural Language Processing (NLP), hypothesis generation/ evaluation, and question answering systems should be available as standalone services, offered as SaaS components that can be integrated into a customer's application on demand.

## Platform as a Service

*Platform as a Service (PaaS)* is an entire infrastructure package that is used to design, implement, and deploy applications and services in either a public or private cloud. PaaS provides an underlying level of middleware services that abstract the complexity away from the developer. In addition, the PaaS environment provides a set of integrated software development tools. In some cases, it is possible to integrate third-party tools into the platform. A well-designed PaaS consists of a orchestrated platform to support the life cycle of both developing and deploying software within the cloud. A PaaS platform is designed to build, manage, and run applications in the cloud.

Unlike traditional software development and deployment environments, the software elements are designed to work together through Application Programming Interfaces (APIs) that support a variety of programming languages and tools. Within the PaaS environment are a set of prebuilt services such as source code management, deployment of workloads, security services, and various database services.

## Managing Workloads

The ability to manage workloads is at the heart of cloud computing. What makes cloud computing so powerful is that it enables an organization to bring together applications that live in the data center with those that reside on public and private clouds. To be operationally effective these various workloads have to act as a single, unified environment. In other words, these services need to be orchestrated together in a consistent manner. One of the fundamental approaches used to achieve this consistency is having the workloads abstracted from the underlying hardware environment.

Workload management in a traditional data center environment has been centrally controlled through job scheduling programs that orchestrated workloads in a serial and scheduled manner. The cloud environment is a different dynamic entirely because workloads are rarely scheduled in a predictable manner. Therefore, cloud workload management depends on load balancing—the process is designed so that complete workloads or components of a workload can be distributed across multiple servers within the cloud.

In a hybrid cloud environment the ability to manage overall performance requires monitoring of the overall service level of the servers, software, storage, and network. Any system, whether on premise or in the cloud, must be managed to achieve the contractual service levels required by customers. However, a cloud environment is more dynamic than an on-premise environment. Therefore, the system has to monitor performance and anticipate changes in compute requirements, the amount of data managed, or the addition of new workloads. A cognitive computing environment requires this type of flexible workload management because there is the requirement for sophisticated analytics of workloads. Data is constantly being evaluated and expanded as new sources of data become available.

## Security and Governance

As cognitive solutions become a strategic platform for businesses, the ability to secure content and results becomes more important. No company will trust a system that may hold the potential for strategic differentiation if the information can be compromised. Therefore, security has to be defined at every level of the environment. Given the nature of the data within a cognitive computing system, it is critical that security is instituted so that unauthorized persons cannot access key data. Therefore, identity management will be key. You will need to work with the cloud provider to indicate which individuals with which roles are entitled to access or change data.

Any cloud environment will require the same levels of security as a traditional data center, including issues ranging from physical security of servers, storage, networks, applications, and data. In addition, there needs to be specific techniques for handling incidents, security of the specific applications, encryption, and key management.

Within a data rich environment, it is critical to be aware of the governance requirements to protect sensitive data. Different industries, markets, and countries have specific requirements for how data about individuals needs to be secured. For example, in the United States there is a regulation called The Health Insurance Portability and Accountability Act of 1996 (HIPAA) that requires that an individual's health information must be kept private. Countries such as Germany and France have specific regulations about where a person's data can be stored. Therefore, although the cloud will have a set of data protections built into the environment, your company is still responsible for the protection of sensitive data. This is further complicated in a hybrid environment in which data may be distributed across a number of different public and private clouds.

Overall governance of data requires a strategy based on understanding the regulations of your industry and understanding how these regulations are implemented and executed in the various cloud applications and services used. Each company will have its own requirements to audit its own security, including its use of public and private clouds. Therefore, every organization needs to have a governance body in place that understands the cloud services used and how those companies comply with regulations. It is prudent, therefore, to create an overall governance plan incorporating every IT service used by your organization.

## Data Integration and Management in the Cloud

Data integration in the cloud offers both huge potential and huge complexities. As with on-premise applications, most organizations have hundreds of different data sources that need to be managed. Although the availability of data in the cloud is a huge help in gaining access to critical information, it also means that there is a need to provide connections and techniques for integrating data sources. Simply connecting data does not solve the problem. Integrating data sources in the cloud requires the ability to correlate the relationships between sources through a catalog that defines the meaning of fields or data sources.

All data integrations are not created equal due to different requirements for each use case. For example, there are situations in which cloud data sources need to be tightly linked together because the sources are interdependent. This can be accomplished through data replication. In some cases, it is important to move several data sources into the same cloud environment for speed. In other situations, the original data source needs to remain in either a cloud data repository or within a data center. In this situation there is the need to provide pointers to move between sources. This typically happens when each source is independent. In fact, in most situations data will increasingly be managed in a distributed manner to process a large number of information sources that need to interact with each other.

## Summary

Cloud computing is a critical deployment and delivery model for applications and data. The capability to distribute huge amounts of data is critical to the development of a cognitive system because it depends on the availability of the right data sources that may physically reside in a hybrid environment. A cognitive system requires the capability to link to and manage the right data sources where they live, when they are needed. The cloud and distributed computing is one of the fundamental models to make it possible for a variety of data sources to be used in this level of decision making.

# CHAPTER 8

# The Business Implications of Cognitive Computing

We are clearly going through a major transformation in the technologies that are available to change the way we live and work. With the declining prices of software and hardware and the ability to create new innovations with few capital resources, industries across the globe are changing. So, if the difference between success and failure is no longer simply based on how big a company is, how will we differentiate one supplier from the next? Cognitive computing may be the factor that can add a new dimension to the competitive race. Can we make smarter products and services? Can we anticipate what customers and partners will need in the future? In this chapter we will explore the disruptive power of cognitive computing.

## Preparing for Change

Businesses have always had more data in their structured databases, document stores, and packaged business applications than they know what to do with. For decades business leaders understood that if they could capture unique insights from that data before their competitors find them, they could have a competitive weapon. Slowly, businesses are beginning to find ways to integrate data across silos so that they can begin taking a holistic approach to gain insights from data. These leaders understand that if they can extract meaningful relationships or patterns from data about customers, partners, suppliers, employees, and overall market dynamics, they can turn that information into knowledge so that they can anticipate changes and even shape the future. But even with all the progress that has been made, companies are still grappling with how to capture insights that are not obvious. The problem goes beyond speed—it is a problem of how to discover relationships that are meaningful, not simply anomalies.

The risks of inaction have never been higher. Emerging companies with little revenue are disrupting entire industries and markets overnight and causing established companies to scramble to create new strategies on-the-fly. Bookstore owners have found that electronic book stores have often destroyed their business model. Cab companies are being threatened by new ride sharing models. Manufacturing companies have found that innovative new automated processes and new supply chains have caused them to rethink their cost structures overnight. New regulations in healthcare have required healthcare providers to create new cost-effective processes that meet the right quality of care.

These three scenarios are only the beginning of the tremendous market upheavals that are facing companies across the globe. Solving these problems is not easy, but fundamental shifts won't come from looking in the traditional places. Making it faster to find a cab or shared ride isn't a sustainable differentiator. Making it cheaper by lowering driver pay or auto quality or better routing won't do it—every competitor can copy those moves. However, knowing more about the customer so that you can pair the right driver and rider based on knowledge of their experiences and preferences just may make the difference. While every company hopes to be able to better understand customer preferences and behavior, it is not effective to just ask them. To gain deep understanding requires that organizations be able observe or capture data from external sources (such as comments on social media and data from customer transactions). But true competitive advantages come from discovering what customers value, even before they can articulate what they will pay for.

## Advantages of New Disruptive Models

On a pure technology level, the advances in deployment models such as cloud and mobile computing are transformational because they enable new disruptive business models. As the market for these types of services has exploded, the cost of computing and storage has dramatically fallen. In addition, emerging deployment models mean that with little capital investment, new companies can create digital assets and gain a foothold in a market in record time. Therefore, companies can no longer assume that a well established installed base or customer loyalty will sustain them in the long run. The answer to this disruption is taking advantage of knowledge in new ways that can support the new realities.

Cognitive computing, as discussed throughout this book, changes the way that data is processed through advanced analytic algorithms and combined with structured, unstructured, and semi-structured data. With cognitive computing, you can discover insights that were previously beyond your ability to achieve through computation. Without a cognitive system, a human is required to manually discover patterns and insights that were buried inside complex documents, reports, journal articles, and videos images. In legal discovery, lawyers often send the opposition so much information that it cannot possibly process the data in a reasonable amount of time, even when keywords can be scanned automatically. The deeper meaning remains hidden. Even with an abundance of time, researchers may miss key patterns and nuances that are hidden in documents. In contrast, if you process this volume of data with a cognitive system, you can gain insights that would have required an army of researchers that are smart enough to see subtleties across information sources. While one researcher with decades of experience might know precisely what to look for, the average researcher will likely miss important data.

## What Does Knowledge Mean to the Business?

Traditionally, companies have relied heavily on past experience in order to predict the future. The fast rate of change in everything from customer preferences to market dynamics to new technology has rendered many of the traditional methods of business forecasting ineffective. Also, traditional approaches are generally inadequate to respond and adapt to external forces, such as extreme weather events that disrupt supply chains or the sudden popularity of an entertainer whose wardrobe will quickly change demand within a specific demographic. All the cues are available in social media data, but traditional systems are not designed to be able to find this data or exploit it so that action can be taken.

In a search for a better way to translate huge amounts of data across business units into a predictable approach to determining outcomes and next best actions, companies are looking at innovative approaches beyond running reports and analyzing data from traditional databases. These businesses are looking for ways to use all types of data to both analyze and continuously learn from that data. Companies are now comfortable using a variety of algorithms to analyze data. The new frontier is being able to take advantage of the variety of data sources—most notably unstructured text data. While it has long been possible to query a text database, leaders want to build a more dynamic and comprehensive knowledge base that can help them anticipate change and take the appropriate action.

The way to find answers to complex issues is changing. The traditional database query is highly structured and takes its direction from the way the database is designed and managed. A SQL query is therefore highly effective when you know that the database includes the data that you need to find. A SQL query is basically a look-up function. When you look for answers in unstructured data, you typically use a search engine when you have an idea of what you want to find, but you don't know where to locate the source of that information. The search engine relies on tagging and keywords to find possible answers. When someone asks a question, it matches the words in the query with the tags and keywords in the unstructured database. It provides the user with documents that match those words but does not provide insight. Selecting the document that can provide the best answer is left up to the searcher.

The answer is not simply a database that enables a user to ask a question. This approach has been attempted for decades with only moderate success. In fact, queries are the right approach when there is a well-constructed and highly structured data source that is designed to manage a specific set of questions. Knowledge-based or expert systems, supported by a rules engine, were a step in the right direction as an approach to capture and leverage the experience of statisticians. These applications, however, cannot carry on a dialogue with users to refine their recommendations or suggest new questions that would increase the confidence in an answer. For example, to determine the best approach when treating diabetes, the typical physician relies on experience and perhaps consultation with specialists. The experienced specialist who has treated so many patients with the same illness may be able to determine a successful treatment in seconds. In contrast, the physician with only one year of experience will have to spend hours searching literature or calling on specialists to make a diagnosis. But this approach is not scalable because that physician cannot easily transfer that knowledge to a newly minted doctor. Therefore, there is an inherent risk when the student relies only on the expertise of one physician. For example, the doctor with only 2 years of clinical experience will spend hours poring over books, looking at journal articles, and asking colleagues for their opinion about what to do. The new doctor may use a technique that seems right based on his limited experience. In some domains, there are only a handful of specialists who have seen multiple cases of rare diseases. They can have a positive global influence if their cases are shared with less-experienced physicians.

Sharing of expertise via cognitive systems may be useful in any domain in which specialized knowledge can be pooled, from oncology to auto repair, as long as the relevant knowledge is captured in a corpus.

## The Difference with a Cognitive Systems Approach

Contrast this with the organization that begins to use a cognitive computing approach. The organization leveraging a cognitive approach will begin by collecting all the data concerning diabetes including treatment options, literature, and clinical trials. That same organization will also leverage the most experienced physicians and begin to codify their knowledge from their years of experience and case files. Unlike a traditional application that had to be written based on previously known processes, the cognitive system is designed to learn and change based on capturing best practices and knowledge into a corpus or ontology. At the same time, these organizations want to be able to use data from sensors to monitor metrics and correct for changes in patient status.

For decades organizations have tried to find a way to automate the entire business and have a single integrated system that could manage it all. This has never worked. What has worked for organizations is to design systems that are focused on bringing together knowledge related to a specific business outcome (domain knowledge). Therefore, applications focused on accounting, for example, can provide the right information about all aspects and processes needed to manage accounting effectively because processes are concrete and the knowledge is mature and well understood. This type of categorization of knowledge is operationalized in everything from marketing and sales to human resources, finance, operations, and customer service.

But these systems have been designed based on a von Neumann architectural approach in which the logic and processes are designed in a linear fashion. Each business area is self-contained. Accounting does not interact with data from manufacturing except at a transactional level. Although this siloed approach provides the business with high-quality business intelligence, it can be difficult for business leaders to look at the relationships of this data and see patterns across parts of the company. One significant challenge to this approach is that conflicting data definitions across functional units often contribute to a lack of trust in the data and inconsistencies in business knowledge. In addition, this traditional approach to building business knowledge has many other limitations in today's dynamic and fast-paced global markets. For example, knowledge about the business tends to be historically based and internally focused. Today, companies are increasingly recognizing the need to integrate external and more dynamic sources of information about customer preferences and changing expectations into the traditional business knowledge base.

The previous discussion is based on the premise that the business problems that existing systems were designed to address are well understood and well defined. In many situations, traditional systems were designed based on the way the business operated in the past. Therefore, as the business changed, these systems could not easily be changed or be adapted to new innovative business processes.

## Meshing Data Together Differently

Traditionally, the systems of record we have been discussing have been designed primarily to support highly structured data. However, the new data environment includes data from unstructured sources that were never considered to be part of a company's systems of record. These new dynamic and varied sources of information include unstructured data and streaming data, such as call center notes, social media data, news or stock market data feeds, log files, and spatial data from sensors. These newer sources of data add new dimensions, insights, and answers to some challenging questions. There are connections between structured and unstructured data that were often understood but could never be used. For example, executives knew that customer support systems contained extensive notes about the problems and future requirements of customers. However, no one had the time to manually search through these systems to see if there were any correlation between specific customer issues and a drop in the sale of a specific item in a retail store. Likewise, companies typically would save terabytes of log data coming from sensors on machines. Although they might save that data for years, it remained dark. It was simply too big to analyze.

The need—and ability—to gain business value from expanded varieties and larger volumes of data add a lot of complexity to the definition of business knowledge. The structured information that represents the traditional knowledge base about the operations of the business is most frequently stored and managed in a relational database management system (RDBMS). The siloed approach to maintaining business knowledge means that a company may manage its data in many different RDBMSs. For example, transaction data may be stored in one database, while customer information could be stored in another. Because the newer types of data that add to business knowledge are more likely to be unstructured, these data types need to be managed in a range of different types of data stores such as a Hadoop Distributed File System (HDFS), graph databases, or spatial databases. These platforms provide the ability to add structure to data and provide a distributed technique for analyzing that data in context. Companies are including these new data management capabilities so that they can analyze patterns in all different types of structured and unstructured data. These new sources and varieties of data can improve everything from monitoring manufacturing processes to the detection of diseases. Businesses can improve business planning and execution and predict outcomes. In the insurance industry, for example, executives are using Big Data to figure out what product offerings are the best for a certain customer with the least amount of risk.

Companies want to add new types of data to the business knowledge base so that this knowledge can be leveraged and exploited in various situations. Advances in cognitive computing are helping businesses to analyze more business-relevant information and to plan more accurately. Although knowledge about past business performance remains critical, it is no longer an adequate or acceptable way for a business to remain competitive in the future. Companies want to anticipate the actions their customers might take. They want to predict and thereby prevent infrastructure failures before they happen. Overall, companies want to find ways to derive business outcomes from analyzing large volumes and diverse types of data that are coming from many different sources. Businesses need to learn from data of all types and use that knowledge to optimize both the operational and customer experience.

Cognitive computing can help companies to redefine business knowledge for their organization. With a cognitive system, companies can move beyond analyzing existing information to making inferences and predictions about the future that will improve with experience. For example, a hospital could use a cognitive system to help reduce re-admissions after patients are released. It is much safer and better for patients' recovery to anticipate if they might be at high risk for readmission and take corrective action to keep those patients out of the hospital. There are a number of factors that could place certain patients at higher risk for re-admission than other patients. Factors ranging from smoking, drug abuse, lack of support at home, or hospital or physician error could have an impact on patients' propensity for readmission. Some of these factors might be known to the physician and recorded in traditional patient records, whereas others may not. In many hospital settings, obvious risk factors are overlooked or are simply unknown. A cognitive system could be designed to analyze past cases and search for patterns of risk factors based on reasons for hospitalization and key patient medical and socio-economic factors. The data would include both structured and unstructured information. At the time of discharge, a patient's record can be compared to the database to determine if he is rated high for re-admission risk. If this is the case, the hospital can implement preventive measures that keep the patient from needing re-admission. Because this is a cognitive system, it is designed to learn and get smarter with each patient case. Aggregated case files may create new value for sharable knowledge. Although the model of risk factors was initially based on historical data, it will be automatically updated and reconfigured each time the system is used.

## Using Business Knowledge to Plan for the Future

As technology advances the relationships between sources of knowledge, we can begin to understand the insights that had previously been inaccessible. Shaping outcomes is the heart of the change offered by a cognitive approach to computing. It is useful to evaluate the four stages of maturity in analytics capabilities to understand where we have come from and where we are going.

## THE FOUR STAGES OF MATURITY IN ANALYTICS

While businesses are discovering the need for advanced analytics to be able to manage change, organizations do not necessarily all have the ability to leverage data in the same ways. Over time, as analysts gain more expertise they will be able to gain new levels of sophistication. Therefore, we have offered four stages of maturity that companies go through in gaining insights from their data.

**Stage 1: Collecting, cleansing, integrating, and reporting on data.** During this stage you can use this data to query and analyze current and past business performance. Before you can make sense of data, it is critical to understand what problem your company is trying to solve. What do you want to do with this data and why? When the organization understands the business goals, it is the right time to put a strategy in place. This stage is important in creating a baseline of consistent and trusted knowledge about the business. You can't begin to accurately predict where your company is headed if you don't have a clear understanding of where you have been. Data cleansing and data integration ensure that senior executives understand that reports from business units such as sales, operations, and finance are accurate. Any predictions of future performance based on current and historical information make the implicit assumption that business operations are stable. This approach assumes a Bayesian approach that begins with a hypothesis and then uses a statistical analysis to reach conclusions. Therefore, the rate of change is considered only for the rate of growth or decline in the overall market.

**Stage 2: Trend analysis for forecasting.** This stage uses basic modeling capabilities to make business forecasts based on an analysis of historical trends. For example, a clothing buyer for a retail chain looks at past sales across the company's stores and forecasts next year's sales by store prior to placing a new order. The model is likely to account for various factors that differ across each of the stores such as climate, store location, and demographic characteristics of shoppers. The buyer may apply what-if analysis to adjust the sales forecast based on changes in selected variables. For example, what if next season has 5 or 10 additional heavy snowfall days? The forecast can be adjusted downward to account for less traffic in the store due to snowstorms. Although creating a forecast for the future based on past performance is a good place to start, these models were not designed to capture and account for change as it is happening. For example, the buyer in this example may end up with a lot of unsold merchandise after overlooking rapid changes in fashion trends among a certain demographic. The outcome from these systems tended to be based on the ability to codify current knowledge and report from those findings. In essence, the results of leveraging these systems were not predictive in nature. Rather, the results are based on a structured and well-defined set of problems.

**Stage 3: Predictive analytics.** This stage is defined by the use of statistical or data-mining solutions that consist of algorithms and techniques that can be applied to both structured and unstructured data. Multiple sources of both structured and unstructured data types can be used individually or together to build comprehensive models. Some of the statistical techniques used in this phase include decision tree analysis, linear and logistic regression analysis, data mining, social network analysis, and time series analysis. A key factor in predictive analytics capabilities is having the ability to incorporate predictive models with business rules into the operational decision-making process. This makes the modeling process more actionable and helps businesses to improve outcomes.

The focus of predictive analytics is on anticipating trends before they happen so that you can act to minimize risk for the business. Although predictive analytics has been used for many years by statisticians in certain industries, advances in software tools combined with increasing compute power has made this technology more accessible and more widely used by business users. Predictive analytics models are designed to analyze the relationships among different variables to make predictions about the likelihood that events will take place. For example, an insurance company may build a model that analyzes the components of fraudulent claims and use this model to flag new claims that have a high probability of being fraudulent. Another common use case for predictive modeling is to help call center agents understand the next best action to take when they are interacting with customers. Based on the individual customer's profile, specific product recommendations can be made at the point of interaction between the agents and customer.

**Stage 4: Prescriptive and cognitive.** Prescriptive and cognitive approaches take predictive analytics to the next level by applying machine learning algorithms, visualization, and natural language processing. Companies want their models to look beyond their internal assumptions about customers and products so that they are better prepared to respond to changing market dynamics.

If models are designed to continuously learn based on each new interaction, the accuracy will improve. For example, a mobile service provider uses analytical models to help customer service agents reduce the level of customer churn. These models analyze information about a particular customer and predict what action the company needs to take to retain this customer. The company's predictive models were updated infrequently and lacking in accuracy and sensitivity to competitive changes in the market. The company significantly improved its customer retention rate by designing a new model that is more prescriptive. The model is designed to be self-learning by feeding each new interaction back into the model, capturing changing market conditions. In addition, the model incorporates social analytics to understand the customer's interactions with and influence on others. These changes improved the model's capability to help drive accurate decision making regarding what the next best action should be to support the customer.

Models that are designed to adapt and change are beginning to be used by companies to predict when a machine is likely to fail so that corrective action can be taken before a catastrophic event occurs. For example, patterns identified in streams of machine data coming from sensors in a train can be used to build models that will anticipate equipment failure before it happens. By using adaptive learning, the model's accuracy can be continuously improved to provide a real-time warning of equipment failure in time for the company to take corrective action.

## Answering Business Questions in New Ways

Cognitive computing can also be thought of as a set of enabling technologies that can be applied to a variety of business problems. Many vendors are providing Application Programming Interfaces (APIs) that can add cognitive capability to a variety of initiatives. For example, one emerging vendor called Expect Labs is adding the ability to take conversations and discussions and discover the key concepts and actions buried in spoken language. This same type of approach can be used to discover patterns of similarities across hundreds of pictures of faces to find a particular person.

This type of discovery of meanings inside data will have a dramatic impact on how business is conducted. We are already seeing what happens when businesses can analyze the content of social media conversations. A company can interact with customers on sites such as Twitter or Facebook to intervene when a customer is unhappy. If a business can fix a problem before the customer gets angry, the company can turn a bad situation into a positive engagement.

In addition to discovering patterns, companies need to be able to impart knowledge to employees with limited expertise. A sophisticated practitioner can use a cognitive computing system to input best practices that can be used by less knowledgeable professionals. This sets the foundation so that the new doctor or engineer can gain a faster understanding of most up to date processes. These systems are fed newer data overtime so that the depth of knowledge is expanded and refined. The promise of knowledge management was always difficult to achieve because it assumed that it would be possible to actively capture what experts knew. In contrast, by using a cognitive approach, a system can ingest written information that can be vetted by experts. In addition, this same system can be trained as new information and new best practices emerge. This new dynamic knowledge source can become a competitive differentiator for a business. Imagine, employees with only a few weeks of experience can have immediate access to the right answers at the time of engagement with customers.

## Building Business Specific Solutions

In addition to the availability of APIs and cognitive services, an emerging set of applications is being developed. In Chapters 11, 12, and 13 you will find details about how cognitive computing applications are being designed to address data driven solutions in various industries. All of these solutions, whether we are looking at healthcare, metropolitan areas, or security and commerce, have common characteristics. The commonalities include:

- A huge amount of data in many different forms
- Industry-specific data (typically unstructured) that is constantly expanding

- A need to correlate a variety of data sources to determine context, patterns, and anomalies

- The requirement to find a way to match the data with deep expertise

- The need to analyze large amounts of data to support decision making, such as next best action

- The ability to have the systems learn and change as business conditions change

Cognitive systems are changing the way people interact with computing systems to help them find new ways of exploring and answering questions about the business. These systems will learn and interact to provide expert assistance to scientists, engineers, lawyers, and other professionals in a fraction of the time it now takes.

## Making Cognitive Computing a Reality

What makes a cognitive computing approach different is that these systems are built to change. The system continues to change based on the ingestion of more data and the capability to identify patterns and linkages between elements. Therefore, companies can look for associations and links between data elements that they might not even know existed beforehand.

The results of creating these types of solutions can be profound. They enable a new level of engagement in which the business leader can have an intuitive interface between the system and the huge volume of data managed in the corpus. Even more important is that these systems are not static. As new data is added, the system learns and determines new ways of understanding situations. For example, new associations may suddenly appear that were not visible or present in the past. Perhaps there is an association between someone who buys books and takes a certain type of vacation. Perhaps there is a relationship between two drugs that can cause a never-before-seen interaction. There may be a new method of treating a serious condition based on a series of new research findings that were published only in the past month in an obscure journal.

The underlying value of a cognitive approach to interacting with technology is that it has the potential to change the way individuals in organizations think about information. How do we ask systems what the data we are seeing means? How can we interact with a system to provide insight when we don't know what direction to take or what question to ask?

It is becoming clear that we have scratched only the surface of the power of information managed in new ways to discover new ways to act and transform organizations.

## How a Cognitive Application Can Change a Market

When industries are in transition with new competitive threats, it is impossible to simply build an application. Traditional applications are intended to automate processes and manage data. When a business is trying to transform a traditional industry such as travel or customer care, innovators need sophisticated technologies that allow leaders to discover new techniques and new knowledge. A travel company that can discover what customers want will have a differentiation. What if a travel company can know what the customer will buy even when the customer has no idea? What if a customer service representative can anticipate that the customer's problem is related to a partner's product within minutes rather than hours?

The new generation of solutions will look beyond codified practices and find the answers that are not obvious. Disrupters in every industry throughout the centuries have done precisely this—they have taken traditional approaches to solving problems and turned them upside down.

## Summary

Cognitive computing is an emerging area that has the potential to change the way humans interact with machines. Creating a corpus of information that collects massive amounts of structured and unstructured information is game changing. Cognitive computing is not designed to be a back-office function such as existing systems of record that keep track of past transactions and interactions. Rather, cognitive computing is intended to provide businesses with solutions that help them move beyond silos of data to expand how they understand the world. In the coming decade, cognitive computing will transform the machine to a human interface and accelerate how we act to solve problems and facilitate change. Although systems of record and engagement won't disappear, cognitive discovery, support, and training systems will enable new and improved ways to understand and serve customers, and raise the performance levels of experts in virtually every knowledge-based industry.

# IBM's Watson as a Cognitive System

One of the best ways to understand the potential for cognitive computing is to take a look at one of the early implementations of a cognitive system. IBM developed Watson as one of its new foundational offerings intended to help customers build a different type of system based on the ingestion of new content. IBM's design focus for Watson was to create solutions based on aggregating data leveraging techniques ranging from machine learning to Natural Language Processing (NLP) and advanced analytics. Watson solutions include a set of foundational services combined with industry-focused best practices and data. The accuracy of results from a cognitive system continuously improves through an iterative training process that combines the knowledge of subject matter experts with a corpus of domain specific data. One of the important capabilities that allows for this machine/human interaction is the ability to leverage NLP to understand the context of a combination of a variety of unstructured and structured data sources. In addition, a cognitive system is not constrained to applications that are deterministic in nature, but can manage probabilistic systems that change and evolve as they are used.

## Watson Defined

Watson is a cognitive system that combines capabilities in NLP, analytics, and machine learning techniques. Watson gains insights and gets smarter with each user interaction and each time that new information is ingested. By combining NLP, dynamic learning, and hypothesis generation and evaluation, Watson is intended to help professionals create hypotheses from data, accelerate findings, and determine the availability of supporting evidence to solve problems. IBM views Watson as a way to improve business outcomes by enabling humans to interact with machines in a natural way.

Individuals have become accustomed to leveraging sophisticated search engines or database query systems to discover information to support decision making. Watson, which also facilitates data-driven search, takes a different approach that is discussed in detail in this chapter. In essence, Watson leverages machine learning, DeepQA, and advanced analytics. IBM Watson's DeepQA architecture, as illustrated in Figure 9-1, is described in this chapter.

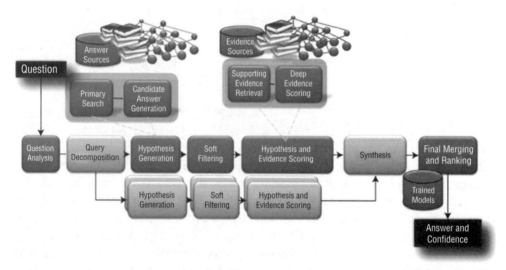

**Figure 9-1:** IBM Watson DeepQA Architecture

Courtesy of International Business Machines Corporation, © International Business Machines Corporation.

## How Watson Is Different from Other Search Engines

One way to understand this unique process is to consider how Watson, as a cognitive computing system, differs from search engines. With a search engine, you enter key words and get results on a topic based on an appropriate ranking. You might also ask a specific question and receive ranked results; however, you will not be able to create a dialogue to continue to refine the results. A typical search engine uses algorithms to rank results based on relevance to the keywords. Secondary rankings may deliver results based on factors such as price or consumer reviews. At this point, humans interact with the list of results and assess which answers or links best fit the question being asked.

With Watson, the individual gets a directed result—either an answer to the question or a follow-up question to help clarify the user's intent. Therefore, the machine is intended to act more like a human expert. For example, the user might ask Watson, "What is the best retirement program for me?" or "What is the best way to lose weight?" If Watson has enough data and enough contextual knowledge related to the subject, the system can understand the language behind the question. This deep level of understanding is driven through the use of statistical analysis and algorithms for developing predictive models. Watson does not simply look for keywords as a search engine would. In addition, Watson, leveraging NLP techniques, has the capability to break a question into subcomponents and evaluate each component for possible answers and solutions. This capability of receiving meaningful, accurate, and timely answers to a direct question is the fundamental difference between most search engines and the question-answering process of cognitive systems.

## Advancing Research with a "Grand Challenge"

Computer scientists have often used games as a way to advance their research agenda and publicly demonstrate innovative computer technology. In keeping with this tradition, IBM has a long history of incorporating games into "grand challenges" for its research teams. Two of IBM's highly publicized "grand challenges" involved the game of checkers in the 1950s and the game of chess in the late 1990s. One of the early pioneers of Artificial Intelligence (AI) programmed an IBM 701 computer to play checkers, and beat one of the top U.S. checkers champions. At the time, this feat was a stunning example of the capabilities of computers. More than 30 years later, IBM's Deep Blue computer was the first to beat a world chess champion. The purpose of a "grand challenge" is to take a theoretical concept and prove it can be done.

IBM's success with its chess grand challenge was based on computers beating humans in the world of mathematics. Researchers at IBM thought that the next challenge should explore and advance the capabilities of computers in human natural language and knowledge. In 2006, IBM outlined a grand challenge that could help transform the way businesses make decisions. One of IBM's researchers suggested that the company build a computer that could compete with human champions and win at *Jeopardy!* The initial focus was to determine if a system could compete against humans by answering questions across a diverse range of topical areas. The biggest issue that IBM researchers faced in succeeding with the grand challenge was establishing the right balance between speed of processing and accuracy of results. Although the goal of the grand challenge was to beat humans at the game of *Jeopardy!* IBM hoped to be able to use the Jeopardy! challenge as a way to begin investigating the potential to create a cognitive systems that could support complex industries.

# Preparing Watson for *Jeopardy!*

IBM brought together an internal team of expert scientists and researchers in fields ranging from machine learning to mathematics, High Performance Computing (HPC), NLP, and knowledge representation to translate the grand challenge into a platform. In order to win at *Jeopardy!*, the team would need to build a system that could answer questions asked in human language faster and more accurately than the top ranked human competitors. IBM determined that Watson would need to answer approximately 70 percent of questions and get the right answer more than 80 percent of the time. Further, this level of accuracy would need to be accomplished in 3 seconds or less for each question.

To accomplish these goals, Watson was designed as a Question-Answering system that uses continuously acquired knowledge to determine answers to questions and confidence scores associated with those questions. Watson understands the context of a sentence by deconstructing each element of the sentence, comparing those elements against previously ingested information, and making inferences as to meaning.

The complexity of the *Jeopardy!* challenge was based on the diversity of question types and the broad base of subject areas included in the game. In addition, there is always one right answer or response to a question in *Jeopardy!* You can't respond to a question with a request for additional information. Contestants need to discern the question based on a set of clues. Clues could be technical information or they could be puns, puzzles, or cultural references. To solve the clue at fast enough speeds to win the game, Watson needed to understand many aspects of language that humans understand instinctively. Humans have a natural ability to understand inference, context, and constraints of time and space.

To ensure that responses are highly accurate, Watson simultaneously generates many hypotheses (potential answers) in a parallel computing environment. These hypotheses need to be generated in a way that casts a broad enough net so that the right answer is among the selections, but not so broad that large numbers of incorrect hypotheses interfere with the overall efficiency of the process. Sophisticated algorithms rank and determine a confidence level for each hypothesis. Advances in natural language processing technologies helped to make this approach a reality. IBM built an architecture that would support the use of machine learning to do extensive experimentation to continuously advance Watson's cognitive capabilities.

The need for computational speed led IBM to use extremely fast and powerful hardware. On the night of the televised *Jeopardy!* competition, Watson included a combination of servers, storage, memory, and networking equipment that placed it in a supercomputer class. Watson included 90 IBM Power 750 servers, each with four processors for a maximum of 32 logical cores per processor. This means that there was a total of 2,880 IBM Power7 Processor Cores. It was the power of the 2,880 cores that allowed Watson to meet the 3-second requirement for delivering an answer to a question. In addition, Watson was designed to store its entire knowledge base in random access memory (RAM) instead of on disk to further speed up processing speeds and deliver fast results. Extremely fast networking technology was included to help move a lot of data between compute nodes at fast speeds.

## Preparing Watson for Commercial Applications

The question-answering process for the game of *Jeopardy!* is different than what you would typically expect in commercial applications. Instead of providing one right answer to a question in *Jeopardy!*, commercial applications require more complex, multidimensional answers. Commercial applications built for industries such as healthcare and finance need to support an ongoing dialogue between humans and machines that would help to drill down to the most meaningful set of responses. In addition, Watson would be expected to ask for more information when needed to help the business users get the most useful and accurate response.

The difference between a typical *Jeopardy!* question and a sample question for a commercial healthcare application is illustrated in Table 9-1. The question from *Jeopardy!* includes a subject domain and a statement about an entity or concept. The entity or concept is not identified in the statement. The subject domain in this question is "delicacies" and the unidentified entity is "pig." In commercial applications for Watson, such as the Watson Discovery Advisor, it is unlikely that there will be just one correct answer. For example, the question shown in the following table asks for a treatment plan for a patient. The intention is for the physician to engage in a collaborative dialogue with Watson.

**Table 9-1:** Answering a *Jeopardy!* Question Compared to Answering a Watson Discovery Advisor Question

| STANDARD *JEOPARDY!* QUESTION AND ANSWER | STANDARD QUESTION AND ANSWER FOR WATSON DISCOVERY ADVISOR |
|---|---|
| Question: DELICACIES: Star chef Mario Batali lays on the lardo, which comes from the back of this animal's neck. | Question: An oncologist is reviewing treatment options with a cancer patient and asks Watson, "What is the recommended treatment for patient X?" |
| Answer: The answer to the question is "pig." | Answer: The answer to the question is multifaceted and is provided as an ongoing dialogue with the oncologist. The answer may include recommendations for additional tests and provide options for various treatments. |

Advanced machine learning techniques are used to train Watson to provide correct answers to many types of questions, including those illustrated in Table 9-1. Watson arrives at the answer by considering many possible responses to the question based on its body of knowledge (corpus). In addition, Watson looks at the context of the question from many different approaches and considers different interpretations and definitions for words and phrases. Each of the possible answers is given a confidence value by Watson. Watson provided the single answer "pig" to the sample *Jeopardy!* question because this was the answer with the highest confidence level. In comparison, Watson may provide several alternative answers to the question about treatment options and show the confidence level for each answer.

IBM is applying many of the technology advancements that helped Watson win at *Jeopardy!* to its commercial applications of cognitive systems. These systems use evidenced-based learning to enable organizations to train systems to get smarter with each new interaction. Training is an important aspect of implementing a Watson system in a commercial environment. The training data includes question and answer pairs on how things are said in that specific industry. Watson can also be trained for a new industry by ingesting resources such as an ontology. For example, in a Watson application for a hospital, the training might include ingesting a deep ontology or coding system specific to medical diagnostic testing or treatments for specific diseases. Ontologies provide a mechanism for determining context by clarifying and defining terminology and creating accurate mappings between resources from different systems. In addition, standards-based guidelines on how to treat specific diseases would be included. Additional training may be based on the clinical expertise of highly knowledgeable and experienced clinicians. Companies can use these cognitive systems to answer new types of questions, make more accurate predictions, and optimize business outcomes.

## Watson's Software Architecture

The design structure of Watson includes software architecture for building Question-Answering systems and a methodology to research, develop, and integrate algorithmic techniques into the system. Although speed and power are critical elements for Watson, the design team initially focused on achieving accuracy and confidence. Without these characteristics, the speed would be meaningless. Therefore, a key design element includes algorithms for assessing and increasing accuracy. The Natural Language Processing technologies incorporated into the Watson architecture—known as DeepQA—include the following:

- Question parsing and classification
- Question decomposition

- Automatic source acquisition and evaluation
- Entity and relation detection
- Logical form generation
- Knowledge representation and reasoning

The DeepQA software architecture is built according to Unstructured Information Management Architecture (UIMA) standards. UIMA was initially created by IBM and then open-sourced to the Apache Software Foundation. It was chosen as the framework for the hundreds of analytic components in DeepQA because of its capability to support the extreme speed, scalability, and accuracy required across a large number of distributed machines. Through experimentation, IBM improved the accuracy of the DeepQA algorithms and, consequently, confidence in Watson's results. The following were DeepQA's core design principles:

- **Massive Parallelism**—A large number of computer processes work in parallel to optimize processing speed and overall performance. Using this technique enables Watson to analyze vast sources of information and evaluate different interpretations and hypotheses at extremely fast speeds.

- **Integration of probabilistic question and content analytics**—Algorithms and models are developed using machine learning to provide correct answers that assume deep levels of expertise across multiple domains. The corpus provides a base of knowledge and the analytics estimate, and understands the relationships and patterns in the information.

- **Confidence estimation**—The architecture is designed in such a way that there are multiple interpretations to a question. There is never a commitment to a single answer. The approach of continually scoring different answers with a confidence level is key to Watson's accuracy. The technology analyzes and combines scores of different interpretations to understand which interpretation is most relevant.

- **Integration of shallow and deep knowledge**—Shallow knowledge is procedural in nature and does not support the ability to make connections between different elements of a particular subject area. You can use shallow knowledge to get the answer to certain types of questions, but there are many limitations. To go deeper than a literal or superficial understanding of question and response, you need to make associations and inferences. To achieve this level of sophistication, you need deep knowledge, which is about understanding the central foundational concepts of a particular subject area—such as investment banking or medical oncology. With deep knowledge you can make complex connections and associations to those central concepts.

The methodology for the development and integration of core algorithmic techniques is called AdaptWatson. The methodology creates core algorithms, measures the results, and then comes up with new ideas. AdaptWatson quickly manages the research, development, integration, and evaluation of the core algorithmic components. The algorithmic components have many roles including:

- Understanding questions
- Creating the confidence level of the answer
- Evaluating and ranking the results
- Analyzing natural language
- Identifying sources
- Finding and generating hypotheses
- Scoring evidence and answers
- Merging and ranking hypotheses

To determine relationships and inferences, Watson uses machine learning and linear regression to rank data based on relevance.

## The Components of DeepQA Architecture

The essential components of the Watson DeepQA architecture include a pipeline process flow that begins with a question and concludes with an answer and confidence level (refer to Figure 9-1). The various answer sources come up with alternative responses, and then each response is evaluated and ranked as to its likelihood of being a correct response. There is an iterative process that needs to take place in seconds but will allow for evidence to be collected and analyzed before the best answer is determined. The components in DeepQA are implemented as UIMA annotators. These annotators are software components that analyze text to create assertions (or annotations) about that text. At each stage, there is a role for an UIMA annotator to help move the process forward. Watson has hundreds of UIMA annotators. The different types of capabilities that need to take place within the pipeline are as follows:

- **Question analysis**—Each question is parsed to extract major features and begin the process of understanding what is asked by the question. This analysis determines how the question will be processed by the system.

- **Primary search**—Content is retrieved from the evidence and answer sources.

- **Candidate answer generation**—Various hypotheses (candidate answers) are extracted from the content. Each potential answer is considered as a candidate for the correct answer. NLP interprets and analyzes the text search results. Answer and evidence sources are examined to provide insight into how to answer the question. Hypotheses or candidate answers are generated by this analysis. Each hypothesis is considered and reviewed independently.

▪ **Shallow answer scoring**—The various candidates for the answer are scored across many dimensions such as geospatial similarity.

▪ **Soft filtering**—After each candidate answer is scored, the soft filtering process scores and selects approximately the top 20 percent of the scored candidates for additional analysis.

▪ **Supporting evidence search**—Additional evidence is researched and applied to the analysis of the top candidates. NLP analysis is performed on the additional supporting evidence. Various hypotheses are tested.

▪ **Deep Evidence Scoring**—Each piece of evidence is evaluated, using multiple algorithms, to determine to what degree the evidence supports that the candidate answer is correct.

▪ **Final merging and ranking**—All the evidence for each candidate answer is combined. Ranks are assigned and confidence scores are computed.

The process flow highlighted depends on the answer and evidence sources as well as the models (refer to Figure 9-1). The major components of this architecture are listed next and will be described in more detail in the remainder of this chapter:

▪ Building the Watson corpus

▪ Question analysis

▪ Hypotheses generation

▪ Scoring and confidence estimation

## Building the Watson Corpus: Answer and Evidence Sources

The Watson corpus provides the base of knowledge used by the system to answer questions and provide responses to queries. The corpus needs to provide a broad base of information as reference sources without adding unnecessary information that might slow down performance. IBM looked at the domain of questions that could be included in *Jeopardy!* and the data sources that would be needed to answer those questions. The hardware was scaled up to provide the computational power required to answer approximately 70 percent of the questions and get the right answer approximately 80 percent of the time. The corpus was developed to provide access to vast amounts of information on a broad range of topics. As Watson was leveraged to meet requirements of commercial applications in areas such as healthcare and financial services, the corpus and ontologies would also need to be developed to provide more domain-specific information. Therefore, IBM developed an approach that would construct the Watson corpus with relevant sources of the right size and breadth to deliver accurate and fast responses. This approach includes three phases:

- **Source acquisition**—Identify the right set of resources for the specific task.
- **Source transformation**—Optimize the format of the textual information for efficient search.
- **Source expansion and updates**—Expansion algorithms are used to determine which additional information would do the best job of filling in gaps and adding nuance to the information sources in the Watson corpus.

Next, each of the three phases is described in more detail.

### Source Acquisition

The appropriate sources for building the Watson corpus will vary based on how Watson will be used. One of the first steps is to analyze the subject matter requirements to understand the types of questions that will be asked. Given the broad domain of knowledge required for *Jeopardy!*, the sources for Watson include a diverse collection of texts including encyclopedias, Wikipedia, dictionaries, historical documents, textbooks, news articles, music databases, and literature. Information sources may also include subject-specific databases, ontologies, and taxonomies. The goal is to collect a rich base of knowledge across multiple domains including science, history, literature, culture, politics, and governments. Building the Watson corpus for commercial applications in areas such as healthcare or finance is different than for *Jeopardy!* For example, building the oncology reference corpus requires ingesting vast amounts of information sources on relevant scientific research, medical textbooks, and journal articles.

The majority of the information sources are unstructured documents in various formats such as XML, PDF, DOCX, or any markup language. These documents need to be ingested into Watson. The system is designed to create indexes for the documents and store them in a distributed filesystem. The Watson instance has access to that shared filesystem. The Watson corpus provides both the answer sources and evidence sources. Answer sources provide the primary search and candidate answer generation (selection of possible answers). Evidence sources provide answer scoring, evidence retrieval, and deep evidence scoring.

### Source Transformation

Textual information sources come in a variety of formats. For example, documents from an encyclopedia are typically title-oriented, meaning that the titles for the documents identify the subject covered in the piece. Other documents such as news articles are likely to include a title that indicates a point of view (identified as nontitle-oriented or opinion-labeled) and may not be a clear indication of the subject matter in the piece. Search algorithms typically do a better job of locating the information in title-oriented documents. Therefore, some nontitle-oriented articles are transformed to help improve the likelihood that the relationship between the content and potential answers can be easily identified.

### Source Expansion and Updates

How do you decide on the right amount of content for the Watson corpus? There needs to be enough information so that Watson can identify patterns and make associations between various elements of information. IBM determined that many of the primary information sources such as encyclopedias and dictionaries provided a good base of knowledge but left many gaps. To fill these gaps, the Watson team developed algorithms that would search the web for additional information with the right context to amplify information in the base or seed documents. These algorithms are designed to score each element of new information relative to the original seed document and include only the new information that appears most relevant.

The Watson corpus also needs to be continuously fine-tuned and updated to ensure accuracy of results. For example, there are approximately 5,000 new articles each week on cancer. Therefore, the Watson corpus for an oncology application needs to be updated constantly with new and relevant information, or it would quickly be out of date. The mechanics of doing incremental ingestion are such that large amounts of documents need to be accessed and continuously ingested into Watson without bringing down the system. In addition, the quality of the ingested information needs to be monitored to eliminate the possibility of corrupting the corpus with erroneous information that could lead to bad answers. For example, consider the question, "What is the best way to lose weight?" There are so many different points of view on this subject. Do you reduce carbohydrates, eliminate sugar, reduce fats, or increase exercise? Is the most recent journal article given more importance, or is the quality and value of the information based on other rating factors such as author expertise?

The process of fine-tuning the corpus to win at a game where there is always a right answer required continuous evaluation to assess Watson's accuracy in relationship to the requirement for extreme speed. IBM used algorithms to test and refine the new resources that should be added to the corpus to increase Watson's accuracy without increasing latency. Technology developed by IBM to increase Watson's speed and accuracy has been used in its commercial applications such as Watson Engagement Advisor and Watson Discovery Advisor.

## Question Analysis

Question Analysis ensures that Watson learns what question is asked and determines how the question is processed by the system. The foundation of the Question Analysis process is based on NLP technology, with a focus on parsing, semantic analysis, and question classification. All these techniques are brought together to enable Watson to understand the type and nature of the questions and to detect relationships between entities in the questions. For example, Watson needs to recognize nouns, pronouns, verbs, and other elements of the sentence to understand what the answer should look like. One reason why the *Jeopardy!* challenge helped to advance IBM's research in NLP is that the domain knowledge required to excel at the game is so diverse. In addition, *Jeopardy!* requires an understanding of many different types of questions, including the capability to recognize humor, puns, and metaphors. IBM worked for many years to refine the algorithms used in Watson's Question Analysis.

Question Analysis requires advanced parsing of the questions from both a syntactic and semantic perspective to extract a logical form. In connection with the parsing, syntactic roles are identified and labeled using algorithms that identify subject, object, and other components of the sentence. In addition, semantic parsing can identify the meaning of phrases and the overall question. The results of the parsing helps Watson to learn what information to search for in the corpus. This is where the associations and pattern matching capabilities become important. Questions are analyzed by identifying the patterns based on the data structures from parsing and semantic analysis. Patterns of words in the text can predict other aspects of the meaning of the content. You need a large enough database of the different types of questions to identify the patterns and recognize the similarities across different logical forms.

Four key elements of the question need to be detected for successful Question Analysis:

- **Focus**—The focus is the part of the question that represents the answer. In order to be able to answer correctly, you need to understand the focus of the question. Determining the focus depends on recognizing the patterns of focus types. For example, one common pattern consists of a noun phrase with a determiner "this" or "these." The following *Jeopardy!* clue illustrates this pattern. "THEATRE: A new play based on this Sir Arthur Conan Doyle canine classic opened on the London stage in 2007." The focus in the clue is "this Sir Arthur Conan Doyle canine classic." The parser needs to connect "this" to the headword "classic." The parser needs to be able to tell the difference between a noun-phrase question and a verb phrase.

- **LAT (Lexical Answer Type)**—Watson uses the LAT to help figure out what type of answer is required. For example, is Watson looking for the name of a film, city, or person?

- **Question Classification**—Watson uses Question Classification to determine the type of question it needs to answer. For example, is the question fact-based, or is it a puzzle, or perhaps a pun? Understanding the question type is important so that Watson can select the right approach for answering the question.

- **QSection**—These are fragments of questions that require a unique approach to find the answer. QSection can identify lexical constraints on the answer (for example, the answer must be only three words) and to decompose a question into multiple subquestions.

### Slot Grammar Parser and Components for Semantic Analysis

Watson uses a series of deep parsing and semantic analysis components to provide the linguistic analysis of the questions and reference content. The Slot Grammar (SG) parser builds a tree that maps out the logical and grammatical structure. There are SGs for many languages including English, French, Spanish, and Italian. The parser used in Watson is the English Slot Grammar (ESG). ("IBM Research Report: Using Slot Grammar," Michael C. McCord, 2010.) The parser was enhanced for Watson according to the specific requirements of the *Jeopardy!* game. The role of the parser is to break up a sentence into its semantic phrases of a sentence. These semantic roles or phrases are called slots. In addition, the term slots can also refer to the names for argument positions for predicates that represent word senses. Some examples of slots are shown in Table 9-2.

**Table 9-2:** Slots—Naming Syntactic Roles or Phrases

| | |
|---|---|
| subj | subject |
| obj | direct object |
| iobj | indirect object |
| comp | predicate complement |
| objprep | object of preposition |
| ndet | noun phrase (NP) determiner |

To derive the meaning of questions, Watson needs a way to recognize the similarities and differences across many different syntactical patterns. It is quite common for the same thought or action to be expressed in slightly different ways. For example, Figure 9-2 shows two sentences with different syntactic components that share the same meaning. Watson uses the SG parser to recognize the subject, object, indirect object, and other elements of the sentence. In sentence (A), Emily fills the subject slot for the verb "gave" and Jason fills the indirect object slot. Each slot represents a syntactic role within the sentence. In sentence (B), Emily still fills the subject slot for the verb "gave." However, in this alternative construct of the sentence, "to Jason" fills the indirect object slot. In other words, the indirect object slot is filled by either the noun phrase "Jason" in sentence A or by the prepositional phrase "to Jason" in sentence B. The syntactic component for the SG needs to understand that these two alternative syntactic examples both have the same meaning. In addition, the SG parse trees need to show both a surface syntactic structure and a deep logical structure. Watson then ranks the various parse trees based on a parse scoring system and selects the parse with the highest ranking.

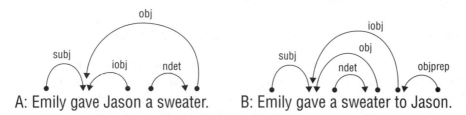

**Figure 9-2:** Parsing two sentences using English Slot Grammar

In addition to the ESG, Watson uses several other components for parsing and semantic analysis:

- The **Predicate-Argument Structure builder** is used to simplify the ESG tree by mapping small variations in syntax to common forms. It is built on top of ESG to support more advanced analytics.

- The **Named Entity Recognizer (NER)** looks for names, quantities, and locations and determines which terms in the phrase are proper nouns that reference people or organizations.

- The **co-reference resolution component** connects referring expressions to their correct subjects and determines the entities to which pronouns relate.

- The **relation extraction component** looks for semantic relationships in the text. This is important if different terms have a similar meaning and is helpful in mapping the relationship between nouns or entities in the question or clue.

### Question Classification

Question Classification is an important element of the Question Analysis process because it helps to identify what type of question is being asked. This process was developed to improve Watson's capability to understand the many different types of clues in *Jeopardy!* You can characterize the clues in *Jeopardy!* by topic, level of difficulty, grammatical construction, answer type, and method to solve the clue. Characterizing the clues based on the method used to answer the question offered the greatest success with developing Question Classification algorithms. Three of the various methods used to find the right answer follow:

- Answer based on factual information.
- Find the answer by decomposing the clue.
- Find the answer by completing a puzzle.

Identifying the question type will trigger different models and strategies in later processing steps. Watson also uses Relation Detection during the Question Analysis process to evaluate the relationships in the question. One of Watson's greatest strengths is in the way it analyzes the question in great depth, including recognizing nuances and searching across the corpus for different possible answers. (See Table 9-3.)

**Table 9-3:** Answering Different Types of *Jeopardy!* Clues

| TYPE OF CLUE | EXAMPLE | HOW YOU ANSWER THE CLUE |
|---|---|---|
| You need to know the facts. | HEAD NORTH: Two states you could be re-entering if you are crossing Florida's northern border.<br><br>Answer: Georgia and Alabama | You answer the question based on factual information about one or more entities. Understand what is being asked and which elements of the clue will help you get the answer. |
| You need to decompose the clue. | DIPLOMATIC RELATIONS: Of the four countries in the world that the United States does not have diplomatic relations with, the one that's farthest North.<br><br>Answer: North Korea | One subclue is nested in the outer clue. After you replace the subclue with its answer, it become easier to answer the outer clue. In this example: The inner subclue is "the four countries in the world that the United States does not have diplomatic relations with." The answer to the subclue is Bhutan, Cuba, Iran, and North Korea. After replacing the subclue with the answer, the new question reads as follows: Of Bhutan, Cuba, Iran, and North Korea, the one that's farthest North. |
| You need to solve a puzzle. | BEFORE and AFTER: 13th Century Venetian traveler who's a Ralph Lauren short sleeve top with a collar.<br><br>Answer: Marco Polo | Two subclues have answers that overlap. |

Why is it important to understand what is asked in the question? Watson needs to learn based on patterns and associations in question and answer resources. The system does not actually understand concepts that would be simple for a child to master. For example, a child can learn that two different types of barking creatures are both dogs even though one is a dalmatian and the other is a golden retriever. Machine learning will help Watson to analyze information in many different ways to figure out that the dalmatian and the golden retriever are both dogs. Alternatively, you could ingest Watson with thousands of Question-Answer combinations, but without machine learning Watson would not be able to answer questions that deviated in any way from the original set. Watson needs to learn to answer new types of questions correctly.

## Hypothesis Generation

How does Watson find the right answer to a question? Watson's key to success with the Question Analysis process is based on the large number of candidate answers that are considered. Hypothesis Generation (Figure 9-3) can identify various hypotheses to answer a question with the expectation that one of them will be the right answer. Although the right answer needs to be among the candidate answers, you don't want there to be too much noise in the selection. If there are too many wrong answers, it decreases the overall efficiency of the Question Analysis process. DeepQA generates the hypotheses using components for search and candidate generation.

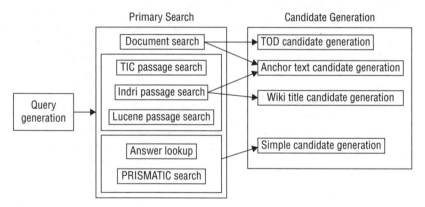

**Figure 9-3:** Hypothesis Generation in Watson's DeepQA Architecture

Following are two components:

- **Search**—Content that is relevant to the question is retrieved from Watson's corpus using search tools such as Apache Lucene. IBM developed highly effective and time-efficient search strategies that leverage the relationship between the content in documents and the titles of those documents. IBM enhanced the native capabilities in the search engines to improve results by extracting syntactic and semantic relations for questions and resource sources.

- **Candidate generation**—Hundreds of potential candidate answers to a question are identified from the search results. Watson uses the knowledge in human-generated text and metadata, as well as syntactic and lexical cues in search results.

Referring to Figure 9-3, you can see that the DeepQA architecture relies on multiple search engines including Indri, PRISMATIC, and Lucene to index and search unstructured text and documents and then generate candidate answers. Each approach has certain benefits, and IBM has optimized results by combining the different approaches. For example, one of the key benefits of Apache Lucene for searching in Watson is flexibility in its architecture that enables its API to be independent of the file format. Apache Lucene is an open source text indexer and search engine written in Java. Text from the different types of sources in Watson's corpus (PDF, HTML, Microsoft Word, and so on) can all be indexed. This approach works for the corpus developed for *Jeopardy!*, as well as for commercial applications.

## Scoring and Confidence Estimation

Scoring and confidence estimation is the final stage in the pipeline. The way Watson uses confidence estimation is a critical element in achieving a high level of accuracy. No single component of the system needs to be perfect. All candidate answers are ranked based on evidence scores, and these scores are used to select the answer with the greatest likelihood of being correct. The various passage-scoring methods used by Watson are combined to improve accuracy. Scores are assigned by matching question terms to passage terms. The net result of this approach to evaluating and ranking the answers ensures that the best answer comes out on top.

There are two methods used for domain relation extraction and scoring in DeepQA: manual pattern specification and statistical methods for pattern specification. The manual approach has a high accuracy rate but takes longer because of the need to find humans with the domain knowledge and statistical experience to create rules for the new relations. Watson looks for the candidate answer by filtering out the noise. There are many different models, including Hidden Markov models, which are used to filter out noise that does not fit the pattern.

There are many scoring algorithms. The four passage scoring (deep evidence scoring) algorithms used in this process are described next:

- **Passage Term Match**—This algorithm assigns a score by matching question terms to passage terms, regardless of grammatical relationship or word order.

- **Skip-Bigram**—This algorithm assigns a score based on relationships observed between specific terms in the question and terms in the evidence passage.

- **Textual Alignment**—This algorithm assigns a score by looking at the relationship between the words and word order of the passage and the question. The focus is replaced by the candidate answer.

- **Logical Form Answer Candidate Scorer (LFACS)**—This algorithm assigns a score based on the relationship between the structure of the question and the structure of the passage. The focus is aligned to the candidate answer.

The candidate answers are scored in parallel across a large cluster of machines, which speeds up the process significantly. This is one of many places within the DeepQA architecture where parallelism comes into play. This ensures that Watson maintains both speed and accuracy. Implementing these scoring strategies together yields better results than if each one was used individually. For example, LFACS is less effective than other algorithms when used individually. However, when used in combination with the other scoring methods, it helps improve overall effectiveness. Ultimately, the way Watson combines the multiple scoring algorithms is by using machine learning and training on questions with known correct answers.

## Summary

IBM's Watson is a cognitive system designed to help expand the boundaries of human cognition. It represents a new era in computing technology by enabling people to begin to interact more naturally with computers. In this new era, humans can leverage and share knowledge in new ways. Watson makes it possible for humans to ask questions in natural language and get answers that enable them to gain new insights from extremely large volumes of information. The research for Watson was based on IBM's extensive experience in NLP, AI, information retrieval, big data, machine learning, and computational linguistics.

A cognitive computing system is not a simple automated processing system. It is intended to create new levels of collaboration between man and machine. Although humans have been codifying information for a long time, there are limitations on the insights and analysis that humans can glean from that information using traditional forms of computing. With a cognitive system like IBM's Watson, the machine can find patterns or outliers in large volumes of unstructured and structured information at fast speeds. A cognitive system gets smarter as each successive interaction improves accuracy and predictive power. The relationship between people and machines is symbiotic in a cognitive system. Good results from a cognitive system require that humans do some mapping and training using machine learning techniques. Humans train Watson by building a corpus of knowledge that may be broad-based or fine-tuned to a specific area such as medicine or finance. The corpus includes information that is codified in books, encyclopedias, research studies, and ontologies. Watson can then search through vast quantities of information and analyze that data in order to provide accurate answers with confidence levels. IBM is applying Watson technologies to multiple industry solutions in fields such as healthcare, finance, and retail.

# CHAPTER 10

# The Process of Building
# a Cognitive Application

Organizations in many different industries are in the early stages of developing cognitive applications. From healthcare to manufacturing to governments, decision makers need to quickly make sense of large volumes and varieties of data. Problem solving often requires the aggregation of a multitude of disconnected data sources including a combination of internal and external data. In addition, it is increasingly likely that the data required to answer problems or deliver new insights is unstructured—such as text, videos, images, sound, or sensor data. Valuable insights may remain hidden because the volume, variety, and velocity (speed) of the data are so hard to manage. Organizations are now beginning to recognize the potential benefits of using cognitive applications to find the patterns in data that can help to improve outcomes.

Chapters 11–13 provide examples of emerging cognitive computing applications across multiple industries. Although the domains and applications described in these chapters differ, certain common attributes of each situation make them a good fit for cognitive applications. Organizations that are implementing cognitive applications typically face similar challenges regarding data and the decision making process such as:

- Large volumes of unstructured data that must be analyzed to make good decisions.

- Decisions must be based on constantly changing data, new sources, and forms of data.

- A significant amount of knowledge about the domain is transferred from senior experts to trainees through a mentoring and training process.

- Decision making requires the analysis of a variety of options and solutions to a problem. Individuals often have to quickly weigh the relative risks and benefits of each alternative and may have to decide based on confidence rather than certainty.

This chapter examines the seven key steps involved in designing a typical cognitive application:

1. Defining the objective

2. Defining the domain

3. Understanding the intended users and their attributes

4. Defining questions and exploring insights

5. Acquiring the relevant data sources

6. Creating and refining the corpora

7. Training and testing

## The Emerging Cognitive Platform

The majority of early cognitive applications have been built from scratch by vendors in collaboration with their customers. The vendors and customers were experimenting and learning together. As the number of cognitive applications under development and deployment grows, vendors are using their experience to codify packaged services, APIs and delivery models that can help customers build cognitive applications more independently and quickly. Most new cognitive applications are developed on a cloud-based cognitive engine that provides the ability to scale processing, storage, and memory. In addition, customers will access a set of well-defined foundational services to speed development of cognitive applications. These foundational services may include a corpus service, analytics service, a data engine such as a graph database, training services, presentation and visualization services, and others. The expectation is that moving forward, cognitive applications will be built on an engine and well-defined APIs that provide some or all these foundational services.

In many ways, vendors are collaborating with partners on these early cognitive applications in a role similar to a systems integrator. Vendors are responsible for the development of the cognitive engine, but much of the development of associated tools and services are created jointly with partners based on their requirements. The partners begin by focusing on defining the domain for their cognitive application, collecting and curating the data sources, and understanding the types of questions and information that their users will be interested in. Typically, the development of the model, including the training and testing of the system, is completed in collaboration with the vendors providing the cognitive platform.

Each phase of developing a cognitive application can be time-intensive and requires the input of domain experts and end users. Many initiatives have required a significant amount of manual intervention in areas such as building and refining the corpus and training and testing the system. If cognitive applications are going to become more accepted and deliver value across many industries, vendors need to provide packages and tools that enable customers to get new applications up and running quickly. One of the most time-consuming aspects of building a cognitive application is selecting, accessing, acquiring, and preparing data for the corpus. Therefore, vendors are beginning to offer corpus services that include industry-specific, pre-ingested, and curated data. For example, in the healthcare industry, these sources might include a healthcare-specific semantic taxonomy and ontology of disease codes and symptoms. Training is critical to the success of the applications and can also be time-intensive. Vendors could provide a pretrained data set for the application in a particular domain or problem area. There will also be extensive use of APIs that abstract some of the challenging aspects of developing and maintaining the application. For example, APIs can simplify the process of importing data for visualization rendering or extracting relationships from data.

## Defining the Objective

Creating a cognitive application has much in common with developing any other enterprise application. You need to understand what the objectives are for your application and how you will achieve those objectives. Therefore, the first step in developing a cognitive application is to understand the types of problems your cognitive application is going to solve. Your objective needs to consider the types of users you will be appealing to and if there will be multiple constituencies in your user base. What issues will your users be interested in, and what do they need to know? One of the unique differences between a cognitive application and traditional applications is that users should expect more than answers to queries. A cognitive application should provide answers to questions but also go deeper and explore context related to how and why something happened.

Building traditional applications often begins with business process. In contrast, in a cognitive application you need to develop an objective based on knowledge and data. Therefore, in the design you need to set some parameters around the type of knowledge that is pivotal to your corpora. In other words, your objective should probably focus on a specific segment of an industry rather than attempt to solve all problems for a particular industry. Several examples of objectives for cognitive healthcare applications follow:

- Provide personalized information and social support to help individuals optimize their health and wellness.

- Help health consumers take a more active role in managing their own health and the health of people they help care for.

- Help determine if the treatment plan selected for the patient is the best and most cost-effective.

- Provide additional knowledge to medical students to support what they learn on their subspecialty rotations.

Cognitive applications are also a good solution in situations in which you would like to provide assistance to a customer service representative or salesperson. Consider a retail organization with a large and diverse group of sellers. This company has a small number of sellers with many years of experience and deep knowledge of the products the company sells. If a customer has specific requests or needs help comparing alternatives, these knowledgeable sellers can answer all their questions and make the sale. However, the company also has high turnover, and many sellers lack the knowledge to provide the right level of support to customers. The company decides to introduce a cognitive application designed to make all the sellers as smart as the most knowledgeable and experienced seller in the company.

## Defining the Domain

The next step is to specify the domain or subject area for your cognitive application. Defining your domain is a prerequisite to identify and assess which data sources you will need for your applications. In addition, your domain definition will be useful in determining the subject matter experts that will be helpful in training the system. Table 10-1 provides a few examples of cognitive application domains and a sample of the data sources and subject matter experts that can create the knowledge base for that domain. As described in the previous section, your stated objective is likely to help narrow the domain focus. For example, a cognitive application designed to train medical students would require medicine as the domain, whereas a cognitive application designed to help clinicians select the right treatment plan for breast cancer patients would require breast oncology as the domain. The medical domain will require comprehensive and broad-based medical taxonomies, ontologies, and catalogues, whereas the breast oncology domain will require segments of the medical ontology as well as additional data specific to the field.

**Table 10-1:** Examples of Cognitive Application Domains

| DOMAIN | SELECTED DATA REQUIREMENTS | SUBJECT MATTER EXPERTS |
|---|---|---|
| Medicine | International Classification of Diseases (ICD) codes, Electronic Medical Records (EMR), and research journals | Senior physicians in medicine and key specialties |
| Airplane Manufacturing and Maintenance | Complete parts list, maintenance records per airplane, and spare parts inventory | Mechanics who know how to anticipate failure and create effective repairs and experienced pilots |
| Retail | Customer and product data | Experienced sales associates |

Although the domain helps to define the data sources you might need, you may also include data sources that are not typically associated with solving problems in that domain. The inclusion of non-typical data sources is needed because cognitive systems support problem solving in a different way from traditional systems. A cognitive application is good at helping users to assimilate knowledge quickly and efficiently. Although some of this knowledge might be found in specific data sources, it may also incorporate information that is typically learned by experience. One of the advantages of a cognitive application is that it can provide every user with proven business practices and industry-specific knowledge that is well known to your most experienced domain experts. A cognitive system's greatest value comes from its ability to combine information from industry data sources with testing and refinement based on interactions with highly experienced experts. For example, when faced with an unusual problem, an airplane mechanic with 30 years of experience might remember similar situations that occurred in the past and recommend something like, "the problem is likely to be A or B and we should take these five steps to get the best result."

## Understanding the Intended Users and Defining their Attributes

You need to understand the types of users who will be accessing your cognitive application. Expectations for user and system interactions will have an impact on the development of the corpus, the design of the user interface, and how the system is trained. The level of accuracy required in a cognitive application will depend on the intended use case. For example, a scientist requires a much more precise level of accuracy than a customer service representative answering questions about replacement parts. However, it is unnecessary and unwise to attempt to anticipate all the questions your users will ask and all the different ways your cognitive application will be used. A cognitive application assumes that the data will grow and change as new data sources are discovered and added. In addition, the machine learning algorithms will refine the way questions are analyzed and answered. You need to build in flexibility so that your application can change as user requirements change. The learning process for a cognitive system is continuous, and as a result, your application will get smarter and deliver greater value to end users the more it is used.

The following best practices can help to ensure that your cognitive application has the flexibility it needs to provide the right level of support for its users:

- **Understand your users' level of understanding of the domain.** Is your cognitive application intended for consumers or domain experts? Will your users understand the meaning of industry-specific terms? Will your cognitive application be used to help train users in a particular domain?

- **Plan for variations in types of questions and analysis required.** Will your application have users with varied backgrounds and levels of expertise? For example, if you are planning for consumers and domain experts, they are likely to ask questions using different words and language styles. Although these users may be looking for insights into a similar topic, they may have widely differing expectations for the level of insight required. The consumer may look for a definition, whereas the domain expert wants to compare alternative solutions to a complex problem.

- **Keep the scope of your application broad enough to support different types of users.** If you are too specific or narrow in your definition of the domain, there may be subject areas that are not covered adequately in the corpus. It is better to err on the side of a little more coverage of your domain than less, as the learning process will successively refine the corpus toward the "right size" with increased usage.

## Defining Questions and Exploring Insights

As discussed in Chapter 1, "The Foundation of Cognitive Computing," a cognitive system delivers insight relative to a domain, a topic, a person, or an issue, based on training and observations from all varieties, volumes, and velocities of data. A cognitive system creates models to represent the domain and generates and scores hypotheses to answer questions or provide insight. To ensure your cognitive application delivers the insights your users are looking for, you need to begin by mapping out the types of questions they may ask. Users of a well-defined and trained cognitive application can benefit in many ways. One significant benefit is the capability to receive alternative answers to questions along with associated confidence levels. These benefits can be achieved only if the right set of data for the domain and the system is ingested into the corpus and then is properly trained and tested. However, before you even begin to train the system, you need to consider the types of questions your users will ask and the types of insight that your users will be looking for.

Many of the early cognitive applications are of two main types: customer engagement, or discovery and exploration. Customer or user engagement applications typically leverage advanced Question-Answer Systems designed to answer questions as part of an ongoing dialogue with the user. Answers to questions may be provided as a set of alternatives with associated confidence levels. Discovery and exploration applications begin with data analysis rather than by asking questions. You may not know what to expect or exactly what questions to ask. Discovery applications are used in situations such as genomic exploration, security analysis, or threat prevention. Typically, in these situations, your cognitive application will begin by looking for patterns and anomalies in the data.

Because the Question-Analysis approach to cognitive applications requires a more rigid structure to understand potential user questions, this process is described next. All questions need to be suitable for evidenced-based analysis; however, the questions do not all need to be initiated by the user. Actually, one of the defining features of a cognitive application is that users can engage in a dialogue with the system. In anticipatory systems, the application is designed to analyze the data and make suggestions or recommendations for the user without the user needing to ask a specific question. As a result, the user can move through paths of analysis not previously anticipated and develop new insights based on the user/application interaction. The cognitive system can make associations between questions, answers, and content to help the user understand the subject matter at a deeper level. The questions users will ask can be placed in two general categories:

- **Question-Answer pairs**—The answers to these questions can be found in a data source. There may be conflicting answers within the data sources, and the cognitive system will analyze the alternatives to provide multiple responses with associated confidence levels.

- **Anticipatory analytics**—The user engages in a dialogue with the cognitive application. The user may ask some questions but not all the questions. The cognitive application will use predictive models to anticipate the user's next question or series of questions.

## Typical Question-Answer Pairs

Developers of question-answer cognitive applications have found that they need to begin with approximately 1,000–2,000 pairs of questions and answers. You have already defined the users of your application, and you need to keep them in mind when creating the question-answer pairs. How will your representative group of users ask questions? Consider not only the content of the question, but also how it will be asked. The questions need to be in the voice of the end user. What style of language will they use? What technical terms are they likely to know? There are often many ways to ask the same question, and you need to consider the alternative styles of questioning when developing these initial questions. Although the answers need to use terms and a language style that will be understood by users, the content of the answer needs to be vetted by subject matter experts.

Table 10-2 provides an example of two questions that might be asked of a medical cognitive application, related to the use of morcellators: a health consumer asks one question and a gynecologist asks the other. The health consumer is looking for a definition, whereas the health professional is looking for more details on risks and benefits of a specific procedure. In a cognitive application, users of both types could engage in a dialogue that would provide more granular information on the topic.

**Table 10-2:** Question-Answer Pairs for Different Types of Users

| QUESTION | ANSWER |
| --- | --- |
| Heath consumer: What is a morcellator? | A morcellator is a device with a spinning blade that is used to shred a fibroid through an incision on a woman's abdomen. The force and speed of the device may cause cellular particles from the fibroid to become dispersed in the abdomen. |
| Gynecologist: What are the risks and benefits of using a morcellator for surgical treatment of fibroids? | Risks include potential spread of an occult uterine sarcoma. Benefits include smaller incisions for the patient, less bleeding, and quicker healing and recovery. |

You should define a sample set of questions prior to selecting the data sources needed to build the corpus. By choosing your information sources based on what is needed to answer a representative set of questions, your system can learn how to answer similar questions in the same domain. If you build the corpus first, you may make the mistake of tailoring your questions for training and testing to the information you already have at hand. When your cognitive application becomes operational, your users may have questions that cannot be answered by the system. It is expected that the corpus will need to be continuously updated during training and operation; however, you want to start out by including as many data sources as required to provide the right level of insight within your chosen domain.

## Anticipatory Analytics

What if the user is not in a position to ask a specific question of the cognitive application? Anticipatory analytics can be used when there are many unknown factors making it difficult for a user to know what questions to ask. For example, in military or security analytics, you may not know when or where a future event will occur or even what event will occur. You need to observe the data and look for patterns without knowing what you are looking for. The data you need to observe and analyze may be unclean or subject to inconsistent definitions and inconsistencies in metrics or measurements around time and place. However, when this data is used for a cognitive security application, unclean data may provide valuable clues to anticipate events or actions. The anomalies or outliers in the data are used to build the models and anticipate changes that can identify security threats or military events in time to take corrective action.

Anticipatory analytics is also used in cognitive applications that are designed to understand an individual's personal needs and help them to make good decisions. Because a user does not need to ask a question to be provided with a recommended action, the creators of the application need to focus on the different personal situations that might be best suited for assistance by a cognitive system. For example, a cognitive assistant could monitor a user's schedule and alert the user if there is a delay in a scheduled air flight or train. By monitoring personal medical devices and applications, a cognitive assistant could alert users they may be getting sick or help them keep on track with dietary goals. Users are increasingly sharing a lot of personal information on a variety of applications and devices—ranging from health monitoring devices to e-mail, travel, and calendar applications. A cognitive application can be trained to integrate this information to learn a lot about you. In addition, a cognitive application can be designed to be aware of what is happening in the world around you through geospatial, travel, health, and other applications. Therefore, a cognitive application that understands your location, your health and medical status, and the context of your questions can make personalized recommendations. An anticipatory cognitive application leverages data to make personal tasks easier and provide information you need before you ask for it.

## COGNITIVE COMMERCE

Cognitive commerce refers to a cognitive application designed to anticipate user needs from a retail or commerce perspective. Organizations with mobile or Internet-based commerce sites are continuously trying to optimize their sites to increase sales. By making it easier for consumers to find what they want faster, these companies can reach their sales goals faster. For example, a company that provides streaming entertainment content could create a cognitive application to make it easier for customers to find the movie they want to watch and make it easier to watch on their mobile device.

Cognitive capabilities are built in to an existing commercial app or other environment. The user has previously provided permission to the commercial

*Continues*

*(continued)*

application to capture personal information (that is, health data, travel itinerary, and exercise tracking). As a result, the application can make suggestions or provide information to the user without the user needing to ask specific questions.

Builders of a cognitive application with commerce capabilities need to plan for the types of questions users will ask as well as the types of capabilities that will have a positive impact on sales. For example, you may expect that users will ask a question about ordering a specific item such as, "Do you have XBrand jeans available in dark wash size 29?" However, you may also want to plan for questions that are more open ended such as, "I saw the perfect silk dress on 'X' character in 'Y' on 'ABC' show. Can you find me something similar in size 4?" You may also want to submit a photographic image of a dress and ask the system to locate the item in a different color or size. A cognitive commerce application could accept complex user queries in natural language and make it much easier and faster for consumers to find the right item to purchase. In addition, by understanding your personal information in context, a cognitive commerce application can anticipate what you might like to buy next before you do.

## Acquiring the Relevant Data Sources

When developing a corpus you should determine the most relevant data sources. This is challenging because you cannot know with certainty what type of insights users might require as their needs change over time. However, taking the time to evaluate data sources you currently own and those you may want to acquire also offers great opportunity. You may discover that you have internal data resources that can provide new insight when leveraged by a cognitive system. Additionally, you may want to include social media data or other external sources. Cognitive systems provide an opportunity to leverage data sources in new ways. To start building the corpus, you need to understand your requirements for a variety of internal and external data sources. As you move through the testing process and your application becomes operational, you need to be prepared to add new sources as they become available and the scope of the application expands.

### The Importance of Leveraging Structured Data Sources

Much of the focus around cognitive computing has been data from unstructured data sources. However, cognitive solutions must gain insights based on the current state of customers or other constituents. Therefore, you need to know what internal data sources are going to be meaningful. For example, if the application is related to travel, the company needs internal data to relate to the details about customers or travel locations. A retail application needs data sources related to merchandise that has been ordered, what products have been sold, and who the customers are. A hospital-based healthcare application needs data on patient status, medical history, and hospital admissions. A manufacturing application may need data that reports on sensor activity from the production floor. These data sources will most likely be stored as structured data in relational databases including customer data from a Customer Relationship Management system or patient data from an Electronic Medical Record for a healthcare application. Additionally, there could be streaming data sources that come from sensor networks.

### Analyzing Dark Data

*Dark data* refers to data that has been stored over many years and sometimes decades. Much of this data has been stored but not previously analyzed. For example, dark data could be data about performance of a company's stock over a decade or data stored at the time of a security breach. With the cognitive system, the dark data can become the benchmark to analyze how things have changed over time. This data may provide new insights by using machine learning to look for patterns in data collected over many years. Given the advent of new analytics technologies, this dark data may now be an important internal data source depending on the domain.

### Leveraging External Data

What external data sources will support users? External data sources may include everything from industry-specific technical journals that are focused on new research findings to industry taxonomies and ontologies. In medical research there are results from clinical trials that might provide insights into drug interactions. Most industries have a wealth of third-party databases with both structured and unstructured data. Increasingly, there are stores of videos, images, and sounds that are of particular interest to either a specific industry or a technical discipline.

Many industries have codified ontologies and taxonomies that are managed and updated by industry consortiums. These sources are critical in creating your corpus. However, you may find that you need to capture only a subset of the available data. These data sources often include the hierarchical classification of entities or concepts within a domain, which are important for determining context and meaning. Table 10-3 provides you with a sample of the types of ontologies and taxonomies available for certain specific industries.

You need to use caution when using these external data sources. For example, what is the origin of the data source? Who owns that data source and how and when was it created? More important, who is responsible for updating the data source on an ongoing basis? Equally important is the security and governance of the data sources. There are data sources that include private information that can be used under strict governance guidelines. If that data is misused, it can cause significant problems for an organization.

**Table 10-3:** Industry-Specific Taxonomies and Ontologies

| INDUSTRY | TAXONOMY/ ONTOLOGY | PUBLISHER | DESCRIPTION |
|---|---|---|---|
| Healthcare | International Classification of Diseases (ICD) | World Health Organization | International codes for diseases, disease symptoms, and medical findings about diseases |
| Healthcare | Semantic taxonomy for the healthcare ecosystem | Developed by companies such as Healthline Corp. | Classifies healthcare information on the web and maps the relationship between consumer and clinical terminology |
| Construction | International Building Code (IBC) | International Conference of Building Officials | Standards and compliance regulations for international building codes |
| Finance | U.S. GAAP Financial Taxonomy | Financial Accounting Standards Board (FASB) | U.S.-based standards for financial accounting and reporting |
| Information Technology | NIST Cloud Computing Taxonomy | National Institute of Standards and Technology (NIST) | Companion to the NIST Cloud Computing Reference Architecture; goal to help communicate the offerings and components of cloud architecture |

## Creating and Refining the Corpora

Building a cognitive application requires extensive collaboration between the technology team and business experts. The initial steps in the development process include defining the objective and user expectations for the application. This stage requires substantial industry or domain expertise. The next series of steps in the application development process relies more heavily on the technology team. The actual creation of the corpus, model development, and training and testing of the system requires skills in areas such as software development, machine learning, and data mining.

The creation of the corpus is not a one-time process. There is an initial effort to build a quality corpus (or corpora) that includes the selected data sources. However, there needs to be continuous re-evaluation of the data sources to determine if new sources need to be added or if enhancements to existing sources are required to improve outcomes from the cognitive application. You need to understand the life cycle for each of the data sources because many of these sources need to be updated at regular intervals. Therefore, you need to set a process in place to ensure that updates to data sources are made on a timely basis.

Although a cognitive application leverages data from the corpora as its primary base of knowledge, not all the data sources used by the system need to be ingested into the corpus. Much of the data may be called as a cloud-based service and used by the application without being included in the corpus. A cognitive application may need to interact with a variety of data management systems including Hadoop, column store, graph, and other environments.

The process of creating the corpus includes preparing the data, ingesting the data, refining the data, and governing that data throughout its life cycle. These steps are described in the following sections.

## Preparing the Data

All data ingested into the corpus must first be validated to ensure that it is readable, searchable, and comprehensible. As detailed in the previous section, structured, semistructured, and unstructured data are likely to be combined in various corpora included in a cognitive system. All data sources need to be evaluated to see if any transformations or enhancements are required prior to ingestion into a corpus. Are your text-based resources such as journal articles, textbooks, and research documents annotated with headings that provide queues to the cognitive system? Tagging should help the system identify and classify the content in specific articles. In addition, tagging can ensure that the cognitive system can quickly make appropriate associations between different data elements.

The requirements to transform the structure of the data can vary based on the cognitive platform you use. The corpora of some early cognitive systems were ingested with primarily unstructured text-based content. As a result, complex structured data sources needed to be transformed into unstructured content prior to ingestion into the corpus. Initially, this transformation was time-consuming. However, services have been developed to help speed up the process of transforming data structures. Vendors are continuing to improve data preparation services for cognitive systems, making it possible for structured data to be automatically transformed within the system. These transformation and other data preparation services can have a positive impact on adoption rates for cognitive applications. Data from structured data sources such as Customer Relationship Management Systems or other database applications needs to be easily and quickly ingested into the system if business users are going to begin using the applications at a greater rate. It is not necessary that the complete database be ingested as is. Actually, it is quite common that only a segment of the existing data source is required to meet the requirements for the domain.

## Ingesting the Data

Managing the data ingestion process efficiently is critical to the success of a cognitive application. Data ingestion is not something that happens just once during the development of the system. Existing data sources are subject to continuous updates and refinements to ensure they are accurate and up to date. The results of the training and testing of the models may indicate weak spots or limitations in the corpora that require the addition and revision of sources. In addition, changing user expectations are likely to result in new additions to the corpora. Delays in making the required updates to the corpora will decrease the effectiveness and accuracy of the system. Therefore, to maintain the viability of the cognitive system, data sources may need to be ingested in near real time. Typically, you will have access to a set of services that are designed to make the ingestion process fast, robust, and flexible. Although there may be some coding required, the ingestion services will include connectors and tools to make the process as seamless as possible.

As in traditional data management efforts, you need to have controls and supports in place to maintain governance and anticipate and correct for errors. For example, you must incorporate real-time traceability into the data ingestion process. If errors result in an unexpected halt in the ingestion process, you need to trace back to understand why the problem occurred and where you were in the ingestion process when it stopped. This is called *checkpointing*, and you can then use this information to restart the ingestion process in the right place. In addition, you may need to monitor the ingestion process to ensure that any records that are deleted or scrubbed to meet security requirements have been handled properly.

## Refining and Expanding the Corpora

As mentioned in the previous section, a corpus needs to be continually refined to ensure that the cognitive application delivers accurate information and provides the right level of insight. Although you have completed extensive preparation for ingesting content needed to provide a good knowledge base for your cognitive application, it is hard to anticipate all data requirements at the outset.

Early in the training process, you may find that the accuracy of the answer to a certain question is below your accepted threshold. By increasing the coverage (adding more data) for certain topic areas in your domain, you should improve accuracy. Plan for multiple iterations of this process of training, observing results, and then adding to the corpus. You need to establish an ongoing process of updating data requirements and adding to the corpus as you proceed through the testing process and after your application becomes operational. You can use expansion algorithms to determine which additional information would do the best job of filling in gaps and adding nuance to the information sources in the corpus. There will be situations in which you need to enrich data by providing lookups to additional sources that might have detailed information about customers or definitions of technical data.

## Governance of Data

The corpora in your cognitive application will include a wide range of data sources. There may be personal data that is subject to the same data privacy rules that apply to data used in other systems in your organization. Therefore, you will need to comply with the same data privacy and security requirements of any system. There will be data that will be ingested into the corpus that might have restrictions on use based on governance requirements. In some situations there might be copyrighted images or content that is part of your corpus. Therefore, you want to make sure that you have a license for use of that content. In healthcare there are patient privacy rules that require that personal information be anonymized. In a retail system it will be important not to expose customers' credit card data. If a corpus includes social media data, you must be sure that you are not violating the privacy of users of those sites. For example, users might decide that they no longer want to allow access to location data. In some countries there are restrictions on where customer data can be stored. A cognitive system may require the highest level of governance and security because over time it will include sensitive data about competitive best practices. Therefore, in designing and operating a cognitive system, governance and security cannot be an afterthought.

# Training and Testing

It is through an iterative process of model development, analysis, training, and testing that the cognitive system begins to learn. Deploying a scalable training and testing strategy can ensure your application works as intended when it becomes operational. You need to measure responses to determine what is the minimal level of accuracy that is acceptable. After this is established through the testing process, you can begin to establish the *ground truth*—a set of data that is the gold standard for accuracy of a model. It may require you to try additional data sets so that the information used for testing is objective. Initially, you create a ground truth that establishes what the system knows and understands. In Question-Answer based cognitive applications, you have a set of question-answer pairs that establish your ground truth. The questions represent the types of questions your users will ask. The answers to those questions are accurate, having been approved by domain experts. These question-answer pairs are developed in clusters around a topic to help with the machine learning process. Algorithms help the system to understand context by looking for associations and patterns in the clusters of question-answer pairs. Your training and testing strategy needs to compare new analysis against the ground truth and add to the base level of truth when needed to improve the accuracy of the system.

This is often an iterative process; each time the data is trained, the accuracy of the application improves.

Cognitive systems are designed to learn from failure and improve through feedback. Your cognitive application may assign a high confidence level to answers that are obviously wrong. As part of the training process, you need to analyze why the system got the answer wrong. Although training the system should be an automated process, there are some aspects that involve manual intervention, particularly by subject matter experts. Figure 10-1 illustrates the steps that help to analyze the reason for the error and what corrective action to take to improve accuracy in the future. These errors are measured against key measures for monitoring cognitive system performance including recall, precision, and accuracy.

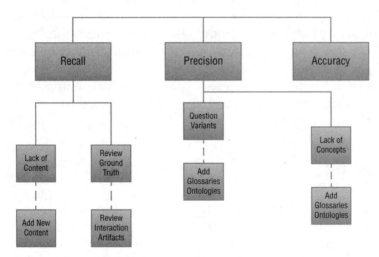

**Figure 10-1:** Improving accuracy of the models

The section "Creating and Refining the Corpora" earlier in this chapter detailed the importance of adding and updating data to ensure the corpus can support the cognitive application. However, lack of data is not the only reason why an application may provide incorrect answers. Subject matter experts may need to review the ground truth and make adjustments to the answers provided to the system. Other errors may occur because the models cannot capture some of the relationships and nuances between similar data sources. One approach to improve this is by adding glossaries and ontologies that provide the system with cues to learn more about key concepts.

Training and testing data can be one of the most time-consuming parts of the process of creating a cognitive system. The smaller the domain, the easier it will be to both create the corpus and find training data to ensure that the information can answer questions and learn over time. In this situation, you can select a sample data set that is representative of the type of questions and type of problems you are addressing. If the domain is larger and more complex, it requires a larger set of sample data. In many situations, you can select sample data that is directly applicable to the problem. For example, the data regarding consumer questions about treatment of diabetes are well understood. However, you may have a situation in which there isn't a lot of certainty regarding outcomes. For example, if you want to understand data from traffic management in a large metropolitan area, you might need a vast amount of sensor data. You may not select the right set of data that is representative of the patterns you want to identify. As you can see, training and then testing results can be complicated by scope and scale issues.

The most important part of the training process is to have enough data so that you are in a position to test your hypothesis. Often the first pass at training provides mixed results. This means that you either might need to refine your hypothesis or provide more data. This process is not unlike learning any new discipline where you start with your assumptions based on incomplete knowledge. As you learn more, you can determine that you need more data from more sources. As you gain more insights from the data, your assumptions will change. At this point you are ready to test your understanding of the domain to see if you have the right amount of knowledge or if you are still required to collect more data and learn more. This is precisely what happens in an automated fashion when you design a cognitive system.

## Summary

Implementing a cognitive solution is a multistep process that begins with understanding the goals and objectives of the project. These steps begin by establishing your objectives: the domain and key user attributes. You also have to define the type of questions you expect users to ask and what insight they may be looking for. You are also required to determine and find the relevant data sources both from internal and external sources. After these stages are complete, you create and refine the corpora. The final stage is the training and testing process. But keep in mind that this is not a serial process. Building a cognitive system is iterative because data continues to change, and the nature and attributes of users changes. A well-designed cognitive system can become a new model for gaining significant insights into business knowledge.

# Building a Cognitive Healthcare Application

The healthcare industry is a large and complex ecosystem that encompasses many different types of organizations that support patient wellness and care. The ecosystem is broad, with a number of well-defined roles including:

- Healthcare providers
- Healthcare payers
- Medical device manufacturers
- Pharmaceutical firms
- Independent research labs
- Health information providers
- Government regulatory agencies

Although there have been enormous technological advances that have enabled organizations to improve health outcomes for patients, the need for continued technical innovation is at a tipping point. Each segment of this ecosystem has typically managed healthcare information in a siloed way making it difficult to share patient and medical research data across the various stakeholders. The volume and variety of healthcare data that needs to be managed, analyzed, shared, and secured is growing at a fast pace. Even when participants are motivated to share information for mutual benefit, the required data is often inconsistent and disconnected, which can slow down progress in medical research and lead to clinical errors that put people's lives at risk. Depending on the methodology used to measure medical mistakes, preventable harm leading to death is either the third leading cause of death in the United States behind heart disease and cancer or the sixth behind accidents and ahead of Alzheimer's disease.

This chapter looks at several healthcare organizations where experts are in the early stages of building cognitive applications that help them to solve well-known healthcare problems in new ways, and begin to solve what was previously intractable. These stakeholders in the healthcare ecosystem are beginning to use cognitive systems to help them find patterns and outliers in data that can help to fast track new treatments, improve efficiencies, and treat patients more effectively.

## Foundations of Cognitive Computing for Healthcare

The healthcare ecosystem creates and manages a huge volume of data such as digital images from CT scans and MRIs, reports from medical devices, patient medical records, clinical trial results, and billing records. This data exists in many different formats ranging from manual paper records and spreadsheets to unstructured, structured, and streaming data managed in a variety of systems. Some of these systems are well integrated, but most are not. As a result, the vast amount of data generated and analyzed by the healthcare industry presents significant challenges. However, as organizations find new ways to manage and share this data, they are finding that there are amazing opportunities for improving health outcomes. For example, healthcare providers have implemented electronic medical record (EMR) systems to maintain integrated, consistent, and accurate patient records that can be shared by a medical team. Although the EMR is still a work in progress for many organizations, there are great benefits to having a complete, accurate, and up-to-date set of problems and treatment for each patient. Treatment decisions can be made more confidently and with greater speed if the medical information is available in a consistent and accurate form.

One of the persistent challenges for healthcare organizations is the need to find the patterns and outliers in both structured and unstructured data that can help them improve patient care. As shown in Figure 11-1, data management in the healthcare ecosystem is moving away from document-centric silos to well-integrated knowledge bases that include both structured and unstructured data.

The management of healthcare data will begin to follow a more standards-based approach to facilitate sharing of data where appropriate. Medical devices and sensors have the capability to generate valuable data about a patient's condition, but this data is not always captured effectively. There are great opportunities to improve screening of patients and anticipate changes in their medical condition by using predictive analytical models on the data streams. Cognitive systems can capture and integrate this new generation of sensor-based data with the entire recorded history of medical research and clinical outcomes captured in natural language text to form a corpus. The system learns from experiences with this corpus, enabling significant improvements in outcomes.

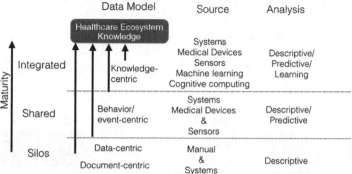

**Figure 11-1:** Foundations of cognitive computing for healthcare

For example, doctors in the neonatal department of a Toronto hospital developed analytical models that provide 24 hours of advance warning on which babies might develop a life-threatening infection. The infection, late-onset neonatal sepsis, is a blood infection that can occur in subsets of newborn babies. Prior to the analytics research done by Dr. Carolyn McGregor, Canada Research Chair in Health Informatics based at the University of Ontario Institute of Technology, the neonatal intensive care unit relied on monitors that collected data on infants' vital signs but stored only 24 hours of data at a time. By capturing the data from the monitors as an ongoing stream of data, the informatics team developed algorithms to analyze the data over time. The algorithm looks for patterns that occur before the infection becomes clinically apparent. With the new system doctors get a digital reading on respiratory rates, heart rates, blood pressure, and blood oxygen saturation, and can monitor infants' vital signs in real time and detect changes in their conditions.

## Constituents in the Healthcare Ecosystem

The healthcare ecosystem has evolved to include a variety of organizations, each of which contributes to the development, financing or delivery of wellness or treatment information, processes, or products. As shown in Figure 11-2, healthcare providers, payers, pharmaceutical companies, independent research groups, data service providers, and medical manufacturers all have access to different sources of relevant healthcare data. Government agencies and even the patients have a role in managing who sees which data. Some of this data is shared, but much of it is controlled by regulations and security requirements. The relationships between the constituents in terms of data sharing are complex and in a state of flux. To move toward a more integrated approach to healthcare ecosystem knowledge that includes more predictive analysis and machine learning, there needs to be continued improvement in the consistency of data shared across the ecosystem.

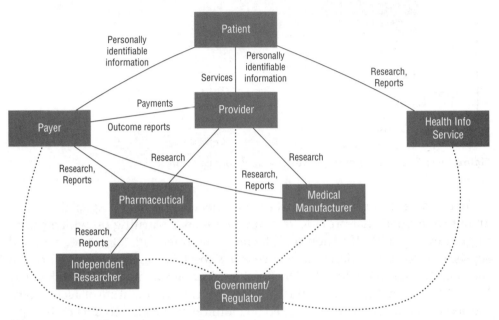

**Figure 11-2:** Healthcare ecosystems data sources

The data managed and leveraged by different constituents in the healthcare ecosystem includes:

- **Patients**—From family history and habits to test results, individuals participating in the healthcare ecosystem produce personally identifiable information, which may be aggregated anonymously, where permitted, to guide care for those with similar attributes.

- **Providers**—Data covers a broad range of unstructured and structured sources. Some examples include patient medical records (EMR, doctors' office notes, and lab data), data from sensors and medical devices, intake records from the hospital, medical text books, journal articles, clinical research studies, regulatory reports, billing data, and operational expense data.

- **Pharmaceutical companies**—Data to support pharmaceutical research, clinical trials, drug effectiveness, competitive data, and drug prescriptions by medical providers.

- **Payers**—Data includes billing data and utilization review data.
- **Government agencies**—Regulatory data.
- **Data service providers**—Prescription drug usage and effectiveness data, healthcare terminology taxonomies, and software solutions to analyze healthcare data.

## Learning from Patterns in Healthcare Data

The benefit of cognitive computing is that healthcare professionals will more easily get the insights they need from all types of data and content to act with confidence and optimize their decision making. The risks of not finding the right relationships and patterns in the data are high in the healthcare industry. In this industry, if important pieces of information are overlooked or misunderstood, patients can suffer long-term harm or even death. By combining technologies such as machine learning, artificial intelligence, and natural language processing, cognitive computing can help healthcare professionals to learn from patterns and relationships discovered in data. The collaboration between human and machine that is inherent in a cognitive system supports a best practices approach that enables healthcare organizations to gain more value from data and solve complex problems.

Gaining more value from data is a multifaceted process that requires both technology and human knowledge. Getting the data right is paramount. The relevant data needs to be accurate, trusted, consistent, and available for access expeditiously. However, having accurate data is only the baseline for improving health outcomes for patients. Physicians need the skill and experience to make sense out of what is often a complex set of symptoms and diagnostic tests. They need to internalize best practices that enable them to ask the right questions and listen for answers from the patient. The solution to a patient's problem is not always obvious in the medical lab results and images. Best practices that focus on connecting all the disparate data points can help physicians, researchers, and others in the healthcare ecosystem to find the right solution.

Learning from patterns in data helps healthcare organizations to solve some of their most challenging problems. For example, The University of Iowa Hospitals and Clinics has identified patterns in a population of surgical patients that help to improve both quality and performance in surgery. The hospital has modeled data from hospital readmission, surgical site infections, and other hospital-acquired infections. The model enables physicians to predict which patients are most at risk for acquiring a surgical site infection while they are still in the operating room and corrective actions can be taken.

Other hospitals use predictive models to reduce costly and dangerous hospital readmission rates as well. The patterns identified from thousands of hospital records are used to build a model that can analyze a patient's medical record to identify risk factors for problems that may occur after discharge from the hospital. Predictive analytics models look at a number of different factors to determine which ones have the greatest impact on hospital readmission rates. As shown in Table 11-1, these factors may be specific to the patient or the physician.

**Table 11-1:** Attributes to Consider for a Predictive Model on Hospital Readmissions

| | |
|---|---|
| Patient Attributes | Smoker, drug abuse, alcohol abuse, lives alone, dietary noncompliance |
| Socio-economic Attributes | Educational status, financial status |
| Physician Factors | Incorrect medicines given, overlooked important information about patient |

Understanding the risk factors can help hospitals to improve processes within the hospital and take corrective measures to decrease hospital readmission rates. The predictive model can help on a case-by case basis by indicating which patients may require more intensive follow up after they are discharged.

## Building on a Foundation of Big Data Analytics

Although there is a great deal of interest and some exciting case examples of cognitive systems in healthcare, these implementations are at an early stage. However, healthcare organizations are not starting from scratch for cognitive computing and big data analytics. There are some high-profile examples of analyzing data and incorporating machine learning in medical environments. The next generation of these healthcare platforms are building on a strong foundation of big data analytics. As healthcare informatics capabilities mature to incorporate cognitive systems, the overall goals for the healthcare organization remain the same. There is a common focus on providing optimal high-quality care to patients and to continually improve healthcare options and outcomes in a cost-effective manner.

Much of the effort in healthcare IT has been focused on developing more integrated systems so that medical information can be safely stored and accessed as needed for research and patient care. For example, healthcare providers have implemented electronic medical records (EMR) to help provide a unified record of medical data for each patient. Much of the patient-related data is unstructured, and large volumes of this data come from digital images, lab tests, pathology reports, and physician reports. As described in the previous section, healthcare organizations are rapidly finding new ways to gain value from this data. In addition to using EMR and other patient-specific data to make decisions for one patient, there is great value in leveraging data across large groups of patients to build predictive models that can improve outcomes for large populations of patients. These analytics efforts need to ensure that requirements for security and privacy are met by removing any personal identifying information from the data.

One healthcare field where big data analytics is rapidly increasing the speed at which new research can be completed is the biopharmaceutical field. Revolutionary advances in DNA sequencing technology makes it possible to collect huge volumes of genomic information for analysis. To keep up the pace of the research, technology is used for sequencing data storage, processing, and downstream analytics. There are huge demands for new computational approaches to store and analyze genomic data. Advanced algorithms, methods, and tools enable scientists to effectively understand the data produced by genomic analyses, and to help answer important biological questions. Advanced modeling efforts are replacing many of the more manual efforts used in the past to analyze genomic data.

## Cognitive Applications across the Healthcare Ecosystem

Many healthcare experts are building on what they have already achieved in big data and analytics initiatives to incorporate machine learning and cognitive computing. The goal is to continue to optimize results in healthcare research and clinical diagnosis and treatment. Gains in speed, innovation, and the quality of outcomes are dependent on how humans interact with the available technology and data. In addition, there is an exceedingly strong requirement within healthcare organizations for those humans with the most experience to put best practices in action and to share those best practices with the next generation of healthcare professionals. This transfer of knowledge takes place continuously through training programs for medical students and residents as well as assistant and mentoring programs in research labs. Introducing a cognitive system to support healthcare professionals as they learn can help drive this process of knowledge transfer forward. Right now the use of cognitive computing is at an early stage; however, the expectation is that over the next decade it will become well integrated into many healthcare processes.

### Two Different Approaches to Emerging Cognitive Healthcare Applications

The implementations of cognitive healthcare applications are proceeding along two different paths: customer or user engagement applications and discovery applications. Customer engagement applications are designed to help find personalized answers to questions. For example, several emerging companies have developed cognitive applications that provide consumers with answers to questions about managing their own health and wellness. Other cognitive systems provide support for healthcare payer customer service agents. With a corpus that contains more relevant information than people could possibly consume and retain, these systems answer relevant questions and provide new insight about their health. Discovery applications are used in situations such as drug discovery or to discover the optimal treatment for a patient. In both types of cases, the healthcare organization needs to begin by defining the end user of the system, the types of questions that will be asked, and the content that is required to build the knowledge base for the system. The cognitive system is used to understand relationships and discover patterns in data that may lead to improved healthcare outcomes.

You need to understand the types of users who access your cognitive healthcare application. What is the medical background and expertise of your users? For example, will the users be medical students, or medical clinicians with many years of experience? Or will your users be health and wellness consumers? Expectations for user/system interaction will have an impact on the development of the corpus, the design of the user interface, and how the system is trained. The user type also has an impact on the confidence levels required and level of accuracy the system needs to achieve. As user requirements and expectations change over time, these changes must be incorporated into the ongoing development of the cognitive system. The learning process for a cognitive system is continuous, and as a result the system gets smarter and delivers greater value to end users the more it is used.

## The Role of Healthcare Ontologies in a Cognitive Application

Healthcare taxonomies and ontologies—a coding system or semantic network of medical terms and the relationships among these terms—are important to the development of a corpus for cognitive healthcare applications. These ontologies are used to map the relationships between terms with similar meanings. There are many ontologies that are already widely used in healthcare to organize terminology related to medical conditions, medical treatments, diagnostic tests, ingredients and dosing for clinical drugs, and drug complications. One example of a medical ontology is the International Classification of Diseases (ICD). The ICD-10 is the current version as endorsed by the World Health Organization. However, it has not yet become the standard in all countries. ICD-10 will become the standard in the United States some time after October 1, 2015. The ICD includes codes for diseases, disease symptoms, and medical findings about diseases. The ICD is only one of many different taxonomies and ontologies in use across the ecosystem. To build an efficient corpus for a healthcare application, you need to find a common language to ensure that data from different sources can be integrated and shared. Without a taxonomy of terms, the cognitive system cannot learn as quickly, and the accuracy of results will be insufficient. Your systems will miss a lot of terms that have the same meaning.

Healthline Corporation has developed one of the largest semantic taxonomies for the healthcare ecosystem. It maps the relationships between consumer and clinical applications, which can help to support new consumer-focused cognitive health applications. Algorithms can reference the taxonomy to improve the semantic understanding of a query to the cognitive system. In addition, cognitive health applications can make more accurate associations between medical concepts by referencing a comprehensive and accurate ontology or taxonomy.

## Starting with a Cognitive Application for Healthcare

Early stage examples of cognitive applications in healthcare are built on top of the cognitive engine or platform. To develop an application you need to begin by defining your target end user and then train the cognitive system to meet the needs of your user base. What is the general subject area for your cognitive application? What do you know about your users' level of knowledge in this area, and what are their expectations or requirements from the cognitive application?

A cognitive system needs to start with a base level of information from which it can begin to find the linkages and patterns that can help it to learn. Although the learning process begins with questions, a trained system can do much more than provide answers to a set of questions. The cognitive system can make associations between questions, answers, and content to help the user understand the subject matter at a deeper level. The basic steps required to build a cognitive application in healthcare follow.

### Define the Questions Users will Ask

You want to begin by assembling the types of questions that will be asked by a representative group of users. After this step is completed, you can assemble the knowledge base required to answer the questions and train the system effectively. Although you may be tempted to begin by reviewing data sources so that you can build your knowledge base or corpus for your system, best practices indicate that you need to take a step back and define your overall application strategy. The risk to beginning with your corpus is that you are likely to target your questions to the sources you have assembled. If you begin with the corpus, you may find you cannot meet the needs of your end users when you move to an operational state.

These initial questions need to represent the various types of questions users will ask. What do users want to ask and how will they ask questions? Are you building a consumer-focused application that will be used by a general population of users, or are you developing a system that will be used by technical experts? Getting the questions right is critical to the future performance of the application. You need to seed the cognitive system with a sufficient number of question and answer pairs to start the machine learning process. Typically, 1000–2000 question/answer pairs seem to be the right number to get the process started. Although the questions need to be in the voice of the end user of the system, the answers need to be determined by subject matter experts.

## Ingest Content to Create the Corpus

The corpus provides the base of knowledge used by the cognitive application to answer questions and provide responses to queries. All the documents the cognitive application needs to access will be included in the corpus. The question/answer pairs you have created help to drive the process of collecting the content. By beginning with the questions, you have a better idea of the content that will be required to build the corpus. What content do you need to answer the questions accurately? You need to identify the resources you have and which resources you may need to acquire to provide the right knowledge base. Examples of content include medical texts, background information on health subjects such as pharmaceutical research, clinical studies, and nutrition, medical journal articles, patient records, and ontologies and taxonomies.

The content you select needs to be validated to ensure that it is readable and comprehensible. Adding meta tags to your content can help with creating associations between documents. For example, you can use tagging to identify that an article pertains to a specific medical condition such as diabetes. In addition, content should have sections and headings to provide cues to the cognitive system. You may need to optimize the format of some of the source data to ensure that it can be properly identified and searched. For example, structured data sources such as a comprehensive nutrition table may need to be transformed into unstructured content prior to ingestion into the corpus. Simple tables can be read by the cognitive system, but more complex and nested tables should be transformed to unstructured text for clarity. The source transformation process is required to ensure that the corpus functions properly.

You need to understand the life cycle of documents you ingest to plan for appropriately scheduled updates. In addition, you may need to establish a process that will ensure you are notified of new and updated content. The corpus needs to be updated continuously throughout the life of the application to make sure it continues to be viable.

## Training the Cognitive System

How does the training process begin? The cognitive system learns through analysis and training (refer to Chapter 1, "The Foundation of Cognitive Computing," for discussion on different types of machine learning and Chapter 3, "Natural Language Processing in Support of a Cognitive System," for details on natural language processing). Just think of how you might approach learning a new subject. Initially you may have a long list of questions. You do some reading and then your questions change in content and scope as you learn more about the subject. The more you read and understand, the fewer questions you have. A cognitive system is similar in that the more question/answer pairs that are analyzed, the more the system learns and understands.

Analyzing the question/answer pairs is a key part of the overall training process. Although it is important for representative users to generate the questions, experts need to generate the answers and finalize the question/answer pairs. The questions need to be consistent with the level of knowledge of the end user. However, the experts need to ensure that the answers are accurate and in line with the content in the corpus. As shown in Table 11-2, you are likely to have some overlapping questions or clusters of questions. These questions may ask about a similar topic using slightly different terms or from a different perspective. Or the questions may be basically the same except one version of the question abbreviates certain terms. The cognitive system learns from these clusters of questions.

**Table 11-2:** Questions Used to Train a Cognitive Application on Health and Wellness

| Question 1 | What is the difference between whole milk and skim milk? |
| Question 2 | Is low fat milk different from whole milk? |
| Question 3 | Is skim milk better than whole milk? |

## Question Enrichment and Adding to the Corpus

The training process for your cognitive application is used to ensure your application works as intended when it becomes operational. Initially, it needs to be repeated multiple times using training data, test data, and blind test data. As each of these tests is completed, you can add content to the corpus to cover areas in which there is inadequate information.

Plan to continually return to the training process after your application goes live so that you establish an ongoing process of updating question/answer pairs and adding to the corpus. Expansion algorithms are used to determine which additional information would do the best job of filling in gaps and adding nuance to the information sources in the corpus.

## Using Cognitive Applications to Improve Health and Wellness

The patient (or healthcare consumer) is central to the healthcare ecosystem (refer to Figure 11-2). This complex ecosystem generates an enormous amount of data that describes the health and well-being of every individual in the system. Many organizations that manage a population of healthcare consumers have implemented various programs to help improve the group's overall health. The challenge is that these programs do not always provide the personalized responses and incentives that their members need to change behavior and optimize health outcomes. The payback of helping individuals to lose weight, increase exercise, eat a well-balanced diet, stop smoking, and make healthy choices overall is huge. Healthcare payers, governments, and organizations all benefit if communities as a whole are healthier and individuals do a better job of managing previously diagnosed conditions. The following list (developed by the Office of the Surgeon General (U.S.); Office of Disease Prevention and Health Promotion (U.S.); Centers for Disease Control and Prevention (U.S.); National Institutes of Health (U.S.); and the Rockville (MD, U.S.) Office of the Surgeon General (U.S.); 2001) shows the many different medical conditions and diseases increased weight is associated with. Even when faced with these facts, it is incredibly hard for many people to make the positive change they need. These conditions and diseases include:

- Premature death
- Type 2 diabetes
- Heart disease
- Stroke
- Hypertension
- Gallbladder disease
- Osteoarthritis
- Sleep apnea
- Asthma and other breathing problems
- Certain types of cancer
- High cholesterol

Finding ways to improve the connections and communication of individuals and the healthcare ecosystem is a priority for a number of emerging companies. Several of these companies are highlighted in the following sections.

## Welltok

Welltok, based in Denver, CO, provides personalized information and social support to help individuals optimize their health with its CaféWell Health Optimization Platform. Welltok works with population health managers, such as health payers, to help decrease healthcare costs by providing a platform that gives people the support, education, and incentives (e.g., gift cards, premium reductions) they need to change their behavior and improve their health.

### Overview of Welltok's Solution

Welltok's CaféWell Concierge is a platform designed to help individuals optimize their health by connecting them with the right resources and programs. It organizes the growing spectrum of health and condition management programs and resources, such as tracking devices, apps, and communities, and creates personalized, adaptive plans for each consumer.

Welltok partnered with IBM Watson to create the CaféWell Concierge app, which leverages cognitive technologies to dialogue with consumers and provide personalized guidance to optimize their health. Vast amounts of internal and external data sources are used to build corpora that form the knowledge base of the system. CaféWell Concierge uses natural language processing, machine learning, and analytics to provide personalized and accurate recommendations and answers to questions asked by individual health consumers.

As a mobile application, health consumers can engage with the CaféWell Concierge at a time and place that is convenient for them. Each individual receives an Intelligent Health Itinerary based on their health benefits, health status, preferences, interests, demographics, and other factors. The itinerary is a personalized action plan with resources, activities, health content, and condition management programs. For example, consumers with controllable health conditions like diabetes or asthma will receive an Intelligent Health Itinerary with educational information and guidelines tailored to them to help them make healthy choices on a daily basis.

Welltok's partners include health payers that make the app available for free to their members. The health payers typically offer incentives or rewards such as entry in a drawing for a gift card for completing a coaching session, or a reduction in health costs for improving your body mass index (BMI). CaféWell uses advanced analytics algorithms to align actions and behaviors with the right incentives and rewards to motivate consumers to get involved in their health. It also learns over time what individuals respond to and what type of incentives or value to offer for targeted behaviors.

Using natural language processing, consumers can dialogue with the application and ask questions related to health and wellness. Welltok followed the steps in the previous section to build a cognitive application that can handle mass personalization, process large volumes of information, and answer open-ended questions in seconds. The architecture and data flow for the question-answer training process for CaféWell is illustrated in Figure 11-3.

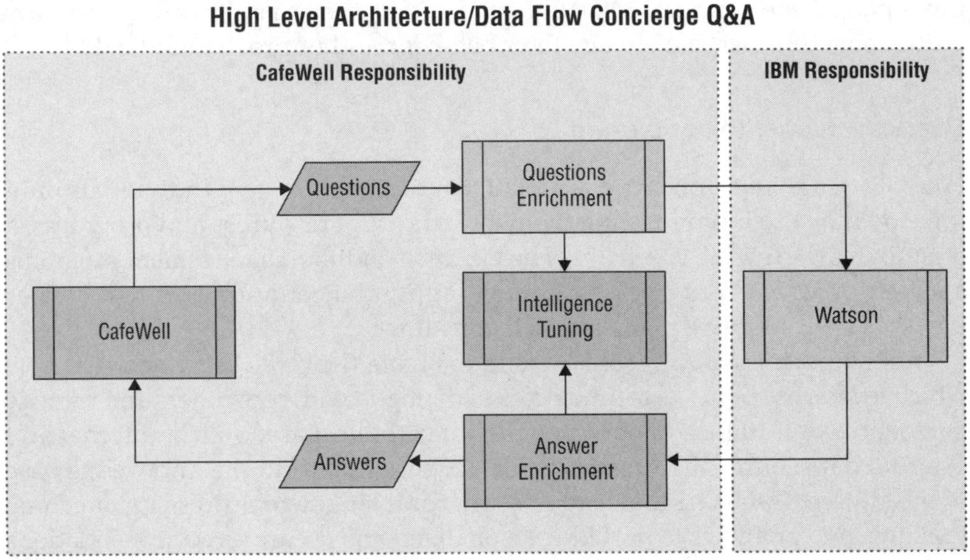

**High Level Architecture/Data Flow Concierge Q&A**

**Figure 11-3:** Welltok training architecture

To develop its question/answer pairs, Welltok collected input from consumers to create questions that would reflect their interests and used subject matter experts to answer the questions logically and accurately. Table 11-3 shows a sample of the thousands of question/answer pairs that Welltok created to begin the training process for CaféWell Concierge. After determining an initial set of question/answer pairs, Welltok developed the corpora (and ontologies) for the application to provide Watson with access to the information sources it needs. Welltok collected unstructured information from third-party healthcare sources to get all the information required for the corpora.

Welltok worked closely with IBM to train Watson for CaféWell Concierge. The iterative process of ingesting data to build the corpus, enrich content, and improve the intelligence of the cognitive system is illustrated in Figure 11-4. By leveraging Watson's cognitive capabilities, CaféWell can understand context and learn about a user's health concerns, goals, and preferences. Watson's machine learning capabilities enables CaféWell to continuously improve the quality of its responses and recommendations. Watson has dozens of different corpora covering many different aspects of health and wellness, including health insurance benefits, nutrition, and fitness. These corpora, in addition to information about the individual, are used to support the advanced analytics algorithms that deliver the personalized recommendations and responses. The application goes beyond providing search results. It builds a relationship with the users—getting to know them, providing personalized recommendations and guiding them to optimal health.

**Table 11-3:** Sample of Welltok Question/Answer Pairs

| | |
|---|---|
| What are some lifestyle changes that I should make if I have high blood pressure? | Lifestyle changes are just as important as taking medications. Reducing your weight by just 10 pounds may be enough to lower your blood pressure. Losing weight can help to enhance the effects of high blood pressure medication and may also reduce other risk factors, such as diabetes and high bad cholesterol. |
| How do you determine the calories burned by your body? | BMR is often calculated using the Harris–Benedict equation. This equation calculates basal metabolic rate based off of 3 variables: weight, height, and age. Using this approach, total energy expenditure can be calculated by multiplying BMR by an activity factor. **Equation For Men:** BMR = 88.362 + (13.397 × weight in kg) + (4.799 × height in cm) − (5.677 × age in years) |
| Do my nutritional needs vary throughout life? | Nutritional needs vary throughout life. From infancy through adulthood, good nutrition is essential to growth and development, and to maintaining health in the later years. |
| Why should I read the food label on packaged foods? | Most packaged foods have a label listing nutrition facts and an ingredient list. In the U.S., the Food and Drug Administration (FDA) oversees the requirements and design of the Nutrition Facts label. The purpose of the label is to help consumers make quick, informed food choices that contribute to a healthy diet. Especially on a low-sodium diet, you need to look at the food label to limit sodium intake. |
| I have a grain allergy, what food should I avoid? What kinds of food are considered grains? | Any food made from wheat, rice, oats, cornmeal, barley, or another cereal grain is a grain product. Bread, pasta, oatmeal, breakfast cereals, tortillas, and grits are examples of grain products. There are whole grains, containing the grain kernel, and refined grains, which have been milled to remove bran and germ. There are many benefits to a diet rich in grains. |

Using Watson's machine learning capabilities, CaféWell Concierge improves the quality of responses users receive with each interaction. And with its spatial and temporal capabilities, the application factors in time and location to provide highly relevant information. For example, it can recommend where and what to eat for lunch based on your location and your specific diet and nutritional requirements.

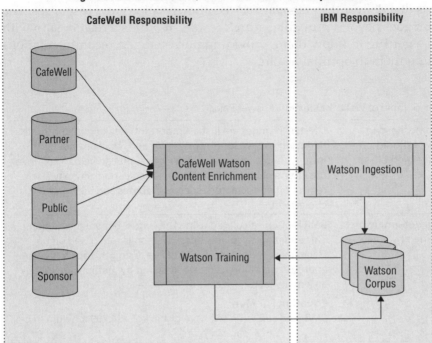

**Figure 11-4:** Welltok high-level architecture and data flow: data flow content acquisition

## CaféWell Concierge in Action

CaféWell Concierge is intended to help individuals understand their health status and receive personalized guidance to help them achieve wanted health and wellness goals, and get rewarded for doing so. The following example shows how an individual with a new medical diagnosis could benefit from interacting with CafeWell Concierge.

Assume you just received a new diagnosis of pre-diabetes from your doctor. You saw your internist in his office last week and after examining you he took some tests. Today, you received a follow-up phone call with your diagnosis and a recommendation to change your diet, lose 20 pounds, and increase your exercise. However, you travel a lot for work leading you to eat a lot of meals at restaurants, and you never have enough time to get to the gym. What do you do next?

Without cognitive computing you might search the Internet for Type 2 diabetes and find information that leaves you confused and scared. Although there are many applications that allow you to search for nutritional information and monitor your weight and exercise activity, they only provide general information about pre-diabetes. A cognitive application can provide you with deeper insight and more personalized high-quality support. CaféWell Concierge creates an Intelligent Health Itinerary for you including programs and resources such as a video coaching session on nutrition, food choices at local restaurants, a fitness tracking device with step goals to help reduce your BMI, and a social community for additional support.

Based on Watson's cognitive capabilities, CaféWell Concierge can integrate and analyze across multiple sources of information so that you can receive tailored and continuous support as you might from a personal concierge.

## GenieMD

GenieMD is also focused on providing a cognitive health application for consumers. The company's mission is to help clients develop more meaningful conversations with their healthcare providers. The overall goal is to help health consumers take a more active role in managing their own health and the health of their loved ones. Users can ask questions in natural language and receive personalized responses and recommendations. These users can access GenieMD through a mobile application. The expectation is that patients will achieve improved health outcomes and that healthcare costs will be lowered. GenieMD aggregates medical information from a range of disconnected sources and makes that information actionable. GenieMD, which is powered by IBM's Watson, is following a development process that is similar to Welltok.

## Consumer Health Data Platforms

Google, Apple, and Samsung are all developing consumer focused heath data platforms. These platforms are in the early stage, and the type and variety of data being collected is narrower than the applications discussed in the preceding sections. Google has a set of Google Fit APIs that it provides to developers to help them manage and combine different types of health data. At this point, the health data collected typically comes from wearable devices such as the FitBit, Nike Fuel Band, and other medical sensors that can detect biometric data. This data includes heart rate, steps taken, and blood sugar level. Nike FuelBand can publish user heath data that it collects to the Google Fit platform.

## Using a Cognitive Application to Enhance the Electronic Medical Record

The electronic medical record (EMR) is a digital record of the medical and clinical data for each patient followed by a provider (independent physician or large medical centers with all physicians in one group). Typically, the EMR is designed to store and retrieve data about a patient that can be used for diagnosis and treatment. It has some basic reporting capabilities such as flagging a lab test as low or high based on predetermined criteria. The EMR can be thought of as having three main functions: Think, Document, and Act. Today, the EMR documents information about a patient and supports the physician's ability to take actions on a patient's behalf. But, the EMR does not help with the "thinking" aspect of determining how to best deliver care to a patient. By incorporating machine learning, analytics, and cognitive capabilities into the EMR, physicians could be guided in understanding how a diagnosis was arrived at and the issues surrounding a treatment plan. Overall, healthcare organizations would like to gain more value from the EMR including finding ways to leverage the information in the EMR to improve coordination between different providers and providing more individualized high-quality care for patients.

Epic Systems, a healthcare software company providing EMR software, holds the medical records of approximately 50 percent of the patients in the United States. The company partnered with IBM to add a content analysis capability to the EMR. This enables physicians to use text-based information on a patient as part of the electronic medical record. IBM's natural language processing software, IBM Content Analytics, enables physicians to extract insights from the unstructured text in real time. The EMR can be used with a cognitive system that enables physicians to get answers to complex questions about patient diagnosis and treatment. The information stored in the EMR could be either incorporated into the corpus of the cognitive system or used as part of an analytics engine that is integrated with the cognitive system. Epic's approach provides for analysis of the physician's text-based notes on a patient and transforms these notes into a format that can be incorporated into the patient record. By automatically applying industry-standard diagnosis and treatment codes, significant improvements in accuracy and efficiency can be achieved.

Hitachi is working on a number of consulting projects with healthcare organizations related to enhancing the business value achieved from the EMR. In one project, Hitachi is working with a hospital and EMR vendor to help determine if the treatment plan selected for the patient is the best and most cost effective. Hitachi provides a clinical repository with an analytics engine and a database extractor tool. The focus is on gaining value from the unstructured content.

The Cleveland Clinic is working with IBM's Watson on a cognitive healthcare system focused on rethinking the capabilities of the EMR. How can the EMR be more accurate and used to help physicians learn about the thought process behind clinical decisions? Dr. Martin Harris, Cleveland Clinic, explained how important it is to create one unified and accurate problem list for all patients. One patient may see four specialists for different medical conditions, but for the benefit of the patient, there must be one problem list that includes all of that patient's medical information. Any omission from the EMR could lead to incomplete knowledge of the patient's conditions, and the impact to the patient can be dangerous.

Although there is some risk that the EMR may be missing an important piece of information, there is typically a lot of information to review in each patient's record. Nothing is deleted in the EMR, and it can be hard to find the information you are looking for. If a patient has a complicated medical condition, the EMR can easily reach 200 pages or more. Given the volume of information in a patient's EMR, some physicians find it more cumbersome to use than the old paper records.

The Cleveland Clinic is building a comprehensive knowledge base using IBM's Watson that can be used to test for omissions and improve the accuracy of its EMR. The Cleveland Clinic ingested information from the EMR into the corpus of the cognitive system along with unstructured data including physician and hospital admission notes. When the unstructured data is compared to the problem list from the EMR, all too often omissions are identified. Using the cognitive system to ask questions would enable the hospital to make sure they are retrieving all information about a patient when needed for analysis. The goal of this project is to develop an EMR assistant that would provide a visual summary of a patient's condition. Users could type in keywords and receive visualizations that would help research a patient's medical history and improve decision making.

## Using a Cognitive Application to Improve Clinical Teaching

The most senior and experienced physicians on the staff of a medical center are responsible for transferring knowledge about clinical diagnosis and treatment to medical students and residents. In addition, senior clinicians and researchers at large teaching medical centers want to share knowledge with staff at smaller community hospitals. Research in many areas such as cancer are advancing so quickly that experts at some of the largest medical teaching centers say that it can take years before the information on the newest treatments is translated to changes in treatment offered at community hospitals. In medicine, one is always a student. Each subspecialty has major conferences across the world where papers on the latest research are presented and medical knowledge is shared. In addition, physicians read journal articles to keep current with new research. One service used by many physicians is UpToDate, a clinical decision support resource that provides edited summaries of recent medical information in addition to evidence-based recommendations for treatment. Even with all these resources, it is extremely challenging to keep up with all the new discoveries in drugs and treatment options.

The training of the next generation of physicians is of the utmost importance to members of a senior medical team. Physician leaders at several top medical institutions are developing cognitive systems that may add new dimensions to the complex task of transferring knowledge about medical best practices and diagnostic skills. The expectation is that these new cognitive systems would be in addition to the traditional methods of personalized instruction followed in teaching medical centers. Physicians who train side by side with senior experts in the field learn lessons that they carry with them throughout their careers. A senior neurologist at a Boston teaching hospital described his role as one of "modeling the behavior that students need to follow in treating patients." A large team of medical students and residents accompany him as he makes rounds in the hospital. Students need to be exposed to a variety of diseases in each subspecialty and learn how to identify the differential diagnosis based on symptoms. However, his teaching goes much deeper than understanding the symptoms and treatments of diseases. He wants the students and residents to learn what questions to ask and how to ask them to get the information they need to deliver optimal care.

The Cleveland Clinic is working with IBM to develop a cognitive system called Watson Paths that will provide additional knowledge to students to support what they learn on their subspecialty rotations. Typically, students rotate through a series of subspecialty rotations, spending one month or more in each rotation. Students' clinical experience varies depending on the cases in the hospital during the time they are in the subspecialty unit in the hospital. Cognitive systems that have been well trained in how to treat a broad spectrum of diseases can change the way medical students are taught.

If a medical student is exposed to the cognitive system before the rotation, then the whole training process can become more powerful and can go deeper. If the student has a better understanding of the process of making a diagnosis on some of the most common conditions, the attending physician can focus more on the less obvious diagnosis. The focus needs to be on having as much information as possible to make a correct diagnosis. Considering that there are approximately 13,000 diagnosis codes in the ICD-9 and more than 68,000 diagnosis codes in the ICD-10, students have a lot to learn. A good internist may know approximately 600 medical diagnoses, whereas a subspecialist may have deep knowledge in 60 diagnoses. Fortunately, a cognitive system can ingest information on a huge scale. Cognitive systems (after training) can produce scenarios for the top 600 diagnoses and provide guidance to medical students to help them learn by showing the step-by-step approach in making a diagnosis. As cognitive systems can keep track of the evidence used to support their hypotheses and conclusions, they can justify the resulting confidence level that the diagnosis is right.

Students will be able to interact with Watson Paths to study different approaches to treating patients with a certain set of problems. The students can interact with a system that offers reference graphs and probabilities of outcomes depending on the treatment approach the doctor and patient decide to follow. Watson Paths will focus on evidence-based learning: validating and calibrating the impact of treatment options that are selected. The system will annotate each decision—helping students to learn the impact of their decisions. As a result of its machine learning capabilities, the more people who interact with Watson paths, the better it gets in accuracy and understanding.

Memorial Sloan Kettering (MSK) is also working with IBM to develop a medical cognitive system powered by Watson. MSK is one of the top cancer research and treatment centers in the world, and its physician leaders are concerned about the length of time it takes for new research to reach the thousands of medical and surgical oncologists that are not based at one of the large cancer centers. MSK identifies the sharing of medical knowledge about cancer diagnosis and treatment as an important part of its mission. The medical center has more than 30 physicians working on the initiative to ingest data from a huge patient database and train Watson.

There is often more than one approach that will work to treat a particular cancer patient. MSK is helping to train Watson so that a physician can get help in assessing the potential outcomes of using one approach versus another. The expectation is that the oncology cognitive system will help to increase the speed at which new treatments can be disseminated. Watson will help with suggestions and support the physician who needs to make decisions about the best approach for his patient.

## Summary

We stated previously in this chapter that it is early for cognitive healthcare applications. It is not easy to project how quickly these applications will evolve and become more integrated with operations across the healthcare ecosystem. However, the significant partnerships that are rapidly forming between healthcare experts and technology leaders in cognitive computing suggest a rapid increase in the pace of development. There are many reasons for the increasing investment of time and money in the development of cognitive healthcare applications. However, the most powerful driver for developing cognitive healthcare applications stems from the challenge of gaining insight from the large and rapidly growing volumes of structured and unstructured data managed by the healthcare ecosystem. There is an overabundance of data generated by the healthcare ecosystem that is not well integrated and not easily shared.

Many of the initial healthcare cognitive computing efforts are focused on how patients engage with their own data. Welltok's Café Well Concierge and GenieMD are excellent examples of this type of application. These applications focus on how the patient communicates with healthcare providers and gains access to information about their medical conditions in a meaningful way. These are practical applications that can help a health consumer adjust his priorities for diet and exercise to improve his overall health. On the other end of the spectrum, there are some interesting applications focused on what can be learned from medical best practices. Clinicians and researchers make decisions that impact people's lives on a daily basis. All too often these decisions are made without the knowledge that comes from a comprehensive understanding of best practices. The goal of many of these emerging cognitive health applications is to ensure that all physicians have the opportunity to evaluate their clinical diagnosis and treatment options in collaboration with a well-trained cognitive system.

# Smarter Cities: Cognitive Computing in Government

One of the great challenges of the 21st century is how to leverage technology to solve a variety of problems that accompany the global trend toward urbanization. In cities everywhere, increasing population density strains physical systems and resources. Individual systems have been developed to collect and manage data for each of functional unit. When critical information cannot be shared across critical services, managers often cannot anticipate safety issues or opportunities to optimize services.

The promise of cognitive computing is to enable metropolitan areas to take advantage of data to evolve and become smarter, and deal with expected and unanticipated events effectively. The objective, therefore, is to learn from experience and patterns of data to improve the way cities function over time. This chapter reviews the problems confronting cities and demonstrates how cognitive computing has the potential to transform the way cities operate.

## How Cities Have Operated

A city is more than the roads, buildings, bridges, parks, and even people found within its borders. Cities around the world have evolved in a similar way for centuries—agencies are created to provide services to the population in response to changing conditions and technologies. These agencies justify their existence based on their ability to collect the right data and manage that data to support their constituents. For example, population density made the rapid spread of disease a public health issue and created a need for public health data tracking. New modes of transportation such as cars and planes required new transportation management departments that required the collection even more data.

Throughout history, these agencies produced paper records, which dominated the way cities managed processes. The problems with paper records are obvious: they are expensive to store, inefficient to retrieve, and subject to damage or loss from water, fire, or even rodents. Even as paper documents could be scanned via optical character recognition (OCR) to make searching text easier, it did not solve the problem. There was still no way to gain insights into the history, meaning, and context of these documents. The basic issue is that documents contain deep structure, which contains virtual knowledge that is not explicitly captured.

When all data was created manually and managed in the form of paper documents, it was difficult or impossible to recognize the relationships and dependencies between these systems. For example, relationships between education and hygiene, hygiene and disease, crime and poverty, are all obvious to us today. However, without a way to analyze data from different agencies or departments to see these patterns, they depended on insight and hypotheses that drove the quest for supporting data. As cities grew with data in departmental silos, it became increasingly difficult to look at data across departments in order to set budget priorities. There was no systematic way to put the pieces together and learn from experience. The real value in the information resided in the brains of these people.

Improved technology provided more efficient ways to collect, manage, and analyze data, the ability to understand and describe scenarios and predict outcomes improved dramatically. In the last few decades there have been significance advances in data-oriented city management. To support changing needs has required the movement from simply managing data more efficiently in databases to adopting analysis tools to make better decisions based on this data.

As shown in Figure 12-1, data management is on a path from document-centric silos to integrated repositories of standards-based structured and unstructured data. From manual systems to a sensor-based generation of relevant data, the progress has been dramatic and opens up new opportunities to develop systems that learn from their own data and experiences.

For example, a modern transportation department can use sensors or transponders, closed-circuit TV (CCTV) for video images, or perhaps mobile phone tower pings to more accurately determine not only how many vehicles pass a certain point at certain intervals. These systems can accurately track where data originates and where it goes. Knowing "who" is much more valuable for planning and operations than simply knowing "how many." When traffic counts were made by mechanical or manual traffic recorders, traffic workers knew only how many cars had passed. With more details about "who" (even anonymized), "where to," and "where from," they can build models that begin to predict flows much more accurately than simulations, and with machine learning algorithms, even begin to control flow by adjusting traffic signals based on actual usage.

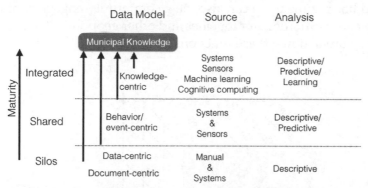

**Figure 12-1:** Foundations of cognitive computing for smarter cities

As similar advances were made in the data collection opportunities for other agencies, from health to safety to areas such as education, new and improved opportunities for analyses have emerged. As data from all these sources—across departments, structured and unstructured—is captured and made available in standard formats that encourage interagency sharing, cities become an ideal, data-rich environment for developing smarter applications.

## The Characteristics of a Smart City

As noted, a city may best be understood as a combination of complex systems that have to work in collaboration with each other—sometimes called a *system of systems*. This is what makes cities and metropolitan areas so difficult to manage. Take a typical large city such as New York or Tokyo. These types of cities include roads and bridges, commercial and residential buildings, public transportation systems, private transportation, water systems, schools, and the public safety infrastructure. Although each of these elements is a universe within itself, they are all interdependent. Operationally, cities rely on smart managers to figure out best practices for managing and improving the way cities work best. But as cities have grown, it is simply impossible for smart managers to approach data driven problems systematically.

A city can become "smarter" if enough data is collected, analyzed, and managed so that critical improvements can be made. What does it mean for a city to be smart? It means that those managing a city collect the right information from a variety of sources and create a unified corpus of data that defines the components that make up a city infrastructure.

Figure 12-2 shows a typical set of government agencies, ranging from the basics of emergency services through utilities, public health, transportation, and human capital management. As individual citizens increasingly have persistent or mobile Internet access and become accustomed to interacting with their government in an ad hoc manner, you can also view community engagement as a function and potential differentiator for cities and other geopolitical units. The following sections break down these functions by task.

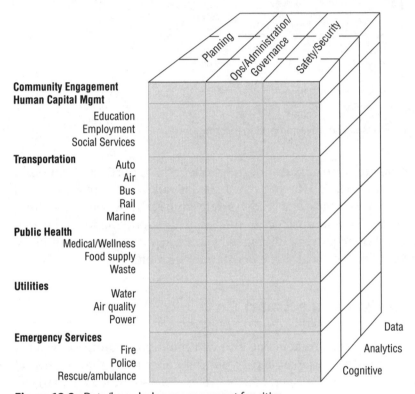

**Figure 12-2:** Data/knowledge management for cities

## Collecting Data for Planning

Each agency in a city collects data for planning, operations, and safety and security, all of which are ongoing activities. The movement toward smarter cities includes better collection and analysis techniques at each stage.

City planning requires that management focus on a broad range of activities in order to promote growth. This growth has to be coordinated with the right scale of operations that allow that growth to be sustainable. At the same time, growth has to be planned so that it can improve and protect the quality of life for citizens. Planners evaluate options and codify them in policies. Planning requires managers to use their intuition and available data to make decisions about the future. The best decision makers are those managers with enough experience to understand what will work and what actions will likely cause problems. However, even the most knowledgeable managers are helped when they get access to better analytical data. What are the trends for extreme weather? What events are happening in the region that might lead to civil unrest, agricultural failures, or drastic population shifts? What are the revenue shifts in industry? What is the outlook for wages? How do all these factors impact the way a metropolitan area can be managed efficiently and effectively? If these professionals managing cities are armed with analytics that can determine patterns and anomalies, they are better prepared for changes.

Cognitive computing applications are well suited to become dynamic planning assistants. Key technologies for cognitive planning systems would include hypotheses generation and evaluation, machine learning, and predictive analytics. The capability of some systems to read vast quantities of unstructured natural language text and analyze it for relevant events and trends will make planners everywhere more effective over time. The cognitive system does not simply analyze data from past events but collects data across anything that impacts the way a city operates. The system looks at the context and relationships between data elements and learns from the data that is ingested and managed over time.

## Managing Operations

When policies are in place, various agencies are required to manage daily operations. The use of data and simple analytics has, of course, changed the way most departments operate. Creating repositories of "open data" by public agencies increases visibility into the processes of government and can improve community engagement. At the same time, this open process creates opportunities for commercial ventures to add value through analysis of the data, or even simply improving the way it is presented to the public.

Internally, this new data becomes even more valuable to civil servants because it makes systems based on prescriptive analytics more effective. City managers and planners are constantly trying to anticipate equipment and infrastructure failures and trying to determine how to provide better services without increasing costs. Cognitive computing approach solutions will soon become a mainstay of city operations centers because these systems can learn the rules of the policies while recognizing the realities of the terrain to "think outside the box." Today, manufacturers of complex and expensive machines like airplanes are already using machine learning to predict mechanical failures and ensure that the replacement parts are in the right vicinity. Tomorrow, no modern city will be without systems to do the smart repair and maintenance management from trucks to supplies, such as salt for icy roads.

## Managing Security and Threats

Virtually all cities assume some responsibility for public safety and security. Beyond emergency services, protection from natural and man-made threats is an ongoing concern. Identifying potential threats that may occur with little or no warning (from gas line leaks or explosions to hurricane forces), internal and external threats must be monitored, assessed, and mitigated or met with managed responses. Cognitive systems are designed to identify trends and events from a variety of unstructured document sources combined with data from sensors, social media, and community sites. Leveraging all of this data is needed to make safety and security initiatives more efficient and targeted.

## Managing Citizen-produced Documentation and Data

For each of the major departments, such as transportation, public health, and emergency services, there is a role for the foundation technologies and cognitive workloads (shown in Chapter 2, "Cognitive Computing Defined," Figure 2-1). Citizens, in these interactions with government, generate a considerable amount of data. All generate or capture data (refer to Figure 12-1), so the foundation structured and unstructured data management workloads are the requirement for advanced systems. At a higher level, senior management in each department has a role in planning and managing operations. By taking advantage of a cognitive assistant that helps to generate and evaluate hypotheses, a manager can gain insights and take corrective actions faster. The wisdom that comes from experience, once held tightly as a job requirement, can be codified in a departmental corpus and used to make workers at all levels more effective.

Any system that gets input from the public or provides assistance to its residents can benefit from natural language processing (NLP) interfaces. However, the most value is created by systems that actually learn from experience as they build a corpus from use by residents and city employees, and increasingly from sensors, as previously discussed. For example, a transportation system that can accept updates about road conditions and traffic flow in real time from sensors, ad hoc natural language input from citizens, and is connected to the maintenance scheduling system for transportation department machines, will be more effective in dispatching the right equipment at the right time to make repairs, start preventative maintenance, or even schedule system upgrades, than a system that is missing any one of these components. Learning from experience—the defining characteristic for all cognitive computing solutions—is the key technology to improve this performance.

## Data Integration Across Government Departments

The importance of interaction between departments cannot be overstated. If water, electrical, or gas lines are to be replaced or maintained, that will often have a major impact on overall infrastructure in other areas. For example, replacing gas lines might mean that a city has to reroute traffic or even resurface major highways. The department responsible for managing utilities will have to share critical information with the transportation planning system so that there is minimal disruption and so that the public is prepared. Predicting major events and planning for alternative routes can help a city manage change. Again, systems that learn from their experiences can better share data among departments to make the overall system more effective. In a major city, no manager can have insights into every planned or unplanned activity. But an integrated cognitive computing system with a common corpus that aggregates data and knowledge from all departments can certainly capture it all and share what needs to be shared between departments.

Chapter 3, "Natural Language Processing in Support of a Cognitive System," (Figure 3-1) discussed the fundamentals of learning systems and the concept of fast thinking versus slow thinking. Fast thinking tasks require intuitive actions that a manager might do without difficult analysis—responding to a citizen complaint or alerting people of an impending weather event. In contrast, slow thinking requires deep thought, analyses, and judgment. In city systems, fast thinking tasks can be automated to make departments more efficient providing deterministic answers to city workers and the public. These systems either require on demand access via the popular 311 information systems in U.S. cities or based on events, such as dispatching alerts to people in a defined perimeter when it's necessary to evacuate for a gas leak, or to remain in place during a police emergency. These answers and notifications can be based on knowledge managed within the cognitive computing system because the system understands the context between elements such as events, people, systems, and the like. The cognitive system is designed to understand relationships and patterns.

For slow-thinking problems requiring consideration of multiple scenarios, or for situations for which there is no single right answer, a cognitive computing system can supply probabilistic responses. Again, knowledge about the user—employee or resident—can make the answers more relevant. For a public health manager trying to determine which course of action to take when facing the possibility of an infectious disease outbreak, confidence-weighted alternatives such as those discussed for healthcare in Chapter 11, "Building a Cognitive Healthcare Application," may help in ensuring that supplies of vaccines or treatments are adequate. Integrating this system with the education system may have a ripple effect on bus planning, which may, in turn, have a ripple effect on transportation logistics. In a city, everything is connected and interdependent. Unified cognitive computing applications, sharing a city corpus and supported by open data, can make those interdependencies a strength rather than a weakness.

## The Rise of the Open Data Movement Will Fuel Cognitive Cities

Nations have long shared data valuable to businesses and individuals when it didn't compromise their own interests. From nautical charts in the 19th century to GPS data in the 20th century, the trend toward openness as a default has grown. In the 21st century, this trend has accelerated among cities, aided by better communications systems, standards, and regulations affecting the distribution of publicly held data.

In March 2012, then Mayor Bloomberg of New York signed the New York City (NYC) Open Data Policy (Introductory Number 29-A) and tasked the Department of IT Telecommunications with developing and posting standards for all agencies to make public data available online.

A goal of the initiative was to provide access to all public data from all agencies through a single web portal by 2018. To date, more than 1,000 public data sets are available from NYC agencies, commissions, and other groups, and available for a variety of private and commercial uses.

NYC also has a program called BigApps to "help teams advance new or existing projects that aim to solve civic challenges and improve the lives of New Yorkers." Teams work with civic organizations to develop applications that use this open data, while vying for cash prizes (totaling more than $100,000 in 2014).

Making data available is the first step, but today the problem isn't a lack of data, or even access to data. The problem is the ability to understand what of value is actually *in* all that data. Using the foundational technologies that are part of the fabric of emerging cognitive computing solutions has the potential for revolutionizing how data can improve the way modern metropolitan areas are dynamically managed.

## The Internet of Everything and Smarter Cities

Previous chapters explore the technologies that make cognitive computing possible. Here you can find answers to two critical questions for public sector cognitive computing: "Where does the data come from?" and "How is value created?"

Now attack the first question. In a modern smart city, or one with smarter aspirations, data comes from three primary sources: citizens, governments, and businesses, through systems and sensors. For businesses, much of the information comes from smarter buildings, which are managed by systems that coordinate information from all the internal systems and sensors for heating, ventilation and air conditioning (HVAC), water, power, transportation (elevators and escalators), and security. The adoption of standards for enabling all sorts of devices to connect to the Internet has made it easy to envision a future where everything that can be connected will be connected. Assigning an Internet Protocol address (IP_address) to a device uniquely identifies it to the rest of the world and allows it to potentially share information with anything else on the Internet. Computers are no longer the only option for Internet communication. Increasingly there are a range of devices that incorporate sensors. Today, devices including refrigerators to smart watches and clothing include the ability to enable machine to machine communication. Summary information is provided to the receiving system or the humans using these sensor-based systems on a need-to-know basis. This so-called "Internet of Things" (IOT) or "Internet of Everything" (soon to be known simply as the Internet) enables businesses and governments to unobtrusively collect or derive all sorts of data about people as they carry on their daily activities. And most of it is given willingly, or without much of a fight. From smart meters that monitor energy usage in the home to transponders that allow us to speed through toll booths without stopping to devices that monitor acceleration and location in our automobiles to closed circuit TV (CCTV) cameras that can monitor group and individual movement, there is no shortage of data being generated.

This city-centric big data, when used to power predictive analytics algorithms or to develop a corpus for a cognitive computing solution, can provide insights that would never be discovered in time to be useful if the data were kept in departmental silos and analyzed by those with no incentive to share with other departments. It is the integration of this data that enables cognitive computing applications for smarter cities of the next decade.

## Understanding the Ownership and Value of Data

In the new cognitive computing era, the traditional questions of who owns such data, who benefits from it, who transforms it into knowledge, and who owns that knowledge takes on new importance as the interconnections create new opportunities to improve the quality of life. At the same time they threaten to take away all semblance of privacy and perhaps security.

Figure 12-3 shows some of the critical relationships between citizens, businesses, and government that enable a virtuous cycle of knowledge creation. With the advent of social media and greater citizen participation in explicit and implicit data reporting, cities get smarter every day. Explicit data reporting includes applications like Street Bump in Boston, a mobile phone app that collects real-time data about city streets by monitoring a user's GPS and accelerometer to identify potential problems such as potholes. (Speed Bump "knows" where the speed bumps are located so it can avoid many false positives.)

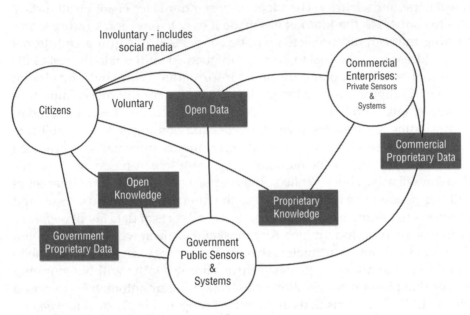

**Figure 12-3:** Modern city data sources and managers

Implicit data reporting includes activities such as making public comments about government activities on social media that are harvested by government agencies. It would also include systems or sensors that are commonly used with little thought given to the information gathering potential, from loyalty programs at retailers to facial recognition software used in public spaces on CCTV networks.

## Cities Are Adopting Smarter Technology Today for Major Functions

This section presents a brief survey of projects in cities that are already working with leading vendors to implement cognitive and precognitive solutions (those based on foundation technologies like predictive analytics that pave the way for future cognitive computing efforts). As the field of cognitive computing is still in the early stages of maturity, most of these projects are ongoing and still being refined as the cities and vendors learn from their experiences. Using the typical urban organizational structure (refer to Figure 12-2), you can focus on a few projects that may form the basis for integrated cognitive computing solutions in the future. In particular, you can consider opportunities to improve the quality of life through analytics and networks that learn from experience.

## Managing Law Enforcement Issues Cognitively

It is not surprising that one of the greatest potential opportunities for smarter cities is in the area of law enforcement. This is an area in which there is a huge volume and variety of data that must be managed and analyzed. It is also an area in which patterns and anomalies play a huge role in solving and preventing crime. Leveraging a cognitive approach can benefit not only a single police department but also has the potential for providing repeatable best practices that can have wide use.

### The Problem of Correlating Crime Data

The biggest problem facing police forces of metropolitan areas is the difficulty in correlating data from hundreds and even thousands of different data sources. Police departments often have access to large databases that capture historical data from local, regional, and national reports of arrests, crimes, and other recorded incidents. These data sources are often stored in relational databases. Other information sources are unstructured and stored in incident reports, paper files, interviews with witnesses, and the like. Still and video images and audio data must also be analyzed. In addition, there may be situations where a large volume of this data is produced on a daily basis from public and private surveillance cameras. Acoustic event detection monitors makes it impossible to manage manually. Recent advances in facial detection algorithms, however (based on recognition of facial parts and their spatial relationships, along with coloring), have helped to automate this task. The problem of analyzing real-time video as it is captured, however, remains a challenge. Big data provides new opportunities, but big cases still demand a lot of human personnel.

Departments, therefore, need enough time and enough skill to fit the pieces of data together to solve crimes. This is complicated because it is not always possible to correlate data manually. An experienced detective will know how to analyze data and will have mastered the process of connecting the dots. In addition, many crimes generate hundreds or thousands of new reports, pictures, bystander videos, and accounts that have to be considered, but which may be received as unstructured natural language voice recordings or text. The sheer volume and complexity of the data can be overwhelming. Even if the "answers" are in the data, finding them in time to prevent further crime can be impossible if a human has to find patterns between data sources.

### The COPLink Project

COPLink is a law enforcement information management system originally developed by the Tucson, AZ police department and researchers at the University of Arizona. It has been commercialized by i2, an IBM company, and deployed in more than 4,500 law enforcement agencies in cities around the United States. This customized project is now being turned into a repeatable cognitive solution under the IBM Watson brand.

COPLink enables individuals, departments, and agencies to gather, share, and analyze historical and current crime information. Users can access data from local and national databases from virtually anywhere, using computers or mobile devices to improve the effectiveness of field personnel. COPLink supports general data standards XML and those commonly used in law enforcement, such as the Logical Entity exchange Specification Search and Retrieve (LEXS-SR), to simplify integration with other applications and to promote data sharing.

The Adaptive Analytic Architecture (A3) enables users to generate leads (hypotheses) for tactical follow-up without extracting data permanently. COPLink also offers agent-based alerts to let officers know when similar searching is made to help coordinate efforts, and can send notifications when new information becomes available based on saved searches.

COPLink uses analytics to actually create suspicious activity reports based on alerts and can share these with the relevant jurisdictions. Simplifying searches and providing this level of database integration makes personnel more efficient. Continuous monitoring of new data and events to improve communications makes them more effective.

There are a number of ways that this type of law enforcement application is being expanded with cognitive extensions, including:

- Providing NLP analyses of unstructured reports as they are created in the field.

- Leveraging hypothesis generation and evaluation technology from Watson to augment the case lead generation process that is currently handled manually by officers.

- Treating the locally generated databases as the foundation for a corpus that can be integrated with cognitive operational systems to plan and manage emergency staff and resources. (COPLink uses analytics to predict crime hotspots, but integrating its corpus—including new knowledge learned from experience with hypothesis testing—with planning tools would enable department managers to benefit from the actual experiences.)

- Integrating sensor data from smart transportation systems in (near) real time to support continuous monitoring of activities that may appear innocuous in isolation, but which may be part of patterns that would otherwise go unnoticed.

## Smart Energy Management: From Visualization to Distribution

The importance of visual reports to help people make discoveries from complex data relationships has been discussed. Visual representations of the state of complex systems can also be used to ensure confidence in an operational system and to enable a human to participate in the management process when anomalies arise. For example, allocating energy production resources for a smart grid, or responding to expected changes in demand based on predictive analytics, may create situations that benefit from operator intervention. Visual abstractions make it easier for the operator to detect patterns than simply seeing relevant numbers scroll past on devices. As power systems integrate subsystems with different characteristics or energy sources, visual interfaces are the only practical way to present all the information as a continuous stream. This is much like the approach taken with an automobile dashboard that abstracts some data into simple color maps—red for danger, yellow for caution, and green for normal operations—but provides more detail for other functions, such as a numerical estimate of the distance that may be traveled before refueling. In a single system that balances power generation from water for hydroelectric generation, wind, nuclear generation, and solar and storage in the form of batteries or supercapacitors, visualization is the key to helping the user understand what requires attention as soon as the system can detect it.

### The Problem of Integrating Regional Utilities Management

A new smart city is being developed in Kashiwa-no-ha, Japan, through a collaboration between public agencies and private sector enterprises with three stated goals: environmental symbiosis, support for health and longevity, and creation of new industries. Creating a new city by design presents an opportunity to build a utilities-based infrastructure that is based on state of the art technologies with minimal constraints from aging systems.

### The Area Energy Management Solutions Project

The Area Energy Management Solutions (AEMS) project in Kashiwa-no-ha, Japan, uses advanced analytics to provide an integrated, comprehensive solution for energy production, provisioning, and optimization. AEMS design and development is led by Hitachi Consulting. Hitachi, the $90BUSD global technology and services provider, has emerged as a leader in the smarter cities movement. Its 2014 Annual Report, titled "Social Innovation: It's Our Future," lays out a vision based on building and leveraging technology to address social challenges, including three that resonate with smart city planners: securing water resources, energy and food; replacement of aging infrastructure systems; and improving transportation systems.

The AEMS project is focused on using analytics to manage energy (including electricity, water, gas, and any other production technology that is ultimately adopted by Kashiwa-no-ha) by forecasting demand and dynamic provisioning based on continuous reporting signals from sensors throughout the city. Creating a solution that incorporates renewable energy sources (solar and wind) with more conventional sources and storing excess capacity through storage batteries allows the system to schedule production when it is convenient and cost effective (daylight for solar and medium-to-high wind for turbines) and puts it into the grid on-demand directly or from batteries that store excess capacity from a period of over-production.

AEMS uses analytics to predict peak loads and evaluate alternative approaches to distribution (from interbuilding sharing of resources, similar to the cloud-based model for sharing physical resources).

By planning for an integrated set of energy systems rather than developing hydroelectric, solar, and other data management systems in isolation, the developers created a design that leverages data from each subsystem and also uses analytics to efficiently load balance the overall system to predict demand, provision resources, and distribute more efficiently. AEMS shares information with building energy management systems in commercial, government, and residential facilities.

### The Cognitive Computing Opportunity

From the published plans and reported progress about Kashiwa-no-ha, it is clear that the planners want to take advantage of all the smarter cities' products and practices that can be applied to the operation of their new home. Kashiwa-no-ha is expected to become a model, or test bed, for emerging cognitive technologies. Further integration, to include systems for each of the major constituencies discussed in this chapter, will be a cornerstone of system design and provide opportunities for collaboration. The Hitachi AEMS is new but expected to be integrated with other smart systems in Kashiwa-no-ha over time. For example, integration with its transportation management system, and even weather forecasting and monitoring, would improve the performance of all the systems by sharing new patterns discovered by machine learning algorithms. Consider a day when the forecast called for mild weather, but the actual weather that day is unseasonably wet and cold. An integrated system that has learned from its shared experiences might see a correlation with changing traffic patterns, resulting in changing power demands from public transportation systems. In this scenario AEMS might predict an increase in the ratio of people working from home, and prepare to reallocate power based on the behavior of residents, not a preset model of consumption. Integration of algorithms and data between these systems could use real-time or just-in-time sensor data about the discrepancy between forecast and actual weather to "know" that power demands would change in time to adjust production or distribution patterns.

## Protecting the Power Grid with Machine Learning

In the United States, power grids are included in the energy sector of critical infrastructure that must be secured against cyber attacks under provisions of the National Cybersecurity and Critical Infrastructure Protection Act of 2014. That requires the Secretary of Homeland Security to conduct activities to "protect from, prevent, mitigate, respond to, and recover from cyber incidents." Energy companies are turning to machine learning algorithms to keep up with the volume of data that must be continuously monitored to mitigate risk and maintain compliance with increasingly stringent regulations. One emerging software company called Spark Cognition in Austin, Texas has developed a cognitive system intended to help secure Internet of Things environments such as power grids.

### The Problem of Identifying Threats from New Patterns

Electrical grids are attractive targets for a variety of physical threats, from vandalism to terrorist attacks. More and more, however, the threats are from cyber attacks that attempt to disrupt service. The scale of the physical infrastructure and complexity of connections and dependencies make automation of threat and breach detection critical and potential threat detection a requirement. As new patterns for threats and vulnerabilities emerge, utilities must prepare responses before they materialize.

### The Grid Cybersecurity Analytics Project

C3 Energy (C3) is an energy information management firm founded by the founders of Siebel Systems with a mission to make energy systems more efficient and secure through analytics. C3, working with researchers at the University of California and a National Science Foundation Cybersecurity Center called TRUST, developed Grid Cybersecurity Analytics (GCA)—a smart grid analytics application that uses machine learning algorithms to identify and detect potential threats. GCA was designed to understand the characteristics of normal operations (communications traffic levels, asset activity, and such) and identify potentially threatening activities or anomalies. The machine learning algorithms enable GCA to adapt and identify emerging threats as they evolve or mutate over time by reading up to 6.5 billion records/hour and providing petabyte-scale analysis. That level of performance is required for large grids serving cities.

### The Cognitive Computing Opportunity

The Grid Cybersecurity Analytics system already leverages machine learning algorithms and the latest research in threat assessment and response. Natural extensions to such a system beyond its application in grid security would center on leveraging data and lessons learned as the system gains experience with threats that have commonalities with potential attacks on other critical infrastructure assets, such as bridges, tunnels, and information networks. A scenario is also envisioned in which systems such as GCA share data with systems such as COPLink and sensor-based smart asset-monitoring systems to help prevent or mitigate attacks by sharing data on individual or groups whose behavior raises a threat alert. On the mundane side, data from the underlying analytics platform could also be shared with a corpus for a resource management system that could be tied to incentives for better energy management and to planning systems to recommend incentives for electric vehicles.

## Improving Public Health with Cognitive Community Services

Public health in cities is concerned with wellness and medical care. Wellness includes access to information and preventative care, feedback on behavior that impacts health, and the availability of a full range of care when prevention is not enough. In some jurisdictions it may also include monitoring or managing risks in the food supply and waste management that can improve or diminish overall health. Some of the earliest adopters of cognitive computing technology have been commercial health management firms that have offered personalized recommendations on activities and nutrition, and sometimes incentives for good behavior. In cities, however, many efforts—such as restricting food sodium content or limiting soft drink sizes—have taken a one-size-fits-all-citizens approach. Cognitive computing technology, which can tailor findings and recommendations for diagnoses and individual wellness plans, is the next logical step.

## Smarter Approaches to Preventative Healthcare

In many established cities, access to preventative care is seen as a social service for economically disadvantaged people or offered as a perk through private or public employers' insurance policies. As the cost of personal health monitoring drops, through the availability of free or modestly priced online educational resources and access to sensor-based feedback devices, local governments can begin to justify community-oriented health services that offer personalized care driven by analytics.

### The Town Health Station Project

Kashiwa-no-ha, Japan, has worked with academia (The University of Tokyo) and businesses such as Mitsui Fudosan to develop the latest in community healthcare supported by cognitive computing solutions to aid in preventative care. Its Town Health Station is a model for public health that is expected to be emulated around the world. The project was designed from the outset to embrace the Internet of things and take advantage of new, continuous sources of health information such as the output of personal devices, from mobile phones to exercise bracelets to workplace and residential sensors. The health station is the center of a partnership between local government, the University of Tokyo Institute of Gerontology, the Center for Preventive Medical Science at Chiba University, and residents, to promote long-term health.

### The Cognitive Computing Opportunity

The Town Health Station project (and ancillary programs such as community exercise activities) are already creating a corpus of individual and community data from sensors and professionals that can be shared with other communities to improve the quality of care locally and remotely. As a planned smart city, Kashiwa-no-ha uses analytics to manage traffic and even plan for shared transportation resources in the spirit of the emerging global sharing economy. Integrating these systems in a common corpus that learns from the experiences and behavior of its residents is a natural evolution for the town, and one that would keep it at the vanguard of smarter cities. Similar to the integration envisioned for the Hitachi AEMS solution, the learning systems that share new knowledge between the town, academia, and the medical community is also expected to share the anonymized unstructured health and wellness data with every system that can use it to improve performance.

## Building a Smarter Transportation Infrastructure

Intracity transportation management is, in many ways, more difficult than regional and national transportation management due to population and structure density. As cities build up, it is increasingly important to manage transportation and traffic flow through better use of information. When it becomes prohibitively expensive and disruptive to add infrastructure such as additional lanes or levels to roads and rails, getting smarter about who can go where, and when, will drive cities to cognitive computing solutions.

## Managing Traffic in Growing Cities

In cities everywhere, traffic congestion leads to frustrated drivers; excess energy consumption, inefficient commerce as people spend more time driving and parking when they could be working and shopping; delayed emergency responses; and higher pollution. It also requires assets to manage peak loads that may be underutilized in general. Almost any change to flow involves trade-offs that inconvenience people and interrupt commerce, while potentially slowing emergency responses. In 2014, lane closures on a heavily traveled bridge between two metropolitan areas in the United States nearly became a political scandal when paramedics took twice as long as usual to respond to an accident with multiple injuries.

## The Adaptive Traffic Signals Controller Project

The city of Toronto, Canada, adopted the Multi-Agent Reinforcement Learning Integrated Network of Adaptive Traffic Signal Controllers (MARLIN-ATSC), a system for smarter traffic management, with impressive results. Toronto reports that downtown delays have already been reduced by 40 percent on an average day by simply managing traffic signals more effectively. Xerox, the $23 billion information and document management company, worked with the University of Toronto's Intelligent Transportation Centre to develop and deploy the system, which incorporates camera images and machine learning chips to enable real-time communication between traffic lights to detect patterns and dynamically adjust their timing. Helsinki has a similar traffic project underway with Xerox, with comparable results and similar opportunities to expand into a cognitive computing environment. As Xerox continues its focus on business transformation and migrates away from a dependence on manufacturing devices, it is building up its credentials in smarter city professional services and integration with projects such as MARLIN-ATSC.

### The Cognitive Computing Opportunity

MARLIN-ATSC is already an example of machine learning and adaptive, integrated devices. In the next several years, many opportunities may be available to integrate systems such as this with other cognitive computing municipal management systems, and to extend its capabilities by collecting data from external systems such as the cars themselves.

For example, the U.S. Transportation Department is working on a "connected vehicle" initiative that would promote the use of car-mounted wireless devices that communicate with each other and with traffic signals to increase the effectiveness of systems such as MARLIN-ATSC. In addition to the obvious issues of individual privacy and security, such a program faces years of testing and changes in legislation before the government would require the use of these devices in new cars. It is, however, technically feasible now.

Transportation management is one of the most developed domains for analytics and cognitive solutions. In part, this is due to the ready availability of sensors and systems to collect and share data. Virtually every component of a transportation system is amenable to measurement, from cars and buses to planes, trains, and boats, plus the highways and ports that support them. Combining data from this type of signal management with data from CCTV or transponders—even anonymously—could further improve the capability of cities to reduce congestion while providing input for security and planning. Integration with security systems such as COPLink to identify patterns after a criminal event could help law enforcement's capability to predict future events. Integration with systems such as the Grid Cybersecurity Analytics may have limited threat improvement opportunities, but offer real potential to improve the use of electric vehicles by better understanding their usage patterns to optimally locate charging stations and introduce variable pricing to encourage usage patterns that minimize infrastructure requirements.

This type of integration may also help speed the way for the adoption of autonomous vehicles (self-driving cars, buses, and so on) by promoting communication between driverless and human-piloted vehicles to make a smoother transition.

## Using Analytics to Close the Workforce Skills Gap

Human capital management in cities requires management of significant interdependencies among employment, education, and social services. Cities also need to find ways to try to lower unemployment, because it can increase crime and lower the tax revenue at a time when assistance is needed the most. Neighborhoods with high concentrations of unemployment face additional problems as lower income disproportionately impacts small businesses and real estate values, too. As businesses tighten their skills and experience requirements for hiring, it is important that new workforce entrants and the unemployed have the right skills when openings appear.

### Identifying Emerging Skills Requirements and Just-in-Time Training

A representative from Boeing, one of the largest aerospace firms noted, "We don't have necessarily a labor challenge, we have a skills challenge." Even with thousands of job openings and thousands of applicants, many jobs at this firm still go unfilled. Preparing residents for opportunities by identifying and training them on appropriate skills before the need arises requires an understanding of emerging skills requirements supported by analytics. Matching skills training to aptitude in an applicant pool is a perfect opportunity for cognitive computing applications.

### The Digital On-Ramps (DOR) Project

Leaders in the city of Philadelphia, PA, with a population of approximately 1.5 million, recognized that their residents were falling behind the digital literacy and technical skills demands of industry and recognized that significant action had to be taken. In 2011, it was estimated that by 2030, it could have 600,000 citizens who were unprepared to compete effectively for new jobs. At that point, only 41 percent of homes in Philadelphia were connected to the Internet, but increasing mobile access was not being leveraged effectively to improve training or education. Working with IBM under a grant from its Smarter Cities Challenge program and support from the Clinton Global Initiative, Philadelphia developed Digital On-Ramps (DOR), a learning delivery system that includes in-person and digital education, tailored to anticipated industry needs and individual aptitudes and learning styles. Similar to the electronic health records (EHR) discussed in Chapter 12, DOR creates a universal ID and "digital record depository" for each learner that tracks school, training, and work experiences and accomplishments. Captured as structured and unstructured data in a personal portfolio, it is used to guide the learner toward a job goal with the advice of a counselor. Today, the counseling is done by human practitioners, but the system is capturing data that is useful for evaluating progress using descriptive analytics. This data should soon be useful as input to predictive analytics when the last two stages in the DORS process—building individual skills and matching a skill set to jobs and networks—have generated sufficient data to build a corpus for a cognitive computing solution.

Early results from DOR indicate that creating individualized programs for future industry needs while leveraging a variety of disparate resources, from the free library to local schools and corporate philanthropic programs, can be a successful endeavor. Human will reinforced by analytics has already enabled Philadelphia to secure a MacArthur Foundation grant to develop a certification process to help guide employers when hiring graduates of the DOR programs.

## The Cognitive Computing Opportunity

A strong workforce attracts businesses, which strengthens the workforce, creating a virtuous cycle. DOR was launched in Philadelphia, PA, but from the outset it was considered to be a model for other cities struggling with the mismatch between skills and jobs in industry. Integrating cognitive computing functionality into DOR will make it more powerful for those in the program, but also for ongoing city planning and management. For example, adding NLP capabilities for interactions between individuals and the system will lower barriers to participation and provide more tailored responses.

As participants become comfortable with sharing information about personal aspirations and experiences with the system (in natural language). It could learn from experience what works and what doesn't (self-training), and begin to make better recommendations and suggestions for midcourse corrections if it detects changing employment conditions. From reading and interpreting labor statistics, job ads, and editorials in unstructured text from around the country and around the world, such a system could provide ongoing personalized guidance to a population that would otherwise be left to its own devices.

Finally, an integrated cognitive computing environment that shares data across all major city systems could use DOR data to improve transportation planning and operations, utilities demand forecasting, and public health as the impact of new jobs propagates throughout the city and region.

## Creating a Cognitive Community Infrastructure

As you have seen, cognitive computing solutions benefit from retaining knowledge created during operation as hypotheses are tested and refined over time. When natural communities—groups of people with similar interests, experiences, or simply geographic proximity—communicate, they raise the collective intelligence of the community. Professional communities that communicate with or through a cognitive computing solution can amplify the learning, as you have seen through medical diagnostics. Physical communities, such as city residents, can likewise benefit from collaboration via cognitive computing.

### The Smart + Connected Communities Initiative

In New Songdo City, South Korea, a partnership between the Korean government and private industry is building a new, green, smart city designed from the outset to make extensive use of sensors and analytics. The $35 billion (U.S. dollars) project is one of the largest new city ventures in the world. Cisco, the $48 billion U.S. dollars global networking and communications firm, has wired every home and business in New Songdo City with video screens and systems to facilitate collaboration and a sense of digital community within a physical community expected to have a population of 65,000 by 2016. This Smart + Connected Communities initiative is the first in what Cisco and the development organization hope is dozens of similar projects throughout Asia. Cisco is a leader in developing devices for the IOT and was an early pioneer of the connected world concept. Cisco is promoting New Songdo City as a showcase for the benefits of networking and remote control of residential and commercial energy management and security. These systems will be integrated from the outset, and machine learning tools such Cisco's Cognitive Threat Analytics—which learns and adapts as new threats are identified—will be deployed as New Songdo City nears completion.

The city, set to be operational in 2015 and home of the largest skyscraper in South Korea by 2016, includes an international school for children of visiting business executives, which is connected at all levels with a sister-school in California. Extensive use of video for collaboration and communication is planned to develop a community of learners within the general population. As video analysis techniques mature, that technology will be integrated to continue the automation of learning support.

The extensive use of telepresence and sensor data to deliver more personalized services to every residential and commercial location should foster communication while discouraging energy-intensive travel. This approach fits with New Songdo City's goal of world-class sustainability.

## The Cognitive Computing Opportunity

New Songdo City is starting with many advantages over existing cities—before the people arrived, the initial wiring was in place to encourage communication and capture sensor-based, video-based, and system-based information. Beyond community sharing, these systems integrate with transportation, energy, and water management systems, providing an unprecedented opportunity for a city whose population is supported by and bound together by cognitive computing technologies.

# The Next Phase of Cognitive Cities

As more of the global population moves into urban areas, the importance of city-oriented cognitive computing will increase. Making better use of the big data generated by the daily activities of individuals, public sector agencies, and businesses will support differentiation for cities as they compete to lure valuable talent and businesses and increase the effectiveness of collaborative efforts for alliances.

For each area, however, you can expect to see an ongoing conflict over private versus public ownership of the data and knowledge, as competition to market intelligent solutions to the densely populated urban residents increases. This is not an issue for cognitive computing per se; rather it reflects the great value that will be created as a result of smarter processing of dumb data at scale.

Most of the examples in this chapter have come from the introduction of analytic and cognitive computing technologies to address straining physical and information infrastructures in established cities. That will continue to be an issue for the foreseeable future, but the desire for urbanization is also driving the creation of new cities to meet the demand. Although planned communities of the last century, from Reston, Virginia, to Celebration, Florida, were built around architectural and open space patterns harvested from the study of centuries of organic city growth, the next generation of planning will be based on communication and collaboration needs, much better suited to cognitive computing analyses than to nostalgic looks at successful town squares.

Kashiwa-No-Ha, Japan, and New Songdo City, Korea, are essentially new cities unencumbered by aging infrastructure and preconceptions. As these two cities mature, and others like them spring up in the next two decades, they will demonstrate the value of integrated analytics and cognitive computing to improve municipal life, and even the most conservative cities will have to adapt or see their relevance erode in the age of cognitive computing.

## Summary

Smarter cities have moved beyond collecting data such as vehicle and animal registrations and tax-based data on homes and income. Now, city managers are collecting data through collaboration between departments with optimization in mind. Some leaders have appointed chief data officers to look for opportunities to share data whenever new systems are created. A new public health record database, for example, may be designed to capture elements that can be shared with an education database, or a security database. Most cities are actively making as much data as possible open for free use by the public and by innovative entrepreneurs who can build new services on this data. Every shared use or new commercial use can potentially produce value for residents.

As smart city managers, including elected officials and civil servants, begin to understand the power of data to transform city life, they are embracing advanced analytics and cognitive computing as a source of added value. Smarter cities make better use of all their resources, and having good data is at the heart of these better decisions. Today, the best systems for creating this type of data are the class of emerging cognitive computing applications that learn from their experiences and can guide their users to better decisions and outcomes. In the future we may take for granted the cognitive computing applications that make cities safer and more efficient, while anticipating our needs as residents. Today, the journey is just beginning but the benefits are already clear.

# Emerging Cognitive Computing Areas

Cognitive computing is beginning to have an impact on a number of different industries. Initially, cognitive computing is starting to transform the healthcare industry, as discussed in Chapter 11, "Building a Cognitive Healthcare Application." Cognitive computing applications are already:

- Making and enabling new discoveries about patterns of symptoms that indicate specific diseases based on the power to read more research and case files than any individual physician

- Explaining the results of findings to medical students to help them refine their own diagnostic abilities

- Democratizing specialized knowledge and making it available to practitioners, who would rarely, if ever, see certain symptoms or conditions

All these capabilities that help drive the adoption of cognitive computing in healthcare will have the same potential in other industries. For example, finding patterns for disease diagnosis and making treatment recommendations are special cases of the general problem of identifying faults and remedies in complex systems. This capability to diagnose problems has applications in industries such as manufacturing—machine maintenance and repair from household appliances to oil rig apparatus, and even call centers for problem resolution. Evidence-based explanations that help to train new professionals can be used in any field where a large or complex body of knowledge is codified. Finally, almost every profession has the potential to thrive by aggregating and analyzing specialized knowledge and packaging and selling that data as a service. Professionals ranging from lawyers to accountants and stockbrokers can be democratized by giving newly-minted professionals and inexperienced users the power to leverage this knowledge with the assistance of a cognitive computing guide.

This chapter identifies attributes of problem domains that make them well suited to similar transformations in other industries, and shows how some functional areas across all industries can also be transformed.

## Characteristics of Ideal Markets for Cognitive Computing

At the heart of every cognitive system is a continuous learning engine that improves with experience and that can return probabilistic results when the data supports multiple candidate answers. Advanced systems make use of natural language processing (NLP) to capture meaning and nuances in text from publications. In addition, these systems can make use of images, gestures, and sound. The systems can increasingly capture streaming data from Internet-enabled sensors. Mapping this functionality to typical business workloads—datacentric tasks found within and across industries—reveals a set of attributes that make some problem domains well suited to cognitive computing applications.

Ideal candidates for cognitive computing include:

- Industries with rapidly increasing or changing volumes of domain-specific knowledge, which make presales advice valuable to buyers but costly to sellers. This would include areas such as retail, where products and offers change constantly, and travel, where options and opportunities change constantly.

- Industries where post-sales support/diagnostics—professional services—are cost centers or revenue opportunities due to complex products. This is especially important when staff turnover is high and changes in product data requires constant training. This includes virtually every industry currently using call centers, from retail to enterprise software support.

- Industries characterized by a lot of specialty knowledge or experience that is highly concentrated in a small group of experts. This includes many professions and complex product presales where configuration decisions are critical.

- Industries that traditionally follow a modern apprentice/intern model for training and certification. This would include most data rich professions such as law, medicine, and financial services.

- Industries in which best practices are known or knowable, and there is a wide variance between the best and least-effective practitioners in the field. (The top experts are differentiated from average performers by their ability to draw on personal experiences or recognize patterns that are unknown or too complex for inexperienced workers.) This would also include most professions.

- Industries in which the sudden availability of sensor data creates opportunities that cannot be exploited by conventional means. This includes industries from transportation to healthcare; wherever sensors can capture meaningful data where real-time analysis by experts has value, cognitive computing applications can be adopted.

- Industries in which success depends on discovering patterns in a large volume of data, particularly unstructured natural language text. Any field that produces a large stream of new research, beyond the ability of practitioners to absorb on their own, is a candidate. This includes most of the natural sciences, pharmaceuticals, and the professions (new case law around the world, changing regulatory requirements, and so on).

As a general rule, the introduction of cognitive computing systems can make an organization smarter by making the top performers more efficient. In fact, even the most sophisticated professional will not be aware of all the new findings in a field. A cognitive system prevents biases from driving decision making. It is quite common for the most experienced professionals to select an approach based on their own best practices without taking into account that there is new data that they have not been exposed to. Less experienced professionals can perform at a much higher level because they can benefit from the shared knowledge.

The cognitive system is not static. It is continually ingesting new information from data and from both successes and failures. The dynamic nature of this environment has the potential to raise the level of expertise of the entire organization.

## Vertical Markets and Industries

This section looks at a few market segments that are already using advanced analytics to improve their performance, and have leaders exploring cognitive computing solutions. The intent is to show how the common characteristics are driving this adoption and acknowledges that there are many other fields with similar attributes and many proof-of-concept projects underway that will change the public perception of cognitive computing and create demand for smarter systems in almost every field.

## Retail

Retail is a notoriously competitive industry. To survive and thrive, retailers have to anticipate what products to purchase based on forecasting trends in advance. They have to understand the impact of changing economic, social, and demographic factors. Retailers also have to make sure that their employees do a good job at both representing the company and the products sold. External factors can also wreak havoc with plans and forecasts. Unseasonable weather, changing gas prices, fluctuating employment rates, and even political unrest can impact buying behavior. Larger firms have used predictive analytics and scenario planning tools for decades. These firms have optimized supply chains to reduce the lag between ordering an item and delivery (lowering the risk of receiving out of fashion or unwanted goods). However, too often retailers miss subtle changes in buying preferences and do not anticipate opportunities to gain advantages over competitors. Cognitive solutions have the potential to help retailers leverage knowledge in inventive ways. For example, a typical large retailer relies heavily on its supply chain automation to deal with customer problems. These systems are weak when unanticipated problems arise. Being able to provide creative ways to deal with problems so that customers remain satisfied and loyal.

### Cognitive Computing Opportunities

Many retailers use predictive analytics tools to detect interesting correlations to discover insights based on loyalty-card data. For example, analytics help retailers to recognize changing habits, buying preferences, and changes in life circumstances (marriages, pregnancy, and such). It is possible to differentiate between an anomaly and a true change in buying preferences. For example, a product may be suddenly popular because of a single event. (A sudden storm causes consumers to purchase snow shovels in a region that gets little snow.) With cognitive computing, these changes may be detected earlier, enabling the retailers to implement innovative new practices and approaches that can change the customer experience. Retailers will be more interactive with customers through natural language dialoging with high-value customers. These retailers will have the ability to learn from the information gleaned from social media and customer interaction with call centers. They will bring together all this data so that it learns from practices of the most successful sales personnel and from the most successful campaigns. Armed with this type of dynamic environment, a retailer could discover new approaches to retail that can change the relationship with customers. Even increasing sales from repeat customers by a small percentage can result in huge profits.

#### Personalized Customer Service

In retail sales, customers are constantly faced with new choices, features, or fashion and must decide which product to buy, when to buy, and from whom to buy. Although recommendations from friends on brands and sellers are important, the customer experience in a store or on a website can make the difference between casual interest and an actual purchase. With that in mind, retailers struggle with the issue of how much personalized attention to provide for each shopper—sometimes sacrificing volume for higher margins. Buyers usually have to choose between stores that offer knowledgeable sales staff and those that don't, whether the purchase is made in a physical store or online. For higher-priced items, from luxury goods to complex home electronics, this creates a tension when good advice in a store often leads to an online purchase based on price. The promise of cognitive computing in this case is to democratize good advice. This requires that retailers offer personalized attention to a buyer's wants and needs by using extensive knowledge about the products. It also requires that retailers gain insights about those customers so that they can make recommendations that are meaningful. Taking advantage of a system that continuously learns and adapts based on collecting and analyzing massive amounts of data can make a huge difference between success and failure.

An early entrant into this market is Fluid, a 15-year-old firm specializing in building online customer experience tools for leading retailers. The company partnered with IBM (who announced an equity investment in Fluid) to build a Watson-based platform that enables customers to communicate with online retail sites to provide customized product recommendations. The goal of this service is to lead the buyer through a dialog that mimics the customer engagement of a personal shopper. Fluid's first customer is NorthFace, a retailer that offers hundreds of products for outdoor activities and caters to "explorers" who are willing to pay a premium for quality.

The Watson-based platform will enable customers to enter a natural language description of their requirements from "I need a sleeping bag for a trip to Argentina in May" to "What should I take on a camping trip with three young children?" By engaging in a conversation with the buyer, the system can leverage information in its corpus about each item in inventory, and each type of activity in its ontology (for example, from camping to hiking). Through this dialoging process, the system narrows the scope of suggestions based on a match between what is available and the knowledge it acquires about the customer from this conversation. The system also stores all the background information from previous customer interactions and queries. The system can also look for similar queries and outcomes from other customers. This is not the same as a simple recommendation engine that provides a series of potential options. In the Watson system, the user can generate questions based on the assumption that the system contains depth of knowledge. As the system collects more information about consumers over time, the level of confidence in those recommendations increases. Retaining information between sessions allows the system to learn from each interaction and provide better advice in subsequent sessions with the same or different users.

### Retail Staff Training and Support

It is critical that in-store personnel provide consistently good advice based on product knowledge and good customer interaction skills. However, retailers typically have high turnover so that average salespeople lack deep knowledge about the products they sell. UK retail technology firm Red Ant commissioned a study of 1,000 retail workers aged 18–55 by an online polling firm. The results were revealing:

- 50 percent of respondents reported feeling embarrassed by their own lack of product knowledge
- 43 percent said they lie to customers every week due to product knowledge deficiencies
- 73 percent said they send customers to another store
- 57 percent said they were given less than 2 hours of training before being sent to help customers

The results clearly indicate that there is a critical need for training. Employees need to understand the products they sell and need access to best practices. Employees often quit or are fired under less than ideal working conditions. It was clear to Red Ant that there was an opportunity to use a cognitive approach to improve the performance of retail workers.

Red Ant specializes in helping retailers improve their processes through analyzing customer and retailer behavior. Therefore, Red Ant is developing a Watson-based retail sales-training application to market. The goal of the product offering is to help sales associates analyze customer demographics and purchasing histories. The application will provide access to product information and market feedback from sentiment analysis to help retail workers make better recommendations to customers. Bringing together customer information with product information while the customer is in the store will enable a more engaging dialog using NLP from Watson and will create a more personalized shopping experience for the consumer. Every interaction with that customer is recorded and can be compared with interactions with similar digital histories. This corpus of data is intended to help predict what will be most effective and record the results. The sales associate may get recommendations via custom on-screen prompts, which could be shared with the customer or via text-to-speech messages through an earpiece.

## Travel

The travel industry has seen tremendous upheaval in the past two decades as information about rates and schedules of transportation, lodging, and leisure activities has been made freely available online. Self-service booking sites have enabled individuals to make their own reservations after searching multiple sites for descriptions, prices, and even reviews, without paying a fee, and other sites have emerged to harvest results from multiple sites with a single search.

That has eliminated the personal touch of an experienced travel agent who could get to know the customer and ask qualifying questions to ensure a good fit between personal goals and desires, and available inventory of transportation, lodging, and experience options.

Although much progress has been made in terms of making information visible, optimizing yield on flights and cruises based on predictive analytics and customer history, what is lost is a store of personal information about the *why* aspects of trip planning, and experience-based recommendations that understand the client's objectives. An individual may have different preferences for pleasure and business travel, and different preferences based on duration, location, and who is paying for the trip or even who is accompanying them, but no single site captures all this information today.

### Cognitive Computing Opportunities for the Travel Industry

It was once common to work with a travel agent who could get to know the preferences of an individual and be on the lookout for new options and new opportunities. Today, the traveler typically has to provide a profile of standard options for each site they use. However, none of these sites provide inferences are made based on observable behavior. This leaves a big opportunity for a cognitive computing travel application that captures information explicitly by capturing patterns of travelers' behavior. There is also the potential for implicitly understanding travelers by monitoring social media streams. There is also an opportunity to allow travelers to interact via an NLP interface with the system.

An example of what you can expect is a company founded by Terry Jones, the founding CEO of Travelocity and an early chairman of Kayak. WayBlazer is a startup founded by Jones with the intention of leveraging cognitive computing services from IBM Watson to add evidence-based advice to its product. WayBlazer is also built on top of a cloud solution built by Cognitive Scale, a company that provides a cognitive-insight-as-a-service platform. The company is collaborating with the Austin, Texas Convention and Visitor's Bureau to create an application that will provide customized recommendations for individuals. Over time, the company intends to expand to provide concierge services to hotels and airlines to improve the overall user experience and provide additional revenue opportunities to these ecosystem partners. WayBlazer is using the NLP and hypothesis generation/evaluation capabilities from Watson to evaluate a corpus initially populated with data from the destination and transportation vendors (suppliers), but which will be augmented by knowledge it acquires by monitoring traveler requests and outcomes. In addition to earning the customary fees from transactions, the system can learn about individuals and group behavior. WayBlazer will collect valuable data that it will be able to sell to the suppliers. The travel industry is fertile territory for a cognitive approach and there will be many competitive services that will provide evidence-based advice to travelers.

## Transportation and Logistics

Transportation and logistics companies face stiff competition, regulatory pressures, and danger from man-made and natural causes, from terrorism to tornados. Keeping the infrastructure safe is an ongoing concern. In addition, there is a need to identify patterns of customer behavior that may foreshadow new revenue opportunities. Logistics firms were among the first to optimize route times with such tricks as minimizing left turns in cities and improving yield with highly optimized hub and spoke terminals. The rise of sensor technology and GPS tools has uncovered further efficiencies, but we are now on the cusp of a new, smarter industry as cognitive computing technologies are applied across the board.

### *Cognitive Computing Opportunities for Transportation and Logistics*

Many changes in technology are transforming the transportation and logistics industries that will be helped by processing and managing complex data. The first change is the rise in the use of sensor data that needs to be interpreted in near real time to identify opportunities to improve efficiency and safety. The second change is the capability of cognitive computing models to provide diagnostic and preventative maintenance recommendations. These recommendations will help make fleet operations and maintenance more effective. For example, these recommendations will help managers schedule preventative maintenance while minimizing disruption.

CSX, a 185-year-old transportation and logistics firm based in Jacksonville, Florida, has implemented this type of system. With more than 21,000 miles of railroad track, connecting virtually all the population and manufacturing hubs in the United States, CSX links more than 240 short line railroads and 70 water ports. The company replaced a manual-intensive track inspection system that required 600 road masters and track inspectors to record track condition information on paper. This information was then manually input into a system for analysis and reporting. The replacement system, called an Integrated Track Inspection System (ITIS), was developed by CSX leveraging analytics technology from SAP. ITIS replaced the manual system with more functionality and mobile access to recording and predictive analytics tools.

CSX and SAP are also developing a complementary planning system that uses natural language processing and sentiment analysis of unstructured customer feedback. Combining data from these systems into a single corpus with data about traffic patterns and sales data will enable CSX to identify new revenue opportunities in a continuous learning environment. As CSX increases its use of sensors to provide real-time data, integration of these systems will create more opportunities to make the lines safer and able to continuously learn from results. This learning will result in new best practices to improve the efficiency of CSX's operations.

## Telecommunications

Telecommunications providers live and die by performance metrics that may be easy to measure but difficult to manage. Customers of these providers are often large companies that resell services to large companies of managed service providers. To be successful they have to provide a predictable level of service. They are often required to provide service-level agreements (SLAs), which specify required performance levels for service delivery. If the telecommunications vendor cannot deliver the service, there are often financial penalties. It is incumbent upon the provider to constantly monitor and manage performance and to demonstrate compliance with the SLA or quickly identify and rectify any subpar performance. Telecommunications providers have matured from providing voice communications channels and basic access to relatively static data, to streaming video to consumers on home and mobile devices, and responding to consumer demand for data on the latest mobile application. As the variety of services offered by telecommunications providers increases, so does variability in demand.

The requirement for continuous performance monitoring, which may have subsecond response time mandates, has led to the deployment of sensors and probes at the edge of the network that can give a real-time view of the actual service level available to the customer. Demand may change due to a variety of events ranging from routine maintenance to a sudden surge in demand because of natural disasters.

### Cognitive Computing Opportunities for Telecommunications

Collecting all this data, even in real time, is the easy part. The hard part is to identify conditions that indicate an impending change in demand in time to reconfigure or reallocate services to ensure ongoing SLA compliance based on weak signals—patterns that have traditionally escaped the notice of even well-trained and experienced network engineers. This is where the benefits of cognitive computing come into play. The problem for telecommunications companies is to evaluate enough historical data to discover and understand patterns and causality, while evaluating signals from the environment about impending events that may trigger demand change.

Hitachi Data Systems has developed a solution aimed at helping telecommunication managed service providers monitor and manage real-time data using a combination of machine learning algorithms, proprietary and open source intellectual property, and third-party offerings integrated through APIs. Hitachi uses a component library built from historical customer data including spatial-temporal event detection, complex event processing, event extraction from unstructured data, and root cause analysis to augment the machine learning algorithms. The system continuously monitors current performance and compares it with historical performance. The system also analyzes unstructured data such as social media streams (weather emergencies or a popular television event that is about to happen) that can impact network performance. By combining real-time data analytics with unstructured data analytics, the system can anticipate changes in demand based on patterns. With continuous learning at its core, such a cognitive computing solution could alert network engineers of impending demand, or even dynamically adjust capacity proactively to prevent a crisis.

## Security and Threat Detection

Commercial network security is a concern for business continuity and general risk management in virtually every industry today. Networks, websites, and applications in the cloud are all attractive targets. Cyber-terrorism attacks made for commercial gain or simply to exploit vulnerabilities to demonstrate the proficiency of the attacker are on the rise and show no signs of abating. Even constant vigilance with conventional technology is not enough to keep up as attackers employ more and more sophisticated approaches to theft and disruption.

### Cognitive Computing Opportunities for Security and Threat Detection

Following are three big drivers for adopting cognitive computing for threat detection:

- The speed at which new threats are developed
- The speed with which damage can be done before an attack can be controlled
- The complexity of networks that are getting beyond the capabilities of conventional systems and network managers to protect

In the past, as new threats were detected, new rules were rolled out to network administrators or individuals with subscriptions to security and antivirus packages. The delay between detection and updates could be hours, days, or weeks.

Fortunately, machine-learning solutions can monitor network access points continuously and compare current activity to historical activity while looking for anomalies—without being told what to look for. Instead of waiting for an update, the system can highlight unexpected activity patterns and even take actions such as quarantining data and network segments while an operator evaluates the situation. For a false positive (an anomaly that simply represents a new but safe activity pattern) the system can learn that the new pattern is benign and update its own knowledge so that future occurrences will be recognized as the new normal and not register as a threat.

The Cognitive Threat Analytics solution from Cisco is an early entrant in this market. It uses machine-learning algorithms to analyze traffic through a secure gateway and look for symptoms—anomalous behavior—without concern for the method of attack. This eliminates the old loop that required threat identification as a first step. Cisco can build a corpus of normal behavior patterns by analyzing the activities of individual users and larger groups of similar users. When an unexpected pattern is found to represent a new, benign activity, the updated corpus can be made available immediately to all users of this cloud-based service. Looking at behavior within the network without the bias of rules that were constructed based on previous threats allows the system to learn based only on relevant evidence.

## Other Areas That Are Impacted by a Cognitive Approach

Although several industries that can be helped by cognitive computing have been mentioned, many others are good candidates. In some of these areas projects are already underway. Other markets will adapt continuous learning solutions in the coming years. This next section indicates which areas will be impacted by a cognitive approach.

### Call Centers

The call center is a cross-industry function that is critical to the reputation and management of an organization. The call center staff is required to have deep knowledge of products and customer issues. However, call centers have notoriously high rates of personnel turnover. When highly skilled staff members leave, their knowledge and best practices leave with them. There is enormous pressure to know intricate details about products and services and to provide the "next best action" to retain customers and sell them other products and services. In addition, call center agents must understand and comply with compliance requirements for their industries.

### Cognitive Computing Opportunities

A considerable amount of data can be applied to creating a cognitive computing solution for call centers. Structured data exists in customer support databases. A considerable amount of data is available in notes and documents related to customer interaction and recommendations that can be added to a corpus for a call center application. Over time, the machine learning process can provide guidance for best practices for addressing customer issues. An NLP interface enables a customer support agent to determine next best actions. In addition, customers can interact directly with an online system to determine solutions without long waits on call center phone lines. Eventually, many inbound tasks—getting input from the customer—should be automated using NLP and hypothesis generation. The refined query can be handed off to a human for action or may be handled directly by a cognitive call center application. (The system may determine whether the caller would prefer a human response by asking or by evidence from previous experiences with the same or similar customers.)

### Solutions in Other Areas

A number of other areas exist in which work has started on creating cognitive computing solutions. These are all areas in which a large amount of both structured and unstructured data exists. Some promising areas include:

- **Financial services**—In a data rich environment such as financial services, it will be possible to gain an understanding of an individual's requirements and the best product offerings. The data will be put in context with a vast volume and variety of data from multiple customers. The cognitive system can learn based on patterns of success to provide best next actions.

- **Legal applications**—The legal industry is heavily focused on unstructured documents that include the details for discovery and compliance. This data comes from records ranging from e-mails to tweets to clinical trial results, which must be kept for years and made available upon demand. These legal activities may be carried out by in-house counsel or outsourced, but they all require electronic discovery. This often requires significant resources to scour relevant documents and filings that were created in unstructured natural language. Advanced NLP systems and pattern recognition algorithms found in continuous learning systems are ideal for these applications. Today, a common practice is to use the Electronic Discovery Reference Model (EDRM, from a coalition of attorneys, IT managers, and other interested parties). In the future, using a cognitive computing system could simplify the process, and people could also be trained to alert the business to new opportunities (investments that fit a profile, for example) or risks (scenarios that foretell legal action) by combining information from the company corpus with updated sentiment analysis of social media data and news feeds that indicate impending litigation before it is filed.

- **Marketing applications**—Most of the applications for marketing analyze results of existing campaigns or use predictive analytics to anticipate future customer requirements. The opportunity exists to actively monitor the information related to customer and prospect interactions. On the outbound side, message and pricing can be structured as hypotheses that can be tested against a corpus of data about the industry, firm, current clients and prospects, and competitors. A well-trained continuous learning system could evaluate alternatives and help marketers refine messaging and pricing by asking the right questions early in the process. Constant monitoring and updating of the corpus with relevant social media and news items—using NLP—would add significant value to that process and to the monitoring of public perceptions of the brand. Sentiment analysis is already used in this context; the cognitive advantage would come from intelligent hypotheses and questioning from the continuous learning component.

## Summary

Early cognitive computing successes in areas such as medical diagnosis, manufacturing fault prediction, and healthcare research have convincingly demonstrated the potential for continuous learning systems to change the way we think about entire industries. In the next decade, these learning systems will likely be applied in every industry or business functional area that is characterized by a rapidly increasing or changing volumes of domain-specific knowledge, a high concentration of specialty knowledge in a small group of experts that has great value to a broader audience, or ones that are undergoing great transformations where uncertainty—that is, there is not one single right answer in most situations—is the rule.

As the cost to deploy these systems becomes an operational rather than capital expense (for example, ecosystem revenue sharing models for cognition as service offerings) the barrier for entry will be lowered even further and adoption should increase rapidly. The trend to offer all sorts of functions as services has already transformed the SMB (Small/Medium Business) market in areas ranging from expense management to productivity suites to customer relationship management applications. The next wave of enterprise-level cognitive computing applications is on the horizon, and the cognition as a service wave for functional areas is not far behind.

# Future Applications for Cognitive Computing

The development of cognitive computing is at the early stages; however, the building blocks to create this new generation of systems are in place. Over the coming decade there will be many advances in both hardware and software that will impact the future of this important technology. So, the future of cognitive computing will be a combination of evolution and revolution. The evolutionary aspects of cognitive computing are foundational technologies such as security, data visualization, machine learning, natural language processing, data cleaning, management, and governance. There will be revolutions in the capability of systems to improve human-to-machine interactions. In addition, some of the biggest revolutions will come in the areas of hardware innovation.

For decades, advances in chip technology were based on increasing levels of component density and systems integration. Although conventional architectures will continue to improve along these lines, fundamentally different architectures are emerging that will have a bigger impact on cognitive computing performance. Neuromorphic architectures, which are "brain inspired" and use processing elements modeled after neurons, will have a profound impact on speed and portability. In particular, neuromorphic hardware will bring a new level of performance for scale up and will allow data to be processed closer to the source, including direct processing on mobile devices. Quantum computing architectures, based on properties of quantum mechanics, offer great promise for fast processing of large data sets that are often found in cognitive computing applications. This new generation of chips and systems will enable demand for context-aware computing to be met. This chapter looks forward to the coming decade and what is coming and what will be possible.

# Requirements for the Next Generation

The need to share knowledge has always been a top requirement for large and small organizations. Myriad attempts have been made over the decades to try to create learning systems that could codify knowledge in a way that does not require years of coding and software development. Emerging technologies that speed the capability to manage and interpret data to gain insights are emerging. A number of important innovations will change the way organizations can translate data into knowledge that is dynamic, sharable, and predictable.

## Leveraging Cognitive Computing to Improve Predictability

Advanced analytics is going to be integrated with cognitive solutions. As cognitive computing matures, companies will find more automated methods of capturing and ingesting massive amounts of data to create solutions. As the corpora of data expand with more experience, it will be possible to incorporate advanced analytics algorithms to a corpus or subset of available data for analysis to determine next best actions or to correlate data to find hidden patterns. This will require a set of tools that can also automate the process of vetting data sources to ensure that data quality is at the level it needs to be. After analysis has been completed, the results can be moved into the cognitive system to update the machine learning models. This will be part of the process of ensuring that a cognitive system can take advantage of the wealth of knowledge and expertise to make better decisions.

## The New Life Cycle for Knowledge Management

In a sense, there will be a new life cycle of knowledge management. You begin by creating a hypothesis for the problem you want to solve; you then ingest all the data that is relevant to that problem area; and then vet the data sources, cleanse them, and verify those sources. You train the data, apply natural language processing (NLP) and visualization, and refine the corpus. After the system is put into use, the data is continuously analyzed with predictive analytic algorithms to understand what is changing. Then the process starts all over again. This life cycle from hypothesis through Big Data analytics creates a sophisticated and dynamic learning environment (see Figure 14-1).

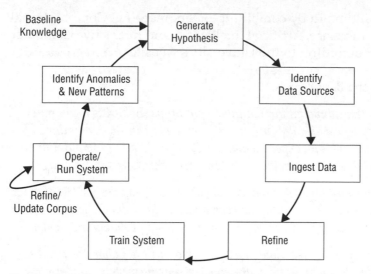

**Figure 14-1:** The life cycle of knowledge management

## Creating Intuitive Human-to-Machine Interfaces

The most sophisticated applications in the first generation of cognitive systems rely heavily on a natural language interface. NLP will continue to be the foundation of how we interact with cognitive systems. However, there will be additional interfaces available for use depending on the nature of the task. For example, there are times when the interface needs to provide visualization so that the researcher can determine where a pattern exists that requires additional exploration. If a biotech researcher is trying to determine the affinity between a disease molecule and a potential therapy, visually detecting patterns will speed the development of a potentially powerful new drug. Other interfaces are also beginning to emerge. For example, improvements in voice recognition technology that can detect emotions such as fear through detection of hesitance could be useful in guiding a user and system through a complex process. When the voice indicates that the instructions are unclear, the system will react with a new explanation. Over time, the system could begin to create new sets of directions that are clearly for a majority of users. A voice recognition system could be helpful in working with the elderly. If the system can detect panic or evidence of a stroke through slurred speech and other cues, it could send help to the elderly individual living at home.

One of the most intriguing experiments with visual interfaces is from an experiment called BabyX developed at the University of Auckland at the Laboratory for Animate Technologies. It is creating "live computational models of the face and brain by combining Bioengineering, Computational and Theoretical Neuroscience, Artificial Intelligence and Interactive Computer Graphics Research," according to the University's website (`http://www.abi.auckland.ac.nz/en/about/our-research/animate-technologies.html`). The University explains the BabyX project:

> *BabyX is an interactive animated virtual infant prototype. BabyX is a computer generated psychobiological simulation under development in the Laboratory of Animate Technologies and is an experimental vehicle incorporating computational models of basic neural systems involved in interactive behaviour and learning.*
>
> *These models are embodied through advanced 3D computer graphics models of the face and upper body of an infant. The system can analyse video and audio inputs in real time to react to the caregiver's or peer's behaviour using behavioural models.*
>
> *BabyX embodies many of the technologies we work on in the Laboratory and is under continuous development, in its neural models, sensing systems and also the realism of its real time computer graphics.*

The laboratory researchers developed a visual modeling technique that enabled programmers to build, visually model, and animate neural systems. The language being developed is called Brain Language (BL). Armed with this language, researchers can interactively work with the simulations and model new behavior. To gain some insights into the potential for this type of interface, you may want to view some of the videos of BabyX (`http://vimeo.com/97186687`).

## Requirements to Increase the Packaging of Best Practices

Most cognitive computing applications are based on custom projects in collaboration with subject matter experts. As with any emerging technology sector, pioneers often blaze their own trail. Over time as there are more and more implementations, it will be possible for these results to be codified into patterns that can be used with other projects looking to solve similar problems. Initially, there will be a set of foundational services that developers can use. However, over time there will be a set of packaged services that has been proven through multiple uses by organizations in similar industries. In a sense there is a corollary with what is now thought of as a packaged application. The difference is that a traditional packaged application is a black box. The user can change data, add rules and business process, but the application itself is sealed from the user.

In a packaged cognitive system, there is a level of transparency. First, it will be critical to understand the assumptions and hypotheses that are built into models as well as the source of the data in the package. In this way, a user could use a subset of the package if the use case is different. There will also be packages that are ubiquitous best practices that will become industry standards. This will have many varied uses for these packaged cognitive applications from training new professionals in a complex field to creating new cognitive applications within a few months rather than a year or more.

## Technical Advancements That Will Change the Future of Cognitive Computing

We have made it clear through this book that we are at the early stages of the evolution and maturation of cognitive computing. Many of the foundational technologies are already in place. However, we still require the evolution of other technologies to get to the predictability and repeatability needed to make systems easy to create and manage. Speed of learning is perhaps the area most in need of innovation. Real-time processing is at the heart of fast learning. On the software side, data has to be analyzed in real time especially to process information in data-rich environments such as video, images, voice, and signals from sensors. These systems will require better clarity, and faster identification of the meaning of these signals. The key to success is improving the time to meaning, not just data acquisition. For example, getting to the point at which the system recognizes and understands the actions of a specific individual within a video fast enough to respond in a threat situation enables more meaningful outcomes. Identifying and then processing the relationships between data in real time can help establish context.

Future innovations in software and hardware will transform what today is complicated and time-consuming for data analytics. Today, to gain this level of expertise requires a lot of manual effort. In the future, machine learning will become more abstracted into the fabric of the development environment. It will be possible to interact with a system in real time as a pattern or connection is detected from the data. This evolution is required as we move from data to information to knowledge. The faster we can process knowledge and understand patterns and context, the sooner we can begin to make discoveries that change the pace of innovation and discoveries across markets and industries.

## What the Future Will Look Like

What will a cognitive system look like in the future? The changes in technology that are needed will not happen all at once. Rather, there are two time horizons to consider: the first five years and then the long term, moving out to the next decade. There are three facets that will define the future of cognitive computing: software innovation, hardware transformation, and availability of refined and trusted data sources. All these are predicated on the development of standards. Before discussing the type of technology that will be at play in the future, take a quick look at what might be expected in five years and then in the more distant future.

## The Next Five Years

There will be considerable change over the next five years. One of the most significant changes will be in the number of well-defined foundational and industry-specific components that are based on foundational and industry-specific elements. For example, there will be a service that can automatically build ontologies based on deep analysis of text in natural language within a domain. Today, the process requires a lot of manual intervention and consensus building. Although people are still expected to have the last word for the foreseeable future, their participation in the process will diminish as ontology building software learns from experience.

Within the travel market, there will be services that might automate the process of building correlations between destinations, predicted weather patterns, and social media data. As interfaces become standardized, it will be possible to automatically link these services together. These functional services will likely be packaged together into workloads using emerging container standards to enable cost-effective cloud deployment.

There will be a series of well-defined services for everything from ingesting specific types of data to analyzing that data in real time and providing visual interfaces that indicate where patterns exist and what they mean. Natural language interfaces will enable users to select the type of interfaces that are most appropriate for the type of analysis being done. One of the newer approaches gaining traction is to move from simply reporting or displaying data to delivering a "story" that explains the data using a narrative interface. Telling a story about how elements of data are related to each other based on wanted outcomes will bring the best clarity in certain situations. Today, many applications rely on graphs and charts to tell a story about the meaning of data.

In other situations when a customer asks a question on a retail selling site, they will be shown a set of products that best matches a keyword. However, what if that engine has a better understanding of the context of consumer's intent? The consumer looking for a sleeping bag might be ready to purchase sleeping bags for the whole family. The successful site would help build a story just for you, based on your needs, your aspirations, and even your financial constraints. Now you have moved from being shown a single item to being shown a story of your future engagement. The world of camping has many nuances, and there could be other products and services that a smart retailer could offer to the consumer. This new type of system will be as cognitive as you allow it to be. Trust and the ability to grant permission for one engagement or over the life of a relationship between a consumer and vendor will be key to the future of engagement.

Imagine a scenario in which the traveler is equipped with a cognitive trip system. The system knows your destination, your preferences for the way you drive, the gas stations along the way, the health of your car, your preferences in food, and the type of hotels you like to stay at. With the right level of input and the right level of security, that system could make your reservations, alert you to alternative routes well in advance, and indicate that you should stop to get your car repaired—although a really smart system might advise you not to leave home on a trip if it can't be completed without predictable auto repairs or maintenance. The system could alert a store that has an item that you need and could even negotiate a price and alert you to the pickup time.

You can apply the same approach to how you deal with your insurance company. You may negotiate a deal with that company based on your habits that will be tracked by a device you wear (assuming that you have granted permission). The information you provide to your insurance company will be aggregated with hundreds of thousands of other insured customers to gain an understanding the level of risk. This could either drive costs down as insurance companies better understand actual risks or create a sharing economy pool of people with similar profiles. It could also lead to new government policies as cognitive systems for human capital management intervene to prevent catastrophic loss for the uninsurable, which could lead to unrest because those things can't be hidden in a transparent, connected society with access to communications and cognitive tools.

## Looking at the Long Term

As the individual technologies that have been discussed continue to mature, we will see them built into the fabric of cognitive systems or platforms rather than assembled from discrete components. Learning will happen in real time and increasingly be influenced by gestures, facial expressions, and seemingly off-hand comments. These systems will, therefore, automatically understand context from events and data from yesterday or from 5 years ago. These systems will store and continuously analyze all social media history in a deep way. Armed with this level of analysis, the cognitive system will anticipate what you might do next and understand why.

Keep in mind, even in ten years permission-based interactions will be the rule. However, there will be more automated techniques that assume your permission level and then ask for confirmation. The system, in fact, is built by analyzing patterns across millions or perhaps billions of interactions. The level of permission the consumer allows will determine the interaction and level of security in this environment. The optimal system will act in the background, making suggestions or recommended actions when necessary but remaining silent most of the time. In essence, you will be dealing with an advanced automated agent that will allow you to create a persona for yourself that is comfortable for you. The agent software gets to know your preferences and personality over time based on the data that you provide directly and the learning system behind it that makes assumptions based on accumulated information. The system will be designed with a set of rules of etiquette based on how humans are comfortable interacting with machines.

In essence, this is the personal digital assistant for the new cognitive era. Rather than the physical device, it may take the form of a representation or personal agent in the cloud with the multiple types of context-appropriate interfaces available at the time of engagement. It could be you and your personal interactions; it could also be the interface to your washing machine. We have already begun to enter an era where the Internet is ubiquitous, but in the coming era, you will always be connected—unless you choose to disconnect. Depending on the situation, the interface is a natural language, a gesture, or a physical action. The cognitive system captures the nuances of your interactions and changes its interaction based on your changing needs and conditions. The system is constantly learning from your behavior and activities behind the scenes. It modifies its actions based on the learning over time. This technique will be widely applied to everything from traffic patterns in a city to security infrastructure.

As more devices with embedded sensors become ubiquitous, the level of data and actions will explode. Professional athletes will be equipped with sensors that know if they suffer a concussion even before a physician examines them. That same type of sensor-based device could warn a construction worker of an obstacle that he should avoid.

These types of cognitive systems will have potential to break down barriers for humans. A sensor-based device with a sophisticated interface can provide a different level of interaction with people who have trouble interacting in social situations. The system is nonjudgmental. Individuals on the autism spectrum could be helped by a system that learns the best ways to interact and has the potential to open lines of communications that have been blocked. The cognitive system adapts to the communication style most effective for different individuals with different disorders. It could be helpful for elderly suffering from Alzheimer's disease.

The most significant change in the coming decade is that cognitive computing will become part of the fabric of computing. Therefore, it will have a profound impact on many industries and many of the tasks that humans do. Machine learning and advanced analytics will be built into every application. Natural language interfaces will continue to be the foundation of how we interact with systems. Eventually, natural language processing will become a utility service rather than a separate market.

## Emerging Innovations

What will it take to get from individual handcrafted systems to the state in which these technologies are deeply embedded in everything you use?

A number of existing technologies that are instrumental in cognitive computing are going to evolve over the next 5 years. That will improve the capability of systems to be created faster with greater capability to solve complex issues. This section discusses the key technologies.

## Deep QA and Hypothesis Generation

Today, Deep QA—which may require a system to generate a series of probing questions for a human to answer for the system to navigate multiple levels of meaning—is rare in practice. In IBM's Watson it is used interactively in a conversational mode with experts to refine their quest for possible answers in complex domains. For example, a doctor may describe a set of symptoms relevant to a patient, and Watson may ask questions that help it to narrow the range of possible answers or increase confidence in one or more diagnoses. It may ask if a particular test has been ordered or ask for more details about a family history. Deep QA requires the system to keep track of all the information that has been provided in previous answers for a session, and only ask further questions when the human answer can help it improve its own performance. It will evaluate the possible answers it may give and assign a confidence level in each, but look at what additional evidence could change that confidence to decide whether to ask for additional information.

If the learning experiences of a lot of systems that answer related questions are shared, that body of knowledge about the process could become a reusable pattern across a domain. In healthcare, for example, there may be enough deep QA analysis to discover the optimal treatment for a specific type of skin cancer because enough data exists— when aggregated—and enough analysis has been done on that data that has been vetted by the best experts in the world. Over time, some hypotheses will have been proven and accepted, so the same query asked at a later date may require less analysis and fewer generated hypotheses as the corpus matures. We may never run out of problems to solve, but for the most part we will see the process of problem solving in complex domains begin to coalesce around cognitive computing. Much like the scientific method guides discovery in the natural sciences, discovery through deep QA and hypothesis generation and testing is likely to become the default approach for many professional disciplines.

## NLP

Advances in NLP have been dramatic in recent years as evidenced by the capability of IBM's Watson to derive meaning from unstructured text under conditions of intentional difficulty. (The QA format of Jeopardy! presents "answers" that may be ambiguous or require context or familiarity with idiomatic speech, and contestants must determine the meaning of the answer before identifying the most appropriate question as a response.) This format is challenging for many humans, but Watson had little difficulty finding the relevant meaning, or alternatively, recognizing when it had low confidence in its answer. The Watson team prepared for the event by studying the way Jeopardy! writers used speech in the past. Those lessons will be valuable as IBM and others extend NLP technology to handle more general cases of slang, colloquialisms, regional dialogues, industry-specific jargon, and the like. A lot of the training is involved with understanding the context of language. NLP systems or services must understand state and conditions that may have been set previously.

Automating translation between natural languages that capture deep meaning remains a difficult problem for NLP. Vocabularies may be mapped from one language to another with reasonable precision (English to French, for example), but natural language communication involves strings or sentences built in to paragraphs and stories that may have explicit and implicit references to meaning expressed in other strings, paragraphs, or even historical references. A key NLP innovation—assuming some common constructs among languages that map to the same underlying deep structures—would be the identification and emulation of the manual process used by expert human translators to discover rules or heuristics they may be applying unconsciously. Analyzing different well-respected translations of books, for example, to identify commonalities and different interpretations, will provide insights into these rules. Today, even some shallow language analysis is so processor-intensive that mobile systems have to send the sentence or string from the device to a cloud-based service before responding. Enabling deep translation on the fly for more than simple statements on mobile devices will require these breakthroughs, or alternatively more powerful NLP chips on the devices themselves.

## Cognitive Training Tools

It is tedious and time-consuming to build a corpus today by training a system based on ingested knowledge. A lot of trial and error and human judgment are involved for every new corpus. Much of the training work that is human-intensive today will become automated as we use current generation cognitive computing systems to examine the process to help build better tools. Similar to the way every generation of high-precision manufacturing tools were built with the previous generation of less sophisticated tools, cognitive computing technology will be used iteratively to discover ways to improve the process of building cognitive computing solutions.

Bias in training is one of the most important issues that will have to be addressed. With a lot of unstructured data and no standards to understand that data, experts make judgments based on their own experiences, which are biased because most have never seen the entire universe of possible interpretations. (Even in narrow medical specialties, for example, the most experienced practitioner has rarely seen every possible set of symptoms or treatment outcomes.) However, they aren't even aware of the bias they are bringing to the situation.

In the future, as cognitive tools become more powerful and apply more cognitive learning, it will be easier to determine the source of a bias and point that out to the expert.

## Data Integration and Representation

Today, connectors, adapters, encapsulation, and interfaces are used to deal with complex data integration. Although this is sufficient if you have a good understanding of the data sources and they are well vetted, it is a different matter when you begin to bring thousands of data sources together. Data integration needs to be automated with a cognitive process so that the system begins to look for patterns across data sources and detect anomalies to see if they represent new, important relationships that were unknown before or problems with a data source being inconsistent.

You saw that ontologies can codify common understanding of complex relationships within a domain, but implementing an ontology is actually a crutch. In a perfect world, a cognitive computing system would not need an ontology because it could dynamically build its own model of the universe by understanding the relationships and context—but that works only if there is enough data and experience and it can process and understand fast enough. Today, we create ontologies so that performance is acceptable with current system constraints. If you could do that processing on the fly, you wouldn't have to predetermine what the ontology would be; you could discover an ontology rather than building one. With sufficient processing power, an ontology would actually be a system state during execution. It would be generated only on demand if it were required for auditing purposes, perhaps to understand why a decision or recommendation was made.

## Emerging Hardware Architectures

Hardware innovations in both the short and long term will have a dramatic impact on the evolution of cognitive computing. Today, it is primarily traditional hardware systems that are used to build cognitive systems. Although parallel structures are used, these systems are still general purpose von Neumann architecture computers, in which all the actual processing takes place in registers within central processing units (CPUs) (or in adjunct processors such as graphical processing units [GPUs]). The real breakthroughs that are on the horizon over the next several years include major changes in chip architectures and programming models.

Complementary to the efforts in software and data architectures, we are seeing two different approaches to hardware architectures evolve. One is based on modeling neurosynaptic behavior (the relationship between neurons and synapses in the brain) directly in hardware. These neuromorphic chips feature many small processing elements that are most tightly interconnected to near neighbors to communicate much like human brain neurons pass signals via chemical or electrical synapses.

The second promising approach is quantum computing, which is based on quantum mechanics (quantum physics), a branch of physics that explores physical properties at nano-scale. Unlike conventional computers whose fundamental unit of storage and processing is the bit (binary digit) which must be a 1 or 0 at any given time, quantum computers use the qubit (quantum bit), which may be in more than one state at any given time. The next two sections explore the prospects for these competing architectural approaches.

### Neurosynaptic Architectures

Why should you look at this new generation of hardware architectures? Simply put, the complexity of identifying and managing relationships between data elements at the scale required for cognitive computing—Big Data—requires enormous computing resources with conventional architectures. Fundamentally, the challenge today is to partition the data effectively to funnel it into an architecture that processes 64 bits of data at a time.

The current basic Intel microarchitecture, for example, used in the Core i7 processor (found in many laptops) and the Xeon family of processors (used in Tianhe-2, currently the world's fastest supercomputer) processes data in increments of 64 bits. Over the past decades, computer scientists have developed elaborate workarounds to compensate for the limitations of hardware. For example, it is relatively easy to add processors to a cluster or system. The individual processors in Tianhe-2 are no faster than those in a modern laptop, but it links together 260,000 of them to harness 3,120,000 cores operating in parallel. The difficult part is to effectively distribute the workload across those similarly architected processors. Some cognitive computing techniques such as hypothesis generation are inherently parallel. Based on the data, it may be desirable to generate hundreds of hypotheses and then process them independently on different processors, cores, or threads.

Another task that would be valuable in a cognitive computing application is real-time image processing in a manner similar to human vision. That also requires mapping millions of bytes of information to look for patterns, which humans do in parallel rather than by breaking up the problem into sequential tasks. For still images, this can take thousands of processors. (The Google experiment mentioned in Chapter 2, "Cognitive Computing Defined," used 16,000 processors just to identify cats.) For video, the problem is much more difficult. A high-definition camcorder typically generates approximately 5 gigabytes of data per minute recording at 30 frames per second. If you want to analyze all the images, you need to analyze each frame and compare it to prior and subsequent frames to find patterns. For example, when evaluating video of a crime scene, detectives look for people whose behavior is not like the rest of the crowd. A human can do that relatively easily with a single video stream, but when multiple streams are involved, it becomes a daunting task that could be automated with sufficient processing power. For most applications today, it is impractical to do large-scale hypothesis generation and evaluation or real-time video analysis.

Now contrast this first to the neurosynaptic hardware approach. The current large-scale leader in this field is IBM's TrueNorth (developed with funding from DARPA), a neurosynaptic chip with 1 million neuron-inspired processing units and 256 million synapses (connections between the processing units, similar to a computer bus but a lot more powerful and faster). Instead of improving performance by adding additional 64-bit register-limited machines, scaling up with a neuromorphic chip builds in the parallelism because while each neural processing unit executes a single function, it communicates with many others. Like neurons in the brain, they are so physically close and connected that they communicate virtually instantaneously. Test systems have already been constructed with multiple TrueNorth chips yielding a system with 16 M neurons and 4 B synapses.

The underlying principle that is modeled in neurosynaptic chips is Hebb's Rule, commonly simplified as "cells that fire together, wire together," —meaning that neurons in close proximity that fire together (actually in rapid sequence) reinforce learning. This was postulated in Donald O. Hebb's 1949 book, *The Organization of Behavior*, which formed the basis for much of the current understanding of associative learning and the development of parallelized pattern matching algorithms. Mapping the behavior of these human brain elements to fundamental constructs in the hardware architecture provides a natural bridge between the way we look at a problem and the way we solve it, which gives neuromorphic computing great appeal (as "brain-inspired" hardware). In the near future you can expect to see billions of processing units per neurosynaptic chip with trillions of synapses. When these chips are assembled into systems, the result will be a new standard for scalable parallelism that has practical applications for pattern matching and learning in cognitive computing systems.

Commercialization of this architecture will require a new programming model, a sophisticated software development environment and an ecosystem of professionals and companies to create a new industry around this model. Efforts to develop these tools and skills are already underway, but in the immediate future you may see hybrid solutions in which neuromorphic approaches will be combined with conventional computers. Similar to the way the average computer today often incorporates special processors for graphics and sound, neuromorphic chips integrated with a conventional system will enable you to take advantage of conventional programming models for much of the required preprocessing.

Why is this architectural approach so important? The emerging architecture enables you to populate each of the millions of neurons in parallel, rather than artificially constraining you to a 64-bit bandwidth for actual processing. When the data is loaded in these neurons, the chip or system can search for patterns in real time. Applications that now are impractical for conventional systems—for example, massively parallel hypothesis processing in medicine and scientific exploration or human-like vision processing become feasible. Parallelism without partitioning is a huge advantage for neuromorphic architectures. The acts of partitioning and reassembling results take time and add complexity. Although there are multiple research efforts to build large-scale neurosynaptic chips, the same approach to mimicking neurosynaptic processing is already being commercialized in smaller scale special purpose chip sets for mobile devices. Qualcomm has a production chip set called Zeroth that is intended to capture patterns of human behavior based on the usage of the mobile device to provide context-aware services. This is planned to be put into production by 2015.

The architectures operate in parallel efficiently so that the total power consumption for a unit of work is lower than that of a register-based architecture. This makes these architectures appealing for mobile devices and at scale will reduce the power and space requirements for data centers. Scalability (up and down) and a simple architectural model will make the adoption of neuromorphic chips inevitable for some cognitive computing applications.

### Quantum Architectures

The fundamental concept behind a quantum computer is to go beyond a binary, two-state (on/off; that is, 1s and 0s) atomic processing unit to a multistate unit called the qubit. A qubit can have multiple states as defined by the physics of quantum mechanics, including being in multiple states simultaneously (superposition). Conceptually, this will be extremely difficult to popularize because it is beyond the mathematical and scientific knowledge and experience of most of the world's population, but it is the most natural way to process quantum algorithms for learning and discovery. Quantum computers can be simulated using conventional computers by mapping each of the possible states to binary states, but, of course, the performance overhead is significant. For example, in a single conventional 64-bit register, you could represent $2^{64}$ values (ranging from a string of all 64 0s to 64 1s, or $1.8 * 10^{19}$). In a qubit with three possible values (0,1, or both) 64 qubits could represent $3^{64}$ values or $3.4 * 10^{30}$, that is, 200 billion times bigger than the binary solutions and impossible to process on a conventional system in anything approaching real time. And in theory, quantum computers can scale without the artificial register restriction, which makes them attractive for massively parallel computations and processing existing quantum algorithms. Like neuromorphic computing, quantum computing will require entirely different programming models, skills, and tools.

Perhaps the most significant barrier to quantum computing is that it requires physical materials to actually be in these superposition states, which requires the processing units to operate at a temperature near absolute zero. That precludes any mobile applications and modestly sized system installations, at least for the time being. Still, the performance potential is too great to ignore. Today, we are seeing significant research and investment in quantum computing by IBM, Google, and DWave (which focuses exclusively on quantum computing). Google has set up a new effort to build its own quantum computer for AI research with academic researchers in the University of California system while continuing to support the independent efforts of DWave.

The energy, space, cooling, and mathematical skills requirements will keep quantum computing from becoming mainstream in the next decade. Although neuromorphic architectures are expected to grow in popularity quickly and be more pervasive at all levels than quantum computing, quantum architectures will continue to attract research funding because it is well understood that a few breakthroughs could lead to fundamentally faster supercomputers.

## Alternative Models for Natural Cognitive Models

Although neuromorphic and quantum computing architectures are based on approaches to established science—neuroscience and quantum mechanics, respectively—that have active research communities in place, they are being challenged by a new approach pioneered by Jeff Hawkins. Hawkins, who changed the way we think about mobile devices when he introduced the Palm Pilot, has an alternative view of human learning. He founded the Redwood Center for Theoretical Neuroscience in 2002 to support research into a layered model of learning based on the functioning of the neocortex. His company Numenta is building applications and an infrastructure for cognitive computing based on his theory of the way the brain stores, processes, and retrieves information about events. His approach is based on the role of the neocortex in human memory as the central organizing principle for computer architecture rather than neurons and synapses. Although it is too early to evaluate the potential for this approach, its Grok for Analytics machine learning anomaly detection product has already demonstrated that it may be useful even if the theory behind it isn't ultimately adopted by the scientific community at large.

## Summary

In the future, cognitive systems will be defined as an integrated environment, which means that software and hardware will work as though they are a single integrated system. This new architecture will scale up and down depending on the use case. For applications such as smarter cities and smarter healthcare, the high-end architectures will enable machine learning in near real time. With personal devices and sensor-based assistants, hardware embedded at the end points will provide processing at the source. This convergence between hardware, software, and connectivity will provide the platform for a huge flood of new use cases and applications for cognitive technologies.

# Glossary

This book includes many technical terms that can be confusing to even the most seasoned technologist. This glossary is a list of terms that may be unfamiliar to you.

**abstraction** — minimizing the complexity of something by hiding the details and just providing the relevant information. It's about providing a high-level specification rather than going into a lot of detail about how something works. In the cloud, for instance, in an IaaS delivery model, the infrastructure is abstracted from the user.

**advanced analytics** — algorithms for complex analyses of either structured or unstructured data, which includes sophisticated statistical models, machine learning, neural networks, text analytics, and other advanced data mining techniques. Advanced analytics does not include database query, reporting, and OLAP cubes.

**algorithm** — a step-by-step description of a specific process, procedure, or method.

**Apache Spark** — an open-source parallel processing framework that enables users to run large-scale data analytics applications across clustered systems.

**Apache Software Foundation** — a nonprofit, community-led organization responsible for coordinating the development and distribution of more than 150 open source software projects.

**API (application programming interface)** — a collection of routines, protocols, and tools that define the interface to a software component, allowing external components access to its functionality without requiring them to know internal implementation details.

**Big Data** — a relative term referring to data that is difficult to process with conventional technology due to extreme values in one or more of three attributes: volume (how much data must be processed), variety (the complexity of the data to be processed) and velocity (the speed at which data is produced or at which it arrives for processing). As data management technologies improve, the threshold for what is considered big data rises. For example, a terabyte of slow-moving simple data was once considered big data, but today that is easily managed. In the future, a yottabyte data set may be manipulated on desktop, but for now it would be considered big data as it requires extraordinary measures to process.

**business rules** — constraints or actions that refer to the actual commercial world but may need to be encapsulated in service management or business applications.

**business service** — an individual function or activity that is directly useful to the business.

**cache** — an efficient memory management approach to ensure that future requests for previously used data can be achieved faster. Cache may be implemented in hardware as a separate high-speed memory component or in software (e.g., in a web browser's cache). In either case, the cache stores the most frequently used data and is the first place searched by an application.

**cloud computing** — a computing model that makes IT resources such as servers, middleware, and applications available as services to business organizations in a self-service manner.

**columnar or column-oriented database** — a database that stores data across columns rather than rows. This is in contrast to a relational database that stores data in rows.

**construction grammar** — an approach to linguistic modeling that uses the "construction" (a pairing of structure and meaning) as the basic unit of language. In NLP, construction grammars are used to search for a semantically defi ned deep structure.

**corpus** — a machine-readable representation of the complete record of a particular individual or topic.

**data at rest** — data at rest is placed in storage rather than used in real time.

**data cleansing** — software used to identify potential data-quality problems. If a customer is listed multiple times in a customer database because of variations in the spelling of her name, the data-cleansing software makes corrections to help standardize the data.

**data federation** — data access to a variety of data stores, using consistent rules and definitions that enable all the data stores to be treated as a single resource.

**data in motion** — data that moves across a network or in-memory for processing in real time.

**data mining** — the process of exploring and analyzing large amounts of data to find patterns.

**data profiling** — a technique or process that helps you understand the content, structure, and relationships of your data. This process also helps you validate your data against technical and business rules.

**data quality** — characteristics of data such as consistency, accuracy, reliability, completeness, timeliness, reasonableness, and validity. Data-quality software ensures that data elements are represented in a consistent way across different data stores or systems, making the data more trustworthy across the enterprise.

**data transformation** — a process by which the format of data is changed so that it can be used by different applications.

**data warehouse** — a large data store containing the organization's historical data, which is used primarily for data analysis and data mining. It is the data system of record.

**database** — a computer system intended to store large amounts of information reliably and in an organized fashion. Most databases provide users convenient access to the data, along with helpful search capabilities.

**Database Management System (DBMS)** — software that controls the storage, access, deletion, security, and integrity of primarily structured data within a database.

**disambiguation** — a technique within NLP for resolving ambiguity in language.

**distributed computing** — the capability to process and manage processing of algorithms across many different nodes in a computing environment.

**distributed filesystem** — a distributed filesystem is needed to manage the decomposition of structured and unstructured data streams.

**elasticity** — the ability to expand or shrink a computing resource in real time, based on scaling a single integrated environment to support a business.

**ETL (Extract, Transform, Load)** — tools for locating and accessing data from a data store (data extraction), changing the structure or format of the data so that it can be used by the business application (data transformation), and sending the data to the business application (data load).

**federation** — the combination of disparate things so that they can act as one—as in federated states, data, or identity management—and to make sure that all the right rules apply.

**framework** — a support structure for developing and managing software.

**graph databases** — makes use of graph structures with nodes and edges to manage and represent data. Unlike a relational database, a graph database does not rely on joins to connect data sources.

**governance** — the process of ensuring compliance with corporate or governmental rules, regulations, and policies. Governance is often associated with risk management and security activities across computing environments.

**Hadoop** — an Apache-managed software framework derived from MapReduce. Big Table Hadoop enables applications based on MapReduce to run on large clusters of commodity hardware. Hadoop is designed to parallelize data processing across computing nodes to speed up computations and hide latency. The two major components of Hadoop are a massively scalable distributed file system that can support petabytes of data and a massively scalable MapReduce engine that computes results in batch.

**Hadoop Distributed File System (HDFS)** — HDFS is a versatile, resilient, clustered approach to managing files in a Big Data environment. HDFS is not the final destination for files. Rather it is a data "service" that offers a unique set of capabilities needed when data volumes and velocity are high.

**Hidden Markov Models (HMMs)** — statistical models used to interpret "noisy" sequences of words or phrases based on probabilistic states.

**hybrid cloud** — a computing model that includes the use of public and private cloud services that are intended to work together.

**information integration** — a process using software to link data sources in various departments or regions of the organization with an overall goal of creating more reliable, consistent, and trusted information.

**infrastructure** — can be either hardware or software elements that are necessary for the operation of anything, such as a country or an IT department. The physical infrastructure that people rely on includes roads, electrical wiring, and water systems. In IT, infrastructure includes basic computer hardware, networks, operating systems, and other software that applications run on top of.

**Infrastructure as a Service (IaaS)** — infrastructure, including a management interface and associated software, provided to companies from the cloud as a service.

**in-memory database** — a database structure in which information is managed and processed in memory rather than on disk.

**latency** — the amount of time lag that enables a service to execute in an environment. Some applications require less latency and need to respond in near real time, whereas other applications are less time-sensitive.

**lexical analysis** — a technique used within the context of language processing that connects each word with its corresponding dictionary meaning.

**machine learning** — a discipline grounded in computer science, statistics, and psychology that includes algorithms that learn or improve their performance based on exposure to patterns in data, rather than by explicit programming.

**markup language** — a way of encoding information that uses plain text containing special tags often delimited by angle brackets (< and >). Specific markup languages are often created based on XML to standardize the interchange of information between different computer systems and services.

**MapReduce** — designed by Google as a way of efficiently executing a set of functions against a large amount of data in batch mode. The "map" component distributes the programming problem or tasks across a large number of systems and handles the placement of the tasks in a way that balances the load and manages recovery from failures. When the distributed computation is completed, another function called "reduce" aggregates all the elements back together to provide a result.

**metadata** — the definitions, mappings, and other characteristics used to describe how to find, access, and use the company's data and software components.

**metadata repository** — a container of consistent definitions of business data and rules for mapping data to its actual physical locations in the system.

**morphology** — the structure of a word. Morphology gives the stem of a word and its additional elements of meaning.

**multitenancy** — refers to the situation in which a single instance of an application runs on a SaaS vendor's servers but serves multiple client organizations (tenants), keeping all their data separate. In a multitenant architecture, a software application partitions its data and configuration so that each customer has a customized virtual application instance.

**neural networks** — neural network algorithms are designed to emulate human/animal brains. The network consists of input nodes, hidden layers, and output nodes. Each of the units is assigned a weight. Using an iterative approach, the algorithm continuously adjusts the weights until it reaches a specific stopping point.

**neuromorphic** — refers to a hardware or software architecture designed with elements or components that simulate neural activities.

**neurosynaptic** — refers to a hardware or software architecture designed with elements or components that simulate the activities of neurons and synapses. (it is a more restrictive term than neuromorphic.)

**NoSQL (Not only SQL)** — NoSQL is a set of technologies that created a broad array of database management systems that are distinct from a relational database systems. One major difference is that SQL is not used as the primary query language. These database management systems are also designed for distributed data stores.

**ontology** — a representation of a specific domain that includes relation-ships between their elements, and often containing rules and relationships between categories and criteria for inclusion within a category.

**phonology** — the study of the physical sounds of a language and how those sounds are uttered in a particular language.

**Platform as a Service (PaaS)** — a cloud service that abstracts the com-puting services, including the operating software and the development, deployment, and management life cycle. It sits on top of Infrastructure as a Service (IaaS).

**pragmatics** — the aspect of linguistics that tackles one of the fundamental requirements for cognitive computing: the capability to understand the context of how words are used.

**process** — a high level end-to-end structure useful for decision making and normalizing how things get done in a company or organization.

**predictive analytics** — a statistical or data mining solution consisting of algorithms and techniques that can be used on both structured and unstructured data (together or individually) to determine future outcomes. It can be deployed for prediction, optimization, forecasting, simulation, and many other uses.

**private cloud** — unlike a public cloud, which is generally available to the general public, a private cloud is a set of computing resources within the corporation that serves only the corporation, but which is set up to be managed as a set of self-service options.

**provisioning** — makes resources available to users and software. A pro-visioning system makes applications available to users and makes server resources available to applications.

**public cloud** — a resource that is available to any consumer either on a fee per transaction service or as a free service.

**quantum computing** — an approach to computation based on properties of quantum mechanics, specifically those dealing with elementary units that may exist in multiple states simultaneously (in contrast with binary computers, whose basic elements always resolve to a 1 or 0).

**real time** — real time processing is used when a computer system accepts and updates data at the same time, feeding back immediate results that influence the data source.

**registry** — a single source for all the metadata needed to gain access to a web service or software component.

**reinforcement learning** — a special case of supervised learning in which the cognitive computing system receives feedback on its performance to guide it to a goal or good outcome.

**repository** — a database for software and components, with an emphasis on revision control and configuration management (where they keep the good stuff, in other words).

**Relational Database Management System (RDBMS)** — a database management system that organizes data in defined tables.

**REST (Representational State Transfer)** — REST is designed specifically for the Internet and is the most commonly used mechanism for connecting one web resource (a server) to another web resource (a client). A RESTful API provides a standardized way to create a temporary relationship (also called "loose coupling") between and among web resources.

**scoring** — the process of assigning a confidence level for a hypothesis.

**semantics** — in computer programming, what the data means as opposed to formatting rules (syntax).

**semi-structured data** — semi-structured data has some structures that are often manifested in images and data from sensors.

**service** — purposeful activity carried out for the benefit of a known target. Services often consist of a group of component services, some of which may also have component services. Services always transform something and complete by delivering an output.

**service catalog** — a directory of IT services provided across the enterprise, including information such as service description, access rights, and ownership.

**SLA (service-level agreement)** — an SLA is a document that captures the understanding between a service user and a service provider as to quality and timeliness. It may be legally binding under certain circumstances.

**service management** — the ability to monitor and optimize a service to ensure that it meets the critical outcomes that the customer values and the stakeholders want to provide.

**silo** — in IT, a silo is an application, data, or service with a single narrow focus, such as human resources management or inventory control, with no intention or preparation for use by others.

**Software as a Service (SaaS)** — software as a Service is the delivery of computer applications over the Internet on a per user per month charge basis.

**Software Defined Environment (SDE)** — an abstraction layer that unifies the components of virtualization in IaaS so that the components can be managed in a unified fashion.

**spatial database** — a spatial database that is optimized for data related to where an object is in a given space.

**SQL (Structured Query Language)** — SQL is the most popular computer language for accessing and manipulating databases.

**SSL (Secure Sockets Layer)** — SSL is a popular method for making secure connections over the Internet, first introduced by Netscape.

**streaming data** — an analytic computing platform that is focused on speed. Data is continuously analyzed and transformed in memory before it is stored on a disk. This platform allows for the analyzing of large volumes of data in real time.

**structured data** — data that has a defined length and format. Examples of structured data include numbers, dates, and groups of words and numbers called strings (for example, for a customer's name, address, and so on).

**supervised learning** — refers to an approach that teaches the system to detect or match patterns in data based on examples it encounters during training with sample data.

**Support Vector Machine (SVM)** — a machine learning algorithm that works with labeled training data and outputs results to an optimal hyper-plane. A *hyperplane* is a subspace of the dimension minus one (that is, a line in a plane).

**syntactical analysis** — helps the system understand the meaning in context with how the term is used in a sentence.

**taxonomy** — provides context within the ontology. Taxonomies are used to capture hierarchical relationships between elements of interest. For example, a taxonomy for the U.S. Generally Accepted Accounting Principles

(GAAP) represents the accounting standards in a hierarchical structure that captures the relationships between them.

**text analytics** — the process of analyzing unstructured text, extracting relevant information, and transforming it into structured information that can be leveraged in various ways.

**unstructured data** — information that does not follow a specified data format. Unstructured data can be text, video, images, and such.

**unsupervised learning** — refers to a machine learning approach that uses inferential statistical modeling algorithms to *discover* rather than *detect* patterns or similarities in data. An unsupervised learning system can identify new patterns, instead of trying to match a set of patterns it encountered during training.

**Watson** — watson is a cognitive system developed by IBM that combines capabilities in NLP, machine learning, and analytics.

**XML** — the eXtensible Markup Language is a language designed to enable the creation of documents readable by humans and computers. It is formally defined as an open standard by a set of rules under the auspices of the World Wide Web Consortium, an international standards organization.

# Index